Cutting

CUTTING

A Guide for the Non-Pro Competitor

Sally Harrison

 **HOWELL BOOK HOUSE**

New York

Maxwell Macmillan Canada
Toronto

Maxwell Macmillan International
New York   Oxford   Singapore   Sydney

Copyright © 1992 by Sally Harrison

All rights reserved. No part of this book may be reproduced or transmitted in any form or by any means, electronic or mechanical, including photocopying, recording, or by any information storage and retrieval system, without permission in writing from the Publisher.

Howell Book House
Macmillan Publishing Company
866 Third Avenue
New York, NY 10022

Maxwell Macmillan Canada, Inc.
1200 Eglinton Avenue East
Suite 200
Don Mills, Ontario M3C 3N1

Macmillan Publishing Company is part of the Maxwell Communication Group of Companies.

Unless otherwise noted, all photographs are by the author.

LIBRARY OF CONGRESS CATALOGING-IN-PUBLICATION DATA

Harrison, Sally.
   Cutting : a guide for the non-pro competitor / Sally Harrison.
     p.   cm.
   Includes bibliographical references and index.
   ISBN 0-87605-845-4
   1. Cutting horse competitions. 2. Cutting horses. 3. Cutting horses—Training. I. Title.
SF296.C87H37 1992   91-25681
791.8'4—dc20   CIP

Macmillan books are available at special discounts for bulk purchases for sales promotions, premiums, fund-raising, or educational use. For details, contact:

Special Sales Director
Macmillan Publishing Company
866 Third Avenue
New York, NY 10022

10 9 8 7 6 5 4 3 2 1
Printed in the United States of America

*Dedicated to
Alan*

Contents

Foreword by Buster Welch — ix

Acknowledgments — xi

Introduction — xiii

ONE *The Heritage* — 1

TWO *The Foundation* — 13

THREE *The Futurity* — 52

FOUR *Selecting the Right Horse* — 82

FIVE *The Basics of Cutting* — 108

SIX *Training Basics* — 137

SEVEN *The First Show* — 167

EIGHT *The Contest* — 176

NINE *Campaigning* — 184

TEN *The Enthusiasts* — 190

Glossary — 211

Index — 219

Foreword

Cutting is the great American horse sport.
I can't think of a better "title" in light of all the good sports my wife, Sheila, and I have met and enjoyed competing with through the years. The people who brought cutting from the open range to the arena and turned the skills of the cowman and cowboy into the contest were real sports.

I like the story about the first recorded contest held with added money. It was held in Haskell, Texas, in 1898 and was advertised to settle once and forever the question of who was the best cutting horse. It was reported that as many as 15,000 people came in buggies, wagons and on horseback.

Sam Graves won on the great old horse Hub. But there is more to the story than who won that day. Boley Brown, a great man and a great sport from Kent County, was the favorite to win on his big sorrel horse. After the gate had been closed on the eleven contestants, a cowboy from Childress rode up and asked to enter.

The gate man wasn't about to let him in, saying the entries were closed. Sam rode over to find out what the trouble was.

"I've got the best horse in the country," the cowboy is supposed to have said, "and I've just lost $150 if they don't let me in."

"If he's that good, I want to see him work," Sam said.

Boley came over and insisted that the cowboy be given a chance.

That fine sportsmanship is still alive and well in cutting today.

Cowboys were gathered from many miles around when West Texas was one big, 50-million-acre pasture. It took lots of cutting horses to sort cattle for brands and four- and five-year-old steers to sell. Cowmen worked within the limits of time, grass and water to hold big herds of cattle. They used large remudas of horses to handle herds of 10,000 to 20,000, in some instances.

The cutting horse was the early cowman's computer, allowing him to work quickly and smoothly, and not chouse and stir the herds until they would be unmanageable. It was important to finish work and move to the next roundup before resources for watering and feeding the cattle and horses were depleted. They moved on, gathering large herds to drive to market, sorting for ownership, branding the year's produce, and turning cattle loose to best use the range.

These men knew cattle, horses and cowboys. They had the grace under pressure to get the job done. The cutting horse belonged to a time when this work was about the only way to make money with the Western range country.

It took great horses. I think J. Frank Dobie said it best when he wrote, "A horse's performance under saddle tells what he is. There was a time when a man on foot was no man at all. A man's best friend was his horse and a horseman unhorsed was *sin pies*—without feet . . . expressing the cooperation between carrier and the carried. Flesh conforming to flesh, spirit blending with spirit, intelligence recognizing intelligence."

A cowman from Texas or the Plains didn't wear silver or anything fancy. His only art was his skill and grace with cattle. He took great pride in it. That's where those great horses came from. I like the time we live in now, but that must have been a wonderful and exciting time to have lived.

As Tom McGuane wrote, "Just as the Plains Indians might memorialize the buffalo hunt in the beauty of their dancing, the rider on a cutting horse can celebrate the life of the open range forever."

There are many different levels of cutting to be enjoyed by people of all ages. Here is hoping we and our children and grandchildren continue to enjoy this great American family sport. This book should be a great help to the beginner. I wish it had been available when I started cutting.

BUSTER WELCH

Acknowledgments

When I was young, my grandmother told me I would be a writer some day. I don't know where she got that idea. It was the furthest thing from my mind.

I never intended to be a writer. I have always just wanted to find out more about the horses and people who fascinate me. Writing about them gave me the chance to satisfy my own desire to learn and to share my findings with other lovers of horses and people.

I guess my grandmother was right, but I still don't *feel* like a writer. I don't feel like I could have completed this book without a lot of help from the following people.

Mike Kelly, Mance Stark and Buster Welch gave me advice and checked the manuscript for accuracy.

Punk Carter set up many of the photographs I shot for the book. Jan Hurley, Ellen Leonard and Kathy Burkett let me use their pictures.

Don Shugart gave me permission to use his action photographs of horses at major NCHA events.

Karl Little, Anita Palmer and George Platt, DVM, made it possible—and fun—to write for the *Cuttin' Hoss Chatter* over the years. Without that background, I never would have attempted a project like this.

My Howell Book House editor, Madelyn Larsen, gave me the chance to write this book.

Pat Steenberge, Melynda Ramos, Henry King and Wayne Morrison also played special roles in the creation of this book.

I am especially grateful to the many cutting horse riders and owners who have shared their stories, knowledge and insight with me over the years.

The prayers and faith of my son Charlie gave me help and inspiration. My daughter Christy buoyed me with her sense of humor and perspective.

My dear friend Alan Gold held herd and lightened the load with enthusiasm, patience and love. I dedicate this book to him.

Introduction

I can't remember when I didn't love horses. The passion mystified everyone but my grandfather. He decided I was a throwback to his Grandpa Stickle, who sent the family pony to a taxidermist after its demise. The old gentleman, a farmer and stockman, received boxcars of wild horses from the West and tamed them for his Ohio neighbors. I loved to hear stories about how Grandpa Stickle hitched renegades to a log, dug his heels into the ground and plowed round and round until his rowdy students saw the light.

My grandfather remembered criss-crossing Grandpa Stickle's pastures bareback atop a grey draft mare. She would dance to avoid stepping on him when he inevitably lost his balance and fell beneath her fat belly. His experience with horses was limited to childhood, but we always attended the county fair and visited the horse stalls to stroke the velvety noses of the tenants.

Once, a young girl was killed when the jumping horse she was riding fell with her. "The horse felt terrible," Grandad solemnly explained. "Horses understand things like that." Then he would tell me again about Grandpa Stickle's broad-backed mare.

Grandad died at eighty-two, shortly after his mind had receded to a time before his children were born. He didn't remember me. "Have we met?" he would ask, puzzled by my intimacy. Once, after I had given up hope of recognition, he smiled and asked, "How are the horses?" Then his expression faded. I answered a stranger.

How are the horses? They are as much a part of my life and work as they were Great-Grandpa Stickle's. They still command the awe and respect instilled by my grandfather. Without design, I became a student of horses and people. By good fortune, I discovered cutting at the 1977 NCHA Futurity.

As a horse-loving Midwesterner transplanted to Fort Worth, Texas, it was inevitable that I would find my way to Will Rogers Coliseum. That's where I watched the 1977 NCHA Futurity, an event that held a special magic for me and a special future for the cutting horse industry.

A bright sorrel colt, nicknamed Little Peppy, was on the brink of a spectacular show and breeding career. His rider and trainer, Buster Welch, a revered master of his trade, collected a record fifth Futurity championship with the win.

Today, Futurity performers are displayed in magnificent slow-motion reruns on a gigantic screen suspended from the coliseum's rafters. But when I saw Little Peppy, he didn't need special effects and a silver screen. He floated through moments of suspended animation, forging a magic bond between human, horse and Hereford.

It's a bond that cannot fail to reach into the heart of a horseman. Linked to the sweat and dust of the Old West, cutting demands a blend of trust, agility, and intelligence unique in the catalog of uses man has found for a horse.

I have watched many great performances since the 1977 Futurity and I have never lost the wonder inspired by that event. I hope this book helps convey the special bond between people and horses that makes cutting such an exciting and rewarding sport.

Cutting

ONE

The Heritage

Mingled sounds from the crowd dropped to a hush. You could hear the cattle breathing. When Miss Silver Pistol entered a cutting arena, only the cows, huddled in false security, were oblivious to the tension.

Miss Silver Pistol was a superhero. She earned over one-half million dollars in one year, more than any other mare in cutting history. But it was spirit, style and sheer energy, rather than winnings, that captivated the grey mare's fans. This was a horse that lived for the game.

Cutting performers have counterparts in baseball, basketball, football, even ballet. But in the world of horse sports, they have no peers. This versatile athlete has the speed of Nolan Ryan's fast ball, the strength of Arnold Schwarzenegger, and the agility of Baryshnikov. Besides being equine "triathletes," cutting horses are intelligent team players. At designated times they comply with riders' directions, but to win it's one-on-one, horse and cow.

In its simplest form, cutting is a contest between a cow and a horse. The horse is guided into the herd by a rider who selects one calf to separate from the others. When the calf is cleared from the herd, the rider relaxes his grip on the reins and the horse is on its own. The lone calf can be compared to a quarterback headed for the end zone. The end zone is the herd of cattle and the horse is the defensive line. If the cow scores, the horse loses.

Cows rarely scored against Miss Silver Pistol. Her resources were limitless. Pouncing into a catlike crouch, she immediately maneuvered into a face-to-face confrontation. From this vantage she could counter every move—wheeling, spinning, crawling, whatever needed to be done to keep the calf in the center of the arena.

Something of a Svengali, Miss Silver Pistol often mesmerized calves into motionlessness. If that happened, she would harry her victim with thrusts of

Wes Shahan rides Quaketta, a cousin to Miss Silver Pistol. Don Shugart photo.

her neck, patting her front feet on the ground in anticipation. She delighted in intimidation and would actually drop to her knees to challenge eyeball to eyeball, nose to nose. This action never failed to send the crowd into a frenzy.

Miss Silver Pistol's abundant agility, cunning and grace was contained in a neat little package. Small in stature compared to many Quarter Horses, she was refined and feminine. Her luminous gun-metal grey coat and silver tail flashed and shimmered with every move she made. Large, dark eyes filled her kind face, topped by keen little ears that were never still, but tuned to her surroundings like radar.

Wes Shahan was a senior at Texas A&M University when he won the 1985 NCHA Non-Pro Futurity riding Miss Silver Pistol. Art, Wes's father, raised her and rode her mother, who was from the Pitchfork Ranch in Texas. For over one hundred years, the Pitchfork has been famous for raising no-nonsense grey horses to work cattle on the open range. Miss Silver Pistol's sire also comes from a family of hardy ranch horses. His dam's sire ran free with a band of mares on the high ranges of southern Colorado.

Miss Silver Pistol and her contemporaries are not hothouse hybrids bred for the spotlight. Their roots are as strong and deep as the centuries-old

The Heritage

Miss Silver Pistol and her Smart Little Lena son.

mesquite trees that draw strength from the western plains. From Chisholm Trail to present day, cutting horses have been irreplaceable partners in the cattle industry.

A Look Back

Fossilized remains of prehistoric horses have been found throughout North America, but there were no native horses when Columbus arrived in the New World.

Spanish conquistadors brought handsome Andalusian horses, descended from Roman army mounts, to the Western Hemisphere in the sixteenth century. Andalusians had been cultivated for centuries from so-called Oriental horses, which were native to northern Africa and the Middle East. Tireless and intelligent cousins of today's Arabian horses, Orientals were valued for their beauty and hardiness. When left to breed and revert to the wild on western American plains, Spanish horses became smaller and sometimes less refined than their statuesque Oriental ancestors, but they never lost their courage and stamina.

Conquistadors rode stallions, but mission settlements kept mares to produce riding stock. When Indians raided seventeenth-century missions, they released horses and cattle. Soon large herds of wild horses roamed the Southwest. By the nineteenth century, Indians had domesticated wild horses, or mustangs as they came to be called, and were using them for warfare.

Imported English horses began arriving in Virginia and Maryland in the mid-eighteenth century. These "blooded" horses, ancestors of today's Thoroughbreds, were also from Oriental—Arabian, Barb and Turkish—stock.

The Thoroughbred Janus sired sprinters that excelled in the quarter-mile races popular with British colonists. Although Quarter Horses were not recognized with a breed registry until 1940, a distinct Quarter-type horse has been popular in this country for over two centuries. Janus-sired horses were the prototype for twentieth-century Quarter Horses. Shorter, with more muscle and hip than their lanky, long-distance English cousins, they could tear the turf from the starting line up to a quarter-mile.

Big-boned Cleveland Bays and draft horses, like the Belgian, were in demand in early urban and farming areas, where they were used as dray and carriage horses. They were taken West, along with Morgans, Saddlebreds and Thoroughbreds, and often crossed with domesticated Spanish mustangs.

Centuries before the conquistadors arrived in America, Spaniards used horses for herding cattle. They also publicly tested the courage, agility and tenacity of their mounts by baiting bulls in small arenas. Horses used in the bull ring were trained to track and dodge cattle and were necessarily quick, smart and aggressive. Process of elimination separated talent from mediocrity in the bull ring in the same way nineteenth-century American range bosses selected cutting horses from run-of-the-mill cowhorses.

English stockmen used dogs for working cattle and kept horses for saddle, harness or sport. This custom was also adopted in the eastern and southern United States. Ranchers of the Southwest, however, needed more than dogs for gathering longhorns in heavy brush and driving them hundreds of miles to market. Texans found native Spanish horses to be well suited for this job, especially if they were crossed with domestic saddle and driving stock. Thoroughbred stallions were bred to Spanish mares to give foals refinement and size. Belgian sires were used to add substance and bone.

Some of the large ranches acquired ready-made saddle horses from eastern

The Heritage

breeders and suppliers by the carload. Yet many western outfits raised their own remudas with Spanish mares and Thoroughbred, Morgan or Arabian stallions and shipped their surplus stock East. Other ranchers preferred to use stocky "Steeldust" or "Billy" stallions, descended from Janus quarter-racing Thoroughbreds, to breed to the Spanish mares.

Cowhorses, as a whole, came to be hybrids with patchwork pedigrees. Turn-of-the-century ranchers could more easily identify mothers and grandsires of their cattle than of their horses. While sires were usually known, broodmares often carried only the names of their owners or sires—"Dr. Rose mare," "Waggoner mare," "daughter of Yellow Wolf." Sometimes they were identified simply by type—"Quarter-type mare," "saddle mare," "Spanish mare."

Ranch horses came in many sizes, shapes and varieties, but they all had to be capable of working cattle in the open, under variable conditions. This meant being able to start fast and stop hard, and keeping a cool head under pressure. There were plenty of racehorses with acceleration, but many lacked the desire to stop, and the patience to work with cattle. Tough and sensible little Spanish mares produced superb cowhorses when bred with combustible runners.

Purebred racehorses were an expensive luxury and a status symbol for wealthy owners, who raced them at prestigious eastern tracks. Mongrelized sprinters, with Thoroughbred and Quarter Horse blood, raced for common folks on unofficial "brush" tracks, scraped out of dusty plains across the Southwest. Owners of "short horses" that were fast at longer distances sometimes purchased falsified papers and raced and advertised them as registered Thoroughbreds. Many of these early runners are ancestors of modern Quarter Horses. Peter McCue is perhaps the most celebrated.

Foaled around 1885, Peter McCue was registered and raced as a Thoroughbred son of Duke of the Highlands, although the American Quarter Horse Association lists the Quarter Horse Dan Tucker as his sire. His owner, who also raced Peter against Quarter runners, advertised Peter McCue as a 16-hand, 1,430-pound horse that could cover a quarter mile in twenty-one seconds flat. If Peter fit his billing, he was a freak as a Quarter Horse or a Thoroughbred. He was, nonetheless, a popular sire that gave Quarter Horse breeders some durable and enduring sons and daughters.

Traveler is an important sire of foundation Quarter Horses whose pedigree is lost to posterity. Photographs portray him as a horse of breeding and refinement. Legend depicts him as a Kentucky Thoroughbred lost in a poker game, later discovered behind a wagon in west Texas, with a mule as a teammate.

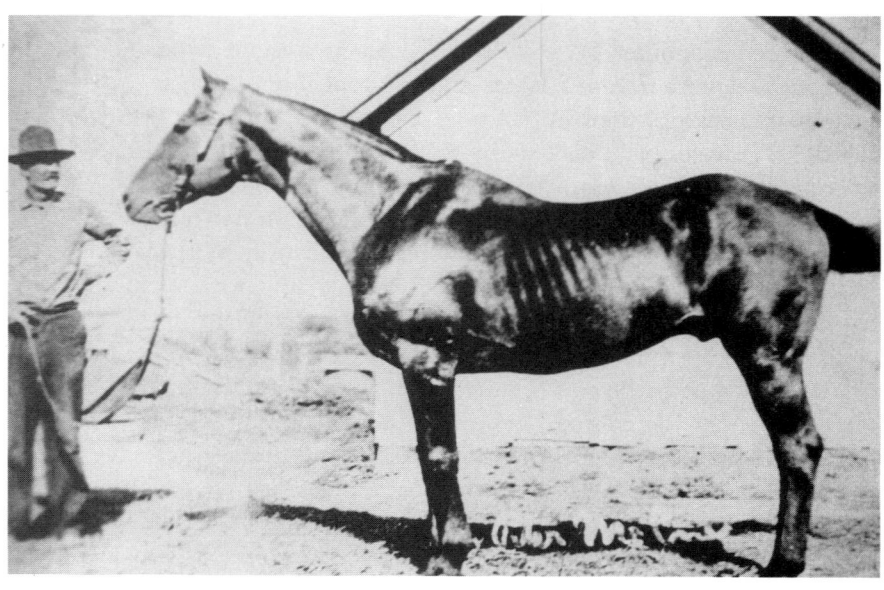

Quarter Horse foundation sire Peter McCue. AQHA photo.

The Old Sorrel. AQHA photo.

Old Fred is another Quarter Horse patriarch of unknown breeding discovered between the traces of a wagon. The big, dappled palomino, with four high, white stockings, looked like he was bred to pull a load, however, as opposed to Traveler, who had the long, lithe lines of a runner. No one ever claimed that Old Fred was a runner, but he did sire Quarter runners and outstanding stock horses.

The first nineteen horses registered by the American Quarter Horse Association were stallions. Wimpy, by Solis, earned the first AQHA certificate when he won the championship of the 1941 Southwestern Exposition and Fat Stock Show in Fort Worth. Twelve of the nineteen stallions, including Wimpy, were sired by Peter McCue or his descendants. Three were sired by Traveler.

Wimpy was owned and bred by the King Ranch of Texas, a great nursery of cattle, cowboys and cowhorses. At one time, King Ranch encompassed over half a million acres of South Texas brush country and raised its own horses to outfit legions of cowboys and vaqueros. Robert Kleberg, Jr., grandson of ranch founder Richard King, was an astute stockman who established the Santa Gertrudis breed of cattle in the 1920s. Under his direction, King Ranch acquired the Old Sorrel in 1918 and founded a dynasty of talented cowhorses.

King Ranch bred the Old Sorrel, a Peter McCue grandson, to Thoroughbred mares hoping to produce quick, sturdy foals for ranch work. The formula worked. Old Sorrel progeny inherited bulk and bone from their sire, and speed and agility from their Thoroughbred dams.

Kleberg, a practical cattleman, understood genetics better than most horsemen, who were often influenced by emotion rather than economics. He culled the Old Sorrel's first crop of foals, keeping mares that satisfied his requirements for type, athletic ability and temperament. All were trained and used on the ranch, where they were evaluated for their working capabilities. He also selected several Old Sorrel sons to breed back to Old Sorrel daughters. Fifty-nine percent of the first two hundred Quarter Horses registered by AQHA were bred or owned by the King Ranch. Many of today's best cutting performers carry the blood of Old Sorrel.

Cutting on the Ranch

Man and horse, the entity, has been surrounded by an ennobling mystique from mounted conquerors to Lady Godiva. Cowboys are laborers hired to tend cattle, but horses and heroics have lifted them above the mundane. Countless songs, stories and Hollywood scenarios tout the glamour of a cow-

A line shack on the Double Mountain River Ranch near Rotan, Texas.

puncher's life. The truth is that cow work is tedious, tiring, lonely and endless. Large herds need constant checking, counting, sorting and culling. Patience is a prerequisite for the job, along with a tough hide and tolerance for privation.

One hundred years ago, ranching outfits built small, one-room shacks along distant and isolated boundary points where lone riders checked herds. One old "line shack" on the Double Mountain River Ranch near Sweetwater, Texas, has scores of cattle brands burned into the wooden fireplace mantel and inscriptions penciled on the whitewashed walls by transitory inhabitants. One forlorn cowboy scrawled: "Jim Latham, batchin it on Thansgiving Day. Lonesome? By God, yes!"

Most cowboys have a string of horses to pick from according to the day's work. Young horses are seasoned by tracking strays and holding herds. More experienced colts are needed for roping calves and sorting cows. Cutting horses are elite members of the ranch team. These soloists have proven their merit for day-to-day tasks, and graduated magna cum laude. Only the most gifted mounts make the transition from ranch horse to cutter.

Young horses need guidance around a herd of cattle. They need to

The Heritage

Buster Welch sorting cattle on NCHA Futurity Champion Clays Little Peppy.

understand patience and learn restraint before they can slip through a herd like fog through rain. Horses are great observers with amazing memories. They are also detail oriented. Smart ones absorb data while tending cows, learning all the nuances of bovine body language. Distance and timing are difficult concepts to teach a horse, but the best cutting horses are born with a natural instinct for maneuvering cattle. This makes a cowboy's job much easier. Instead of reining and spurring through a herd, then chasing cows and playing catch-up, the rider with a good cutting horse can relax and do the job right.

Sorting cattle on the open range takes coordination and planning. Once the herd is bunched, riders circle the perimeter to maintain the shape and discourage slipaways. Other riders man the cuts. "Cuts" refers to the location of cows that have been cut from the herd.

The rider who is cutting enters the herd slowly and deliberately, taking care not to disturb the cows. If one animal bolts, the whole herd might follow. When a cow is selected for the cut, it is slowly driven to the edge of the herd. A competent horse and rider will deliver it to the herd holders, who head it for the cuts. If a cow tries to return to the herd, the horse must be there to meet it and send it back to the cuts.

Haidas Becky and Buster Welch drive cattle with slow, deliberate skill.

Cutting horses are developed, not trained. Horses can be taught to dance and dip in front of a cow, while a skilled rider coordinates the steps. Training will not, however, compensate for cow sense and desire.

Tom Saunders, president of NCHA in 1949, reminisced about some of the great, old Texas ranch horses of the twenties and thirties, in the December 1958 issue of the *Cuttin' Hoss Chatter*.

> There was an Art Waggoner in our remuda that hands from the Matadors, J J's and X's called tops as a cutting horse. Nobody trained him, or groomed him, nor did he ever know what the inside of a stall looked like. He was truly a natural, and so particular about his ability to do it his own way, if you tried to cue or handle him too much, he'd unload you. He sensed his responsibility and showed it upon entering a herd by quickening his cat-like steps, just as though he were walking on eggs. Staying far enough back to counter every move an animal made, he could shuffle, weave and bob, duck, dodge, drop low with fore legs well apart, gather up and step sideways, head and turn back with lightning quickness of a jack rabbit. If you didn't want to drag the toe of your boot when he came back through himself, you'd better raise it high and grab a part of that elm. . . .

The Heritage

George W. Saunders, famed Texas character and first president of the Old Trail Drivers Association, had on his ranch a gotch-eared horse about which Will Rogers always said, "It was worth the trip to the brush country just to sit above ol' Gotch and feel his shoulders roll, watch his ears work and his head drop low when he looked an ol' steer in the eye and dared him to try to get back to the herd."

A century ago, when cowhands were long on work and short on entertainment, they liked to sit around the chuck wagon at night and trade stories about cutting horses. There were "brag" horses like Rooster, a cutting horse so adept at driving cattle his owner wagered the gelding could drive a rooster into a burlap bag. Rooster sacked plenty of poultry and greenbacks and became a legend on West Texas ranches.

Cutting as a Contest

Cutting contests were conjured up by cowboys to provide an ultimate answer to the question, "Who's the best?" Eventually, exhibitions were offered to public audiences.

Buster Welch grew up listening to tales of renowned cutting horses. "I remember when I was a little kid, they didn't have hardly any contests, but they talked and bragged about cutting horses constantly," says Welch. "People didn't sell them then. That would be like selling your windmills. You just wouldn't sell your cutting horse."

There was no official format for early cutting horse contests. Some were speed events where the riders cut as many calves from the herd as possible in a given amount of time. Other rules required riders to drive a cow into a small pen, or to cut a designated steer from the herd.

The first advertised cutting event offering a monetary reward was in Haskell, Texas, at the 1898 Cowboy Reunion. Sam Graves and Old Hub, a twenty-year-old pensioner from the 8 Ranch, cut and delivered eight calves in five minutes and won a $150 jackpot, at a time when $40 would buy a good saddle.

Seeds for the National Cutting Horse Association were planted by thirteen ranchers and cowboys at the 1946 Fort Worth Fat Stock Show. Their objective was to develop a standard format for cutting horse contests, including rules for judging. Before this time, contestants were rewarded for completing specific tasks in a certain time period. Technique was secondary to the end result. NCHA rules and procedures focused on technique and brought a new dimension to the fledgling sport.

Today, cutting horse competition appeals to a broad spectrum of sports and horse enthusiasts, from ranchers to corporate executives. NCHA has 13,000 members in 50 states and 13 foreign countries and over 1,500 annually sanctioned contests. Besides being the nation's richest equine arena event, with single purses exceeding $1 million, cutting is also the nation's most popular equine family sport.

TWO

The Foundation

Cow cents has been the bottom line on every King Ranch horse for over a century. While the legendary South Texas ranching empire is famous for handy riding stock, the King Ranch economy was built on cattle. At one time, 95,000 head roamed more than 1 million acres.

The Old Sorrel

By 1975, the famous Running W brand of horses and cattle had become the symbol of generations of intensive line breeding, relentless culling and scrupulous selection. King Ranch horses were instruments of labor, bred for utility. The Old Sorrel, foaled in 1915, was the King Ranch wellspring. His progeny bred true for agility, speed, cow sense and heart. According to Robert Denhardt in *The King Ranch Quarter Horses* (c. 1970), "more than 90 percent of the cow horses on the [King] ranch are Old Sorrel on both top lines of their pedigrees."

Wimpy, who holds first place in the American Quarter Horse Association registry, was a double Old Sorrel grandson bred and owned by King Ranch. Of the nineteen horses designated foundation sires and honored with the first American Quarter Horse Association registration numbers in 1940, twelve were descended from Peter McCue, the Old Sorrel's grandsire. Little Richard and Tomate Laurales, both Old Sorrel sons, were among this elite group.

King Ranch acquired the Old Sorrel as a young colt from a South Texas breeder of Quarter-type racing and roping stock. The heritage of his dam is unknown, but his sire was Hickory Bill, a Peter McCue son.

Reputedly sired by Dan Tucker, a quarter-mile racehorse, Peter McCue was registered with the American Jockey Club as a Thoroughbred sired by Duke of the Highlands. Samuel Watkins of Petersburg, Illinois, bred and raced strapping Peter McCue in the company of Thoroughbreds until he was four. Later, under the ownership of John Wilkins and Milo Burlingame, he ran on quarter-mile tracks in south Texas. Burlingame insisted that on more than one occasion the big stallion clocked a quarter-mile in twenty-one seconds. Since the advertised accounting of Peter McCue's pedigree differed from that of the Jockey Club, it is impossible to know the truth about his race record. Looking at his photograph (see page 6), it is hard to imagine the huge, long-barreled horse on the same track with either Thoroughbreds or Quarter Horses.

In 1911, at the age of sixteen, Peter McCue was retired to stud. Whatever the truth about his parentage, Wilkins' stallion had a profound effect on the Quarter Horse breed.

Shortly before the onset of World War I, Robert Kleberg, Jr., began looking for a stallion to improve the ranch remudas. Because he knew about Peter McCue "short horses," and liked Hickory Bill stock horses, Kleberg thought the Old Sorrel might meet his demands for a sire of quick, yet sturdy ranch horses.

George Clegg was the name the Old Sorrel carried to the King Ranch, but when his prowess as a working horse and sire of deep sorrel lookalikes became legend, the cowboys and ranch hands began referring to him simply as the Old Sorrel.

Because he was the cornerstone of a new breed of dark red cowhorses, the Old Sorrel's moniker endured. Just as Kleberg had engineered a vigorous breed of beef cattle, called Santa Gertrudis, so he envisioned a superior line of ranch horses from the Old Sorrel. By breeding Old Sorrel daughters back to Old Sorrel, Kleberg used selective inbreeding to achieve his goal. A few of Old Sorrel's best sons were kept as stallions to produce third and fourth generations. Thus we have Wimpy, who was out of the Old Sorrel daughter Panda, and sired by the Old Sorrel son Solis.

Looking back over three-quarters of a century of King Ranch horses, Stephen "Tio" Kleberg wonders at the success of his great-uncle's plan. "If you were only selecting for one thing, it would be easy," says Kleberg. "The difficulty is that we want conformation, soundness, disposition, good looks, physical ability and cow sense. It takes a lot of years of breeding to get it done.

"Thoroughbred people breed for one thing—speed. Soundness helps, but there are horses that have conformation defects and run like hell."

The Foundation

Robert Kleberg, Jr., of the King Ranch. AQHA photo.

Kleberg, former president of AQHA, extols Quarter Horses, but he knows Thoroughbreds better than most horsemen. His great-uncle Robert bred and raced Thoroughbred Triple Crown winner Assault.

Robert Kleberg valued the Old Sorrel line for stamina, dependability, intelligence and cow sense—a combination of qualities not intrinsic to running horses. He did, however, occasionally outcross Quarter mares to specially selected Thoroughbred stallions. Old Sorrel, whose dam was thought to be a Thoroughbred, was also bred to Thoroughbred mares.

Rey Jay

After the formation of the American Quarter Horse Association in 1940, Old Sorrel–bred horses were in demand throughout the Southwest. Many became distinguished arena cutting horses. One of the best was Rey Jay, the "one-eyed wonder."

Horseman Curly Talmage of Azle, Texas, liked King Ranch horses. He had trained an Old Sorrel grandson in the early fifties and remembered him as an outstanding cowhorse. He also preferred a horse of medium stature and muscling, as opposed to the stocky "bulldog" Quarter Horses that were popular

Rey Jay, the "One-Eyed Wonder." AQHA photo.

at that time. Third- and fourth-generation Old Sorrel horses of the 1940s and 1950s were as much as 75 percent Thoroughbred, and they were built to Talmage's specifications.

Rey Jay was two years old when Talmage first saw him in 1957. "He was in an old garage," remembers Talmage. "It was all boarded up, and when I looked through a crack, the first thing I could see was this white spot in his eye. It glared at me and I thought, 'What is that ugly thing?' Then I looked at him closer and I liked him. I went ahead and bought him, spot and all."

An opaque lesion, the result of an injury, discolored Rey Jay's eye and impaired his vision. He could see movement, but images were blurred and indistinct. Because of this impairment, Talmage paid only $350 for Rey Jay at a time when other Rey Del Rancho sons were selling for five times that amount.

Rey Jay's pedigree is a study in King Ranch breeding. His sire, Rey Del Rancho, was by Ranchero, who was by Solis, by the Old Sorrel. Ranchero was out of Borega, by the Old Sorrel. Solis was bred to many of his Old Sorrel–sired half-sisters in an attempt to fix the Old Sorrel type. This seemed

The Foundation

to work better for King Ranch than breeding Old Sorrel to his daughters.

Rey Del Rancho's dam Panda De La Tordia was also sired by Ranchero, and was out of a Babe Grande daughter. Babe Grande was another Old Sorrel son. Calandria K, Rey Jay's dam, was sired by Tino, one of the few bay sons of Old Sorrel. Old Sorrel was so prepotent for his sorrel color that King Ranch had selected for that trait along with other desirable characteristics.

Rey Jay traveled from the King Ranch to Fort Worth in a shipment of horses purchased by Loyd Jinkens, who traded the one-eyed colt to a dairy-farming neighbor of Talmage's for a few Holstein cows. Lanham Riley, another neighbor, rode Rey Jay several weeks to get him used to a saddle and bit, and from then until Talmage bought him, Rey Jay was used to gather dairy cows from the pasture.

When Talmage began riding him, he found the colt to be a great cowhorse some days, and a bungler on others. Detective work solved the problem.

"If dust got in his good eye, he would hold it closed and miss cows," says Talmage. "We used to haul horses in open trailers and use protective goggles to keep the bugs out of their eyes. So I bought a three-dollar pair of goggles and cut the plastic out of the good eye and kept it on the bad eye and it worked."

Not long after Talmage got Rey Jay, he purchased a pretty, Thoroughbred-looking mare with King Ranch bloodlines on the top of her pedigree and Waggoner Ranch breeding on the bottom. Talmage registered the mare as Georgia Cody and bred her to Rey Jay. In 1958 Georgia Cody produced her first foal, Gay Jay, a sorrel filly with a white star and hind socks.

While Gay Jay grazed Talmage's pasture with her dam, her sire was earning trophies and admirers in cutting arenas around the country. One fan, Tommy Lee of Fort Wayne, Indiana, talked Talmage into trading his stallion for $4,000 and a palomino mare.

"I've had people ask me if I didn't kick myself for selling Rey Jay," says Talmage. "But I never felt that way. Most everybody sells horses if they can make a profit."

Talmage did later regret selling Gay Jay, his only Rey Jay foal, for $400. "I sold her to a man in Fort Worth for his daughter," recalls Talmage. "I also sold him a gelding for his son. They were Christmas presents, and I had to deliver them to his house on Christmas Eve and tie them in the back yard."

Gay Jay changed owners several times in the next few years, but Talmage always kept track of her. When Texas horseman B. F. Phillips, Jr., offered her in a sale in the mid-sixties, Talmage went prepared to bid.

"I went to the sale and said that I was going to buy my mare back," remembers Talmage, who had turned Gay Jay down a few years earlier because he couldn't afford the $1,000 asking price. "At this time I had a little money in my pocket. But Marion Flynt sat down in the front row and bought Gay Jay for $17,000 and I went home with an empty trailer."

Flynt, a West Texas businessman and rancher who served twelve years as NCHA president, owned the great cutting mare Marion's Girl, as well as Jewel's Leo Bars, known to cutters as Freckles. In 1965, Flynt had purchased Rey Jay from Tommy Lee for $25,000, hoping to raise fillies to breed to Freckles. Flynt's best-producing Rey Jay daughter would prove to be Gay Jay, however. From Gay Jay and Freckles, Flynt got Freckles Playboy, Jay Freckles and Freckles Hustler, all leading money earners.

Freckles Playboy, AQHA World Champion Junior Cutting Horse and 1976 NCHA Futurity Reserve Champion, has been at the top of cutting's leading sire lists for over a decade. Smart Play, 1990 NCHA Reserve Futurity Champion; Playboys Lynnea, 1990 NCHA Non-Pro Futurity Champion; and Playboys Ruby, 1991 Memphis and Augusta Futurity Champion, are a few in a long list of Freckles Playboy standouts.

Rey Jay's Pete, Rey Jay's most famous son, was out of an unregistered buckskin mare that was used as a turnback horse on Tom Lee's Indiana farm. Kenneth Peters bought and trained the gelding and Buster Welch rode him to win the 1966 NCHA Futurity Championship. S. J. Agnew purchased Rey Jay's Pete after the Futurity, and he placed in NCHA standings for several years, along with two other Rey Jay offspring, Rey Lad and Little Boy Rey. Ollie Rey, an NCHA Top Ten contender, was one of the few Rey Jay sons that was not gelded.

It is mostly his daughters and their sons that have assured Rey Jay's immortality in the cutting world. Christy Jay, by Rey Jay, produced 1976 NCHA Futurity Champion Colonel Freckles, who, in turn, sired 1981 NCHA Futurity winner Colonel Lil. Other champion-producing Rey Jay daughters include Miss Cocoa Jay, Jay Moss, Alice's Rey Jay and Chickasha Gay.

Mr San Peppy

In 1975, Stephen Kleberg, vice-president of King Ranch, made the decision to actively court the burgeoning cutting horse show market. To implement a program as quickly as possible, King Ranch needed a currently hot stallion prospect and a seasoned NCHA trainer.

"At that time," explains Kleberg, "our mares were of good quality, but the stallions we had were not continuing to improve the quality of the foals. They were at the same level as the mares, and we felt we needed a better stallion than the mares, in order to improve the offspring."

The Foundation

Mr San Peppy. AQHA photo.

King Ranch hit pay dirt in Sweetwater, Texas, home of Buster Welch and 1974 NCHA World Champion Mr San Peppy.

Bred and raised by Gordon Howell of Dallas, Mr San Peppy had won the 1972 NCHA Derby with Welch in the saddle, and the 1974 World Championship in the name of Welch and S. J. Agnew. In addition to his show record, Mr San Peppy carried considerable clout through his pedigree, as an outcross for line-bred King Ranch mares, while still delivering the Old Sorrel through his dam's sire.

Mr San Peppy, by Leo San, is out of Peppy Belle, by Pep Up, a line-bred Old Sorrel stallion. Peppy San, 1967 NCHA World Champion and full brother to Mr San Peppy, had established the siring potential of this pedigree when his daughter Peppy's Desire won both the Open and Non-Pro World Championships in 1975.

Mr San Peppy passed the test for Kleberg on all counts, not the least of which was durability.

"Soundness is primary in all our horses," explains Kleberg. "Every horse has been ridden and we know what they'll do. They have to be sound, and then we go for ability and disposition.

"That's one thing that impressed us about Mr San Peppy. He has never taken a lame step. He's an exceptionally well-made horse. The key to soundness is overall good conformation. The cutting horse has to have good conformation or he will not hold up."

King Ranch purchased Mr San Peppy in 1975 and Welch came aboard as adviser and trainer. Although Mr San Peppy was traveling to compete in the 1973 NCHA Top Ten, he also bred a dozen mares, including Sugar Badger, a Grey Badger II daughter owned by Joe Kirk Fulton of Lubbock, Texas.

In 1977, Fulton was grooming Sugar Badger's three-year-old colt, Peppy San Badger, for the Futurity and brought him to King Ranch for Welch's assessment. "I never was as impressed with a horse in my life," remembers Welch about his first ride aboard Peppy San Badger, the horse that would give him his fifth Futurity win, in 1977. Welch was convinced that the sorrel colt might be Mr San Peppy's greatest son, and King Ranch purchased him for the Futurity.

Peppy San Badger so closely resembled his sire that he was nicknamed "Little Peppy." But father and son were worlds apart in style. "Mr San Peppy was a fierce working horse," says Welch. "Little Peppy had that ability, but he also had a lot of balletlike movements.

"A lot of times he might balance himself when a cow was coming to him and just drag his front feet around and never touch the ground with them. He'd just use his back end and be real low in front. His front feet wouldn't be two inches off the ground.

"He had a unique way about him. He could be a real classy, pretty horse, with lots and lots of style, and then he could immediately turn into a fierce working horse and hold bad, bad cows."

Kleberg attributes Little Peppy's athletic ability to his conformation. "He has so much strength in his back end, and he is so well balanced," explains Kleberg. "If you could draw the perfect horse as far as balance, it would be Little Peppy."

Balance gave Little Peppy an edge, but it was brain power that endeared the horse to Welch. "He was a brilliant horse anywhere you put him," says Welch. "He was one of the most thinking horses that I ever rode. I used him to work cattle on the ranch. If we were dragging calves, he would figure out where the branding fire was and the shortest way to get there. It never took him long to figure out what the plan was in anything he was doing.

"He was a quiet horse, too. He never fretted, yet he always seemed to have energy for whatever was needed. He never took a step that felt tired, no matter how long he had been ridden or how many go-rounds he had completed."

King—Grandson of "the Mexican Man o' War"

Over six hundred horses were registered with the American Quarter Horse Association in 1940, the year of its formation. Many carried descriptive names like Yellow Boy, Red Dog, Old Sorrel, Long Mane, or Seal Brown. Others were named after people and places—Oklahoma Star, Del Rio Joe, Tom Burnett, Fanny Rhea, Triangle Lady 13 and Sadie O'Brien. Still more were named for their talents—Calf Roper, Cowpen Annie, Fleet, Long Gone.

These were no-nonsense names for horses that packed saddles from sunup till sundown. Sheik, Chief, Duchess and Little King may have hinted at royalty, but there was only one King.

King began life as Buttons, on the ranch of Manuel Benevides Volpe, near Laredo, Texas. Volpe was a fast-horse fancier who owned one of the best. Zantanon, known as "the Mexican Man o' War," was purchased by Volpe at fourteen years of age for $500. Although the stallion was in such poor condition he could barely stand to eat, Volpe had seen him race in Mexico and was willing to pay the price, a considerable sum in 1927. Volpe

King P-234. AQHA photo.

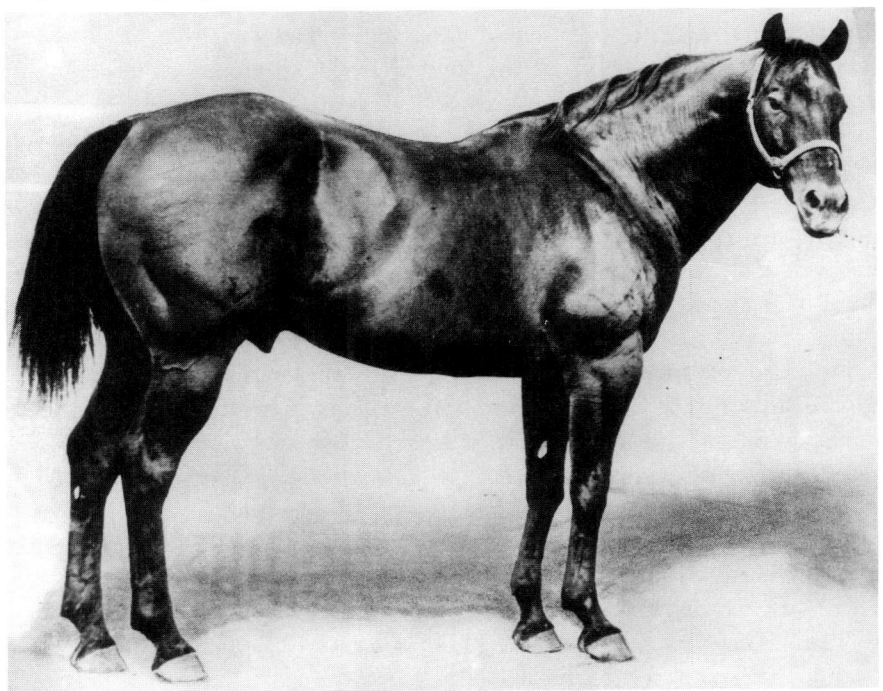

also coveted the blood of Zantanon's sire Little Joe, who had died two years previously. He nursed the stallion back to health and began breeding him in the early 1930s.

Button's dam was a mare that Volpe had collected on a wager. Although she is named Jabalina in AQHA Stud Books, Volpe referred to her as a brown, hog-backed mare and called her Javalina. Javalinas are ill-tempered wild hogs with long tusks, whose stuffed and mounted heads adorn many hunting lodges in the South.

Volpe sold the hog-backed mare's bay colt at weaning for $150. He was trained and matched at 200-yard sprint races, then sold to New York Giants baseball player Byrne James, who used him for roping and stock work. It was James who started calling the stocky stallion King.

Judging from photographs, Zantanon was a well-balanced horse with a long hip, medium muscling and light bone. King was balanced and refined, but he was heavily muscled with great depth in the shoulder and hip. It was not surprising that he was a better stock horse than match racer.

Jess Hankins and his brothers, J. O. and Lowell, lived within a few miles of each other in Rocksprings, Texas. Although cattle, goats and sheep were their main stock-in-trade, each brother had some broodmares. Lowell and J. O. loved a good match race. Jess just loved good horses.

The first time Jess saw King, whom Byrne had sold to Winn DuBose, he bred a mare to him. But he was so impressed with the bay stallion's glossy good looks, he couldn't wait for the foal. When DuBose hinted King might be for sale, Hankins jumped at the chance. He borrowed money from Lowell to meet DuBose's $800 price, a substantial amount in 1937, a day of $20 stud fees.

Lowell Hankins had also noticed something special about King. "His hair was finer than most horses," he remembers. "There was a sheen to it, and it was real fine. It *shined* like new money."

Although King had a sterling reputation as a roping horse, his siring ability was unknown. The first breeding season, Jess set King's stud fee at $15. The resulting foals looked good enough to raise the rate to $25 the second year. By the time Jess's first King foals were two-year-olds, he was receiving $50 per mare. Each year the fee climbed, peaking at $500. Even then Jess had to turn mares away.

Most of King's foals inherited his sturdy physique, which was popular among Quarter Horse breeders of the forties and fifties.

"King was what you call an old, true bulldog type," says Lowell. "The way I remember him, he wasn't real bulgy muscles like some of them. Most of those horses get a little bit coarse. He was real refined."

The Foundation

Another attribute shared by King foals was an agreeable disposition.

"There may be other horses with dispositions like King, but I kind of doubt it," says Lowell. "I think I could have bred a mare with a double twine string on the halter and I don't believe he would have broken it.

"We used to have enough labor to spend a lot of time with our colts, and they'd be just as gentle as dogs by the time we got them to the sale. I've had people ask how on earth we got them that gentle. I told them it was in the breeding.

"We used to sell horses to some fellows in the Carolinas. They'd have a trailer that would haul about six grown horses, and they'd put ten to twelve yearlings in it. One time, we got them loaded and they wouldn't all quite go in. We had to take them out and do them over. I remember them commenting that they'd never seen a bunch of horses that gentle. It was the breeding, mostly. As long as you don't abuse them and they've got the right bloodline in them, they'll do that way."

The best King-sired progeny were Hankins bred. While Jess favored halter and performance colts, Lowell and J. O. bred for speed. J. O. bought Queen H in 1936 and began breeding her to King each year. From this cross he got the stakes winner Squaw H, and Hank H, whose daughter Hanka produced the champion running horse and leading sire Tonto Bars Hank. Hank H is also found in the pedigree of 1986 NCHA Futurity Reserve Champion High Brow Hickory and Bar Socks Babe, a leading dam of NCHA champions.

J. O. owned a black filly by the Thoroughbred Hygro, out of a King daughter. Hyglo won many races and equaled the world record at 400 yards. When she was bred to her grandsire King, she produced King Glo, sire of the first two NCHA Futurity winners: Money's Glo and Chickasha Glo. King Glo also sired NCHA Futurity winner Chickasha Dan and Annie Glo, 1979 World Champion Mare. King Glo is also found in the pedigrees of 1980 NCHA Futurity Champion Mis Royal Mahogany, 1988 World Champion Hyglo Freckles and 1986 leading money earner Oak Aglow.

Lowell is not surprised at the success of King Glo progeny. "Probably the best, or second best, horse that King ever sired was right there," he says of King Glo. "Of course, he wasn't known like Poco Bueno. Poco Bueno did more because he was bred to more mares."

Lowell owned a black mare called Miss Alice, who was half-sister to 1949 AQHA Running Champion Diamond Bob. When Lowell bred Miss Alice to King, he got four more champions, including Black Gold King, sire of Mackay Alice. Mackay Alice was a leading cutting horse performer. Her daughter Alice's Rey Jay was a top cutter and is the dam of three leading NCHA money earners.

Gay Widow was a Hankins bred King daughter who covered all bases. She earned a Register of Merit (ROM) racing, and was an AQHA champion in performance and halter. Her son, Gay Bar King, by Three Bars, became a leading sire of broodmares, whose progeny include Non-Pro World Champion Gay Bars Gen and AQHA Champion Gay Bar Lady, dam of Reserve AQHA World Champion Doc Ware and Super Stakes Reserve Champion Sugs Gay Lady.

Full brothers Power Command and King Command, by King, appear in the pedigrees of Commander King, Hesa Commander, Dun Commander, Commando King, Doc Per and Doc Athena. King's Pistol, by King, was the first stallion to become an NCHA World Champion. He is the dam's sire of Miss Silver Pistol, NCHA Non-Pro Futurity Champion and the first cutting mare to earn over $500,000.

Jess Hank, by King, sired Susie L, who was the dam of Susie's Bay. Susie's Bay, by Poco Tivio, is the dam of World Champion Doc's Marmoset and her full brothers Doc's Oak and Doc's Solano.

Poco Bueno and Royal King, however, are the two King sons that helped bring cutting into the show arena. It would be hard to find a cutting pedigree today without one or the other.

Royal King

Although he inherited his sire King's gentle nature, it was Royal King's gritty determination that earned points in cutting contests. His foals displayed the same tenacity, right down to flattening their ears back against their necks when they faced a cow.

Little is known of Rocket Landing, Royal King's dam, except that she was sired by a horse called Dolph and out of Cricket by Coldy. She did produce a full brother to Royal King, Rockey Red, who was also owned by Earl Albin and who was an NCHA Top Ten Finalist in 1952.

Albin, a rancher from East Texas, owned Royal King most of his life and began breeding him as a two-year-old. One of his best foals came from that first crop. Miss Nancy Bailey, foaled in 1946, was NCHA World Champion Cutting Mare in 1952, 1953 and 1957. Royal King, who was campaigned at the same time, was Reserve World Champion Cutting Horse and World Champion Stallion in 1953.

Although Royal King produced some outstanding sons, like World Champion Gelding Royal Chess, his greatest gift to cutting was his daughters. Royal Jazzy was a leading competitor in the early sixties. Although she did not live

The Foundation

Royal King and Earl Albin's children. AQHA photo.

to produce, her full sister Royal Jazabell founded a dynasty for Spencer Harden of Millsap, Texas.

"I think these horses get the style they have from Royal King," Harden says of his champions. "A lot of horses will drop their front ends, but these horses will drop all over. The Royal Kings that I have had always had that drop and look and a lot of shake and shiver to them."

Royal Jazzy, who was owned and shown by Bubba Cascio, had the same style. "When she'd stop a cow," remembers Cascio, "she'd go to getting lower and lower, and pounding her feet, and just kind of trembling all over."

Royal Jazabell produced 1976 NCHA World Champion Mare Bill's Jazabell, by Cutter Bill. Bill's Jazabell's only foal was Jazabell Quixote, 1982 NCHA Non-Pro Futurity Champion. Jazabell Quixote has produced 1988 NCHA Non-Pro Futurity winner Jazalena, 1989 NCHA Open Futurity Champion July Jazz and 1990 NCHA Futurity Non-Pro Reserve Champion All That Jazz.

Jazzy Socks was another Royal King daughter out of a half-sister to Royal

Jazzy and Jazabell Quixote. Spencer Harden also owned Jazzy Socks and was a Non-Pro NCHA Futurity Finalist, riding her in 1969. Jazzy Socks produced Doc Wilson and Son Ofa Doc, both leading sires of NCHA money earners.

Many horsemen frown on the practice of inbreeding. Jess Hankins never had any qualms about perpetuating King's qualities through this method. In fact, he was so successful, other breeders with King blood followed suit. Jazzote, 1986 NCHA World Champion Cutting Horse, was the result of such a cross. His dam, Queen Vicky, was sired by a full brother to Jazzy Socks, by Royal King. Queen Vicky's dam was sired by an inbred King son, and out of a Royal King daughter.

Two other performers whose records support Hankins' faith in line breeding are Royal Blue Boon and Sir Royal Lynx, Co-Reserve Champions in the 1984 NCHA Super Stakes. Both of these cutters are out of Royal King daughters, who are out of Royal King granddaughters.

Royal King is the maternal grandsire of both the sire and dam of Mis Royal Mahogany, 1980 NCHA Futurity Champion. King Glo, by King, is her dam's paternal grandsire. Royal Silver King, 1986 NCHA Futurity Champion, carries Royal King through his sire Brinks Royal Lee.

Miss Royal Fleet, by Royal King, is the second dam of 1978 NCHA Futurity Champion Lynx Melody.

Royal King's greatest influence on present-day pedigrees comes through his daughter Royal Smart. She is the dam of World Champion Gelding Royal Santana, by Peppy San, and his full sister Peppy Smart. Peppy Smart is the dam of Triple Crown Champion Smart Little Lena, a leading sire of NCHA aged event money earners since 1987.

Smart Little Lena's sire, Doc O'Lena, was the 1970 NCHA Futurity Champion and one of only two foals out of cutting's most celebrated mare, Poco Lena. Poco Lena is the daughter of Poco Bueno, King's most celebrated son.

Poco Bueno—The Charismatic Cutter

The Waggoners liked good horses. Dan fashioned a cattle empire on the back of a horse, and his son W. T. expanded the horizon. Once asked if he intended to buy all of North Texas, W. T. Waggoner quipped, "Only what joins me."

Cattle and horses were W. T.'s passion and he cursed his luck during a drought when oil gushed from wells sunk in search of water. During the Depression, after oil had made Waggoner the richest man west of the Mississippi, he indulged his love of horses by building one of the nation's finest

The Foundation 27

Poco Bueno. AQHA photo.

race tracks near Fort Worth. It is said that he offered Sam Riddle $1 million for Man o' War, then signed a blank check when Riddle refused the offer.

E. Paul Waggoner, W. T.'s son, shared his father's love for horses. Instead of lithe Thoroughbreds, however, he was interested in the sturdy stock horses that helped build his father's cattle empire. The American Quarter Horse Association's first Stud Book was full of good Waggoner ranch horses, and Paul decided to make the 3D Stock Farm in Arlington, Texas, his Quarter Horse headquarters.

In 1945, Waggoner purchased the yearling colt Poco Bueno to stand with Jessie James and Pretty Boy at the 3D Ranch. Poco Bueno was sired by King, and out of Miss Taylor, by Old Poco Bueno. Old Poco Bueno, like

King, was a Zantanon son. Bob Burton started Poco Bueno's training, but Pine Johnson handled the stallion throughout his show career.

Johnson, who developed his expertise with horses and cattle on the famous Pitchfork Ranch of Texas, preferred quick and nimble Thoroughbred–Quarter-cross horses like the ones Pitchfork hands used for ranch work. He chose light and lean horses over stocky ones, believing them to have more stamina for working cattle.

Compact and muscular Poco Bueno was all Quarter Horse in type. While Johnson liked the colt's looks, he was skeptical about his ability to perform with speed and agility. Johnson's stocky student was not long proving his ability, however, and in a way Johnson never forgot.

"He taught me to hold on to the saddle horn," said Johnson. "Back then it was an insult to ride with your hand on the saddle. You'll notice in photos that we rode with our arms up.

"That changed for me after one contest when Poco Bueno turned out from under me so quick that I landed on my feet, standing up. A lot of people thought I had stepped off of him. But I didn't. He just dropped down and turned, and I never even tripped."

His aggressive, hard-working style made Poco Bueno a crowd pleaser wherever he was shown. Capitalizing on his audience appeal, Waggoner entered the stallion in contests and cutting exhibitions around the country. During breeding season, however, he came home to the ranch and was turned out with a band of thirty mares.

Powerfully built, Poco Bueno soon became a standard for Quarter Horse conformation. When lookalike foals began arriving, out of Waggoner-bred ranch mares, Johnson had little trouble selling them as weanlings for $1,000 each—in the days when a Coke cost a nickel.

Poco Bueno foals were known for stylish good looks and athletic ability, but Johnson thought it was attitude that set them apart from other performers.

"A million dollars will buy a dog, but only love can make him wag his tail," said Johnson. "Some horses don't care enough to be trained. I don't care what you teach them. They aren't going to absorb it, because they're looking for a way to quit. But Poco Bueno horses don't have any quit in them.

"Most of your intelligent, brilliant horses love to work. But the first thing you have to do is teach them to trust you. Poco Bueno didn't like some people. I'd be holding him and some people would walk up and he'd lay his ears back.

"The Poco Bueno horses were kind of shy-type horses. If they hadn't been raised gentle, they would be extremely wild."

Many of Poco Bueno's best performers were Waggoner-bred, out of Pretty Boy daughters, and were trained by Pine Johnson. Although he had a soft spot in his heart for all of them, Johnson's favorite was a bay filly named Poco Lena.

Poco Lena

In the fall of 1950, besides the stallions Poco Bueno, Pretty Boy and Jessie James, only one horse remained at the 3D Ranch. She was a rangy weanling by Poco Bueno, out of Sheilwin, by Pretty Boy.

"Poco Lena was a quick, growthy kind of colt that looked sort of strung out," recalled Johnson. "Everybody then was looking for a Quarter Horse. They wanted compact muscling and pretty heads. She didn't have any of those things. She was sort of a string bean."

Poco Bueno was a standard for Quarter Horse type, but Poco Lena's dam, Sheilwin, left much to be desired. "She didn't have a muscle on her body," said Johnson, "and she was plain in the head. I would have culled her as a broodmare."

Poco Lena was introduced to cattle as a yearling. From the beginning, her intensity was commanding.

"She always seemed like she had control of a cow," said Johnson. "You never had to go in and pick a cow. You just went in and cut a cow and she'd handle it. And if you really asked her to put out a lot, instead of coming apart and losing her training, she'd just get more intense and try harder."

The bay filly's working style was like her sire's, and Johnson rode with one hand fixed on the saddle horn. "When she went to turn, she'd drop straight down, seemed to me like six or eight inches to the ground, and then glide away," remembered Johnson. "She never did turn standing up."

Don Dodge, of California, bought Poco Lena when she was a long two-year-old. Dodge had owned and shown Poco Lena's full brother, Poco Tivio, as well as the Waggoner-bred world champion Snipper W. In the six years that he owned her, Poco Lena earned nearly $50,000, as well as several AQHA halter championships for Dodge.

In 1959, wealthy Texas oilman B. A. "Barney" Skipper paid Dodge $18,000 for Poco Lena—a record price for a ten-year-old mare. Skipper had ridden Poco Lena's three-quarter sister, Poco Mona, and was sold on the bloodline.

A large, heavy man, Skipper rode with a car seat belt strapped under his chaps and attached to the saddle. He also had the habit of constantly spurring his horses.

"Poco Lena was very sensitive," recalls Johnson. "She responded to the lightest touch. When I heard that Skipper had bought her, I thought that she would never be able to stand it. But she just hung in there."

Although Skipper was a non-pro, Poco Lena was a professional. She adjusted to weight, balance and spurs, never missing a beat. She was NCHA Reserve World Champion under Skipper's saddle for three consecutive years—1959 through 1961.

For ten consecutive years of her career, Poco Lena was never out of the NCHA Top Ten Standings. She was Reserve World Champion five times, a record which may never be equaled. She was NCHA World Champion Mare three times, and placed in 395 cutting events. When she was retired, she had earned $99,782—twice as much as her closest challenger. She remained cutting's all-time leading money earner until surpassed by Mr San Peppy in 1976.

After winning a show in Arizona on September 30, 1962, Skipper flew back to Texas, sending the mare home in a trailer. Skipper was killed when his plane crashed during the early hours of October 1. Poco Lena was not located until October 5. She had been confined to the trailer for three days without food and water. When she was led from the trailer she could barely walk. Severe and chronic laminitis would plague her for the rest of her life. Poco Lena's show career was ended.

Although she was thirteen years old, Poco Lena had never been bred. So great was her reputation, however, Dr. Stephen Jensen of Paicines, California, purchased Poco Lena from Skipper's estate, sight unseen, to breed to his stallion Doc Bar.

"My parents were absolutely horrified at the condition she was in when she arrived," remembers Stephanie Ward, the Jensens' daughter. "She was so horribly crippled the radiologist said he had never seen a coffin bone that wanted to come through the bottom [of the foot] as much as hers had. Her coffin bones were rotated perpendicular."

Later, the Jensens learned the truth about the mare's condition.

"She got foundered with Skipper," says Don Dodge. "He brought her by my place. He fed the hell out of her. He didn't know much about horses and he foundered the mare—and he still kept going."

With the best veterinary care, and after a year and a half of concentrated effort, Poco Lena was pronounced in foal. Little progress was made on her crippled feet, however. She was never completely out of pain, and lived her final years on the lawn of Doc Bar Ranch because, as Stephanie Ward explains, "It was the softest place."

Poco Lena's first foal, a 1967 bay colt, was named Doc O'Lena, in honor

The Foundation 31

Poco Lena with Dry Doc. J. Jensen photo.

of his sire and dam. Her second foal, a 1968 bay colt named Dry Doc, was her last.

"She was a good mother," Stephanie remembers. "If the colts would get away from her, she would get up and hobble over to them. She would rear back on her back legs, and just barely touch her front feet to the ground.

"We had a board fence around the pasture, and when Dry Doc got older and wanted to run, we took the two bottom boards off and he could run out in the pasture with the other mares and foals, and then come back to the lawn with his mother."

Doc O'Lena and Dry Doc learned to nurse while Poco Lena was lying down. Although she was a devoted mother, the pain was often too great for her to stand. She developed huge shoe boils on her elbows and hip from lying on the ground.

Poco Lena's condition declined rapidly after Dry Doc was born. She was put to sleep shortly after he was weaned.

Doc O'Lena, Poco Lena's first son, won the NCHA Futurity in 1970, sweeping the go-rounds, a feat that has never been duplicated. His Finals' score of 223 points was also a Futurity record. Dry Doc followed his brother by winning the 1971 Futurity.

In 1974, Doc O'Lena daughter, Leantoo, won the NCHA Non-Pro

Futurity, and was the first NCHA Futurity Champion to be sired by a champion. In 1975, Lenaette, by Doc O'Lena, won the Futurity with 224 points, breaking her sire's record.

Smart Little Lena, by Doc O'Lena, was the first horse to win the NCHA Futurity, Derby and Super Stakes—the NCHA Triple Crown. In his first three crops of performers, Smart Little Lena sired two Futurity Champions and a Reserve Champion.

Poco Lena, first in the ranks of NCHA Hall of Fame and first in the hearts of many cutting enthusiasts, endured and endures. Don Dodge, who is not free with superlatives, keens in on her fiber and heart: "She could stand the hauling and the doing," says Dodge. "She was a tough mare."

Poco Tivio

Before Poco Lena, there was Poco Tivio. Like his full sister, Poco Tivio was born on the Waggoner Ranch, trained by Pine Johnson and ridden into the leading ranks of NCHA and AQHA cutting performers by Don Dodge.

Poco Tivio set the stage for Poco Bueno foals in 1951 and 1952 when

Poco Tivio. AQHA photo.

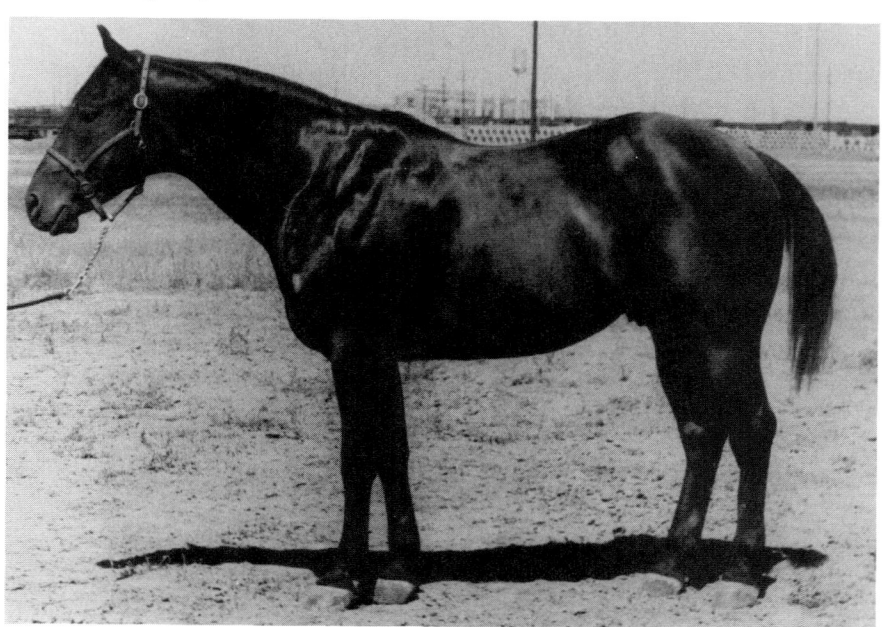

he ranked in the NCHA Top Ten. "Poco Tivio was a nice little horse," remembers Dodge. "But he couldn't compare to Poco Lena. She was a tough mare. I saw Poco Bueno perform when I was riding Poco Tivio. He was a real nice kind of horse. But there were none of those that were equal to her."

Johnson also thought Poco Tivio lacked his sire's presence. "Poco Tivio didn't have the refined, handsome look that Poco Bueno had," said Johnson. "He was a plainer-looking horse—kind of coarse looking. He was kind of temperamental, and he was very strong and aggressive."

By 1953, when Poco Tivio was six, Dodge was on the way to a World Championship with Snipper W and was turning heads with four-year-old Poco Lena. Since he was in the business of showing and selling horses, rather than breeding, he was happy to sell Poco Tivio to fellow Californian Charley Araujo.

Araujo was an astute breeder and showman who believed in the relationship between form and function. He wanted the bulky Poco Bueno son to breed roping and stock horses, which were popular on the West Coast.

Jack and Tom Finley of Gilbert, Arizona, were friends of Araujo's who bred racehorses.

Their goal was to breed a Quarter Horse that would meet all demands. A Finley-bred horse was pretty to look at and hell to outrun. Little Egypt, sired by the Finley stallion Texas Dandy, was a track record setter and a Halter champion. Annie Echols, owned by the Finleys, produced an AQHA Grand Champion; three Halter Champions; and the stakes winner and producer, Fancy Three. Annie Echols was also the dam of Par Three, the sire of AQHA World Champion Halter Horse Zan Parr Bar.

Doc Bar, out of a Texas Dandy mare, was the Finley's greatest gift to the cutting world, although they had tried to make a racehorse out of him. Araujo brought Doc Bar to California and was the alchemist for the Doc Bar and Poco Tivio breeding phenomenon. Since 1970, Doc Bar sons out of Poco Tivio daughters have had a major impact as performers and sires in the cutting world.

Poco Tivio's most successful daughters, all foaled between 1954 and 1957, are Teresa Tivio, dam of Cal Bar, Fizzabar, Nu Bar, Doc's Remedy, Boon Bar, Doc's Haida and Doc Bar Gem; Jameen Tivio, dam of Doc's Lynx, Doc's Prescription, Doc's Hotrodder and Doc's Tom Thumb; Susie's Bay, dam of Doc's Oak, Doc's Solano and Doc's Marmoset; and Bonita Tivio, dam of Peponita.

Puro Tivio, Poco Tivio's son out of Red Jane C, a full sister to Poco Bueno, is the sire of Doc Tari and Doc's Jack Sprat. Johnny Tivio, by Poco Tivio, is the sire of Jimmette Too, the dam of Docs Okie Quixote. And Doc's Haida, out of Teresa Tivio, is the dam of Haidas Little Pep.

Poco Champ

Pine Johnson's favorite foal by Poco Bueno out of Sheilwin was the 1950 bay colt Poco Champ.

"Poco Champ would have been a great horse," said Johnson. "But he ended up without an opportunity. He was very pleasant to work with—even-tempered, and he didn't mind what you were doing, or where you were doing it. If you wanted to gallop, fine. If you wanted to walk, or stand, it didn't matter. He seemed to be at home whatever he was doing.

"Sheilwin's foals were very sensitive and couldn't stand a lot of pain and hurt. Poco Champ was a different temperament than any of the others. He was a lot quieter. The last time I saw him, they had his head tied down with baling wire, and this guy was riding him and whipping him with it. And he said, 'I've about got him where you can do something with him.' Poco Champ couldn't have raised his head if he had wanted to. He wasn't even built to raise his head up.

"I never did abuse a horse. Once in a while, I'll take my gloves off and whoop them with my gloves, if they refuse too much. Poco Bueno, if he would lose a cow, which he didn't lose many, I'd just kind of scold him and say, 'Aw, you know better than that.' And, boy, when he'd cut another cow, I'll tell you, he sure worked."

Pine Johnson was smiling in 1988, when Cols Little Pepper, out of Pepper Champ, by Poco Champ, won all go-rounds of the NCHA Futurity and tied Smart Little Senor in the Finals.

Joe Reed II

The racket was distracting. While stable hands rolled the dice and called on Lady Luck, Della Moore kicked her stall and called to the Thoroughbred down the aisle. Finally, someone turned the chestnut stallion into the big mare's stall. Soon quiet prevailed and the game continued. Della Moore, sprint queen of the Louisiana bayous, came to San Antonio for a match race in 1920 and left with Joe Blair's foal growing in her belly.

Although Joe Blair was one of the fastest short distance Thoroughbreds in the Southwest, Della Moore's owner could make more money racing his big bay mare than by raising a foal. The baby, a colt named Joe Reed, was hardly weaned when his dam was sent back to the track.

Joe Reed was a handsome chestnut, with four white stockings and a blaze, who resembled his sire enough to be registered with the Jockey Club.

The Foundation

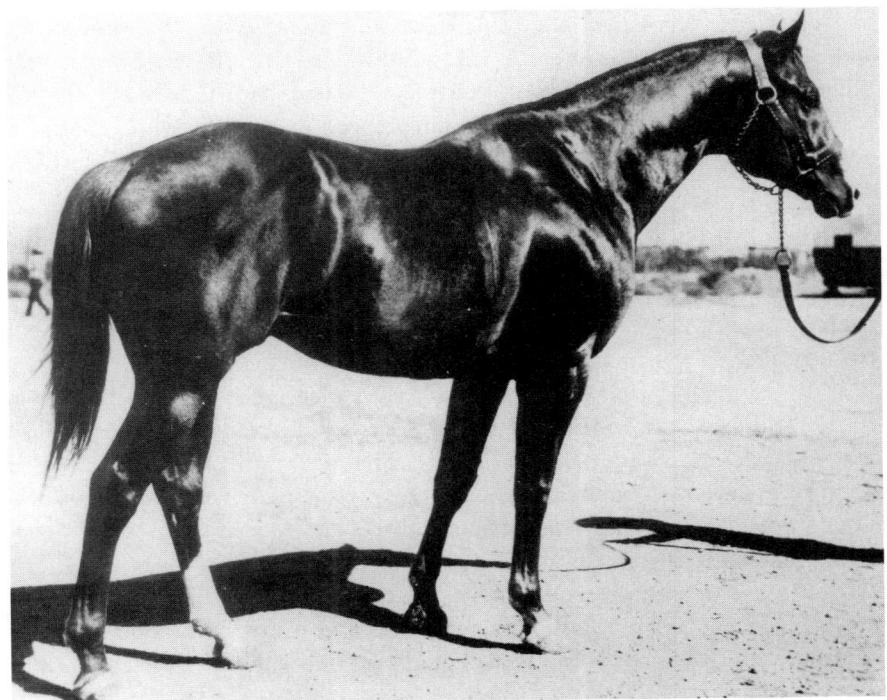

Joe Reed II. AQHA photo.

Although he was a disappointment when raced against Thoroughbreds, he was fast up to the quarter-mile and earned his oats for J. W. House of Cameron, Texas, by siring "short horses" that thundered down Texas straightaway tracks. When bred to mares like Little Red Nell, a descendant of Steel Dust, the early-day prototype for Quarter Horses, Joe got runners like Red Joe of Arizona. Red Joe sired Nelly Bly, the third dam of modern cutting's super sire Doc Bar. When Nellene, a half-sister to Red Joe of Arizona, was bred to Joe Reed, she produced Joe Reed II.

Bert Wood was an Arizona cowboy with an affinity for fast horses. As a youth, Wood earned a few dollars exercising Joe Blair and never forgot the chestnut stallion who was quick enough to challenge Panzarita, the world record holder, at five-eighths of a mile. On a visit to Texas in 1941, Wood discovered five-year-old Joe Reed II, unraced and unbroken, and took him back to Arizona on a freight train. Little Fanny, a Joe Reed daughter who had just weaned Leo, was also part of the sales package, but Leo stayed in Texas.

Ranching was a livelihood for Wood and his wife Dorothy, who raised and trained their horses for cattle work, but hauled them to nearby Hacienda Moltacqua, at Tucson, for weekend races. Wood had high hopes for Joe Reed II as a racehorse, until the stallion stepped on a bottle while chasing a renegade cow down a ravine. Wood tried everything to heal the cut, but even surgery didn't help.

Early in the stallion's seventh year, in spite of his damaged foot, Wood decided to try him in Tucson against some of the nation's fastest quarter-milers. Every Sunday afternoon for three weeks, Joe Reed II ran and won. Exercise between races was out of the question because of his game foot, but Joe flew first to the finish every time the starting gates opened. Clabber, a World Champion runner dubbed the "Iron Horse," chased Joe's tail down the track. Even immortal Shue Fly couldn't top Joe's time in the speed trials.

Joe's victories were costly, however. The crack in his foot widened and he was in pain. He went home undefeated—with the coveted title of World Champion Running Stallion. After his three-win sweep, Joe Reed II never raced again, although he did win several halter championships.

With his reputation established as Joe Reed's best son, Joe Reed II settled into the life of breeding stallion, ranch hand and family pet. Dorothy Wood shared ranch duties with Bert and remembers that she often held Joe's lead shank during breeding, while Bert managed the mares.

"Joe was very gentle," says Dorothy. "Our kids used to ride him bareback and crawl over him and under him. I have a movie where my two-year-old is crawling under his belly with a brush, and sitting between his hind legs. He had a beautiful disposition."

The Woods bred fifty mares a year to their champion at $100 each. Because of his good looks, kind temperament and impressive racing title, Joe Reed II was popular as a sire of both race and show horses.

"Back then they used to talk about the bulldog type [horse] for working cattle and then the racing type," explains Dorothy. "But to me, Joe always personified all in one. He could run but he was also equally as good with cattle."

Quarter Horse breeders of that era were divided into two camps—bulldog advocates and Thoroughbred enthusiasts. But Joe Reed II met both groups' demands.

"He was a lot prettier horse than his sire," remembers Dorothy. "He had beautiful conformation and one of the prettiest heads I've ever seen on a stallion. It was so refined."

Joe seemed to produce good foals from all types of mares, but the Woods' favorite cross was with Little Fanny, a pretty bay mare who was sired by Joe's sire—Joe Reed, by Joe Blair.

The Foundation

"We did quite a lot of line breeding," Dorothy explains about their strategy for breeding Joe Reed II to his half-sisters—the same program House used to get Leo from Little Fanny. "I think that Joe was so strong and had so many good qualities, he overcame things a weaker horse might have shown [in his foals]."

Leo, the first son of Joe Reed II and Little Fanny, heads the list of leading maternal grandsires of Register of Merit qualifiers. Firebrand Reed, another Joe Reed II son out of Little Fanny, sired Star Brandy, the all-time leading dam of fifteen ROM.

Little Sister W and Gusdusted were coal black siblings by Joe Reed II out of Little Fanny. Little Sister W was a track record holder and stakes winner of twenty-two races. Gusdusted was a successful show horse who sired Cutting Champion Black Wasp, the grandam of World Champion Halter Horse Wild Four.

There seemed to be a special affinity between Joe Reed II and Little Fanny that went beyond the breeding shed. Dorothy remembers hearing Fanny call to Joe many mornings: "When Little Fanny was in the pasture she'd come up to the corral fence and call him every day. If he was in the stall, she'd nicker to him and get him to come out and say hi to her."

Little Fanny wasn't the only mare who produced winners when bred to Joe Reed II. From Navie Girl came Joak, a leading maternal sire of show and race ROM. Nevermiss produced Bull's Eye, a leading maternal sire by Joe Reed II. Bull's Eye sired the dam of Doc Quixote, the sire of 1990 NCHA World Champion Cash Quixote Rio.

Even television's most celebrated equine star, Mr. Ed, was sired by Joe Reed II, out of his daughter Anniversary. Anniversary, who produced top runners, was foaled on Bert and Dorothy Wood's wedding anniversary. In 1991 they celebrated their fifty-second anniversary, thirty years after the death of Joe Reed II.

Leo

Much has been made of the fact that Bud Warren of Perry, Oklahoma, paid $2,500 for a seven-year-old stallion with arthritic knees in 1947. But Warren, a savvy horseman and knowledgeable breeder, knew he had a bargain in Leo. He'd heard tales about the "Pawhuska Powerhouse" who won twenty out of twenty-two match races in one season. He also owned two of his daughters—Leota W and Flit. Leota W was one of the fastest Quarter Horses of her era and had won at every official distance from 200 yards to 440. She was from

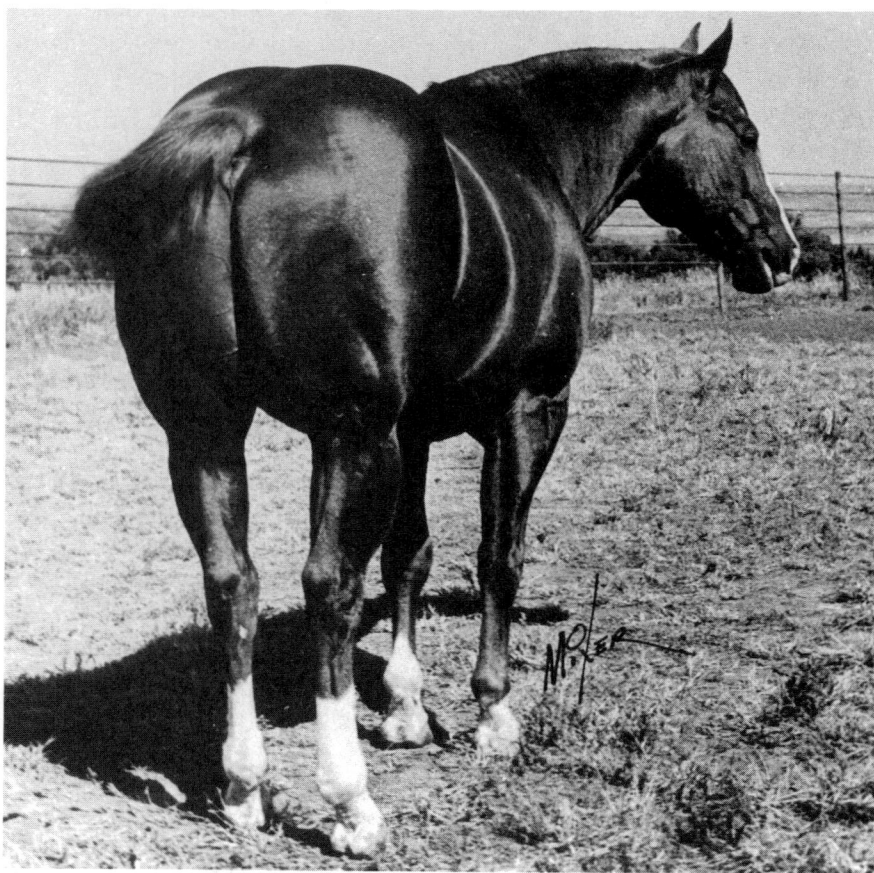

Leo, the "Pawhuska Powerhouse." *AQHA photo.*

Leo's first foal crop, purchased in utero with her dam. Warren put up $1,000 to match eighteen-month Leota W against Miss Bandplay, a short distance speedster that cost Oscar Jeffers $4,000 as a yearling. It must have seemed a steal when Warren bought Leota W's sire for $2,500.

Leota W was all the advertisement Warren needed for his new stallion, and by the early fifties Leo was a leading sire of racing ROM. Everyone wanted a Leo foal. Wilbur Wilson, breeder of Lady Thomas Wilson, the all-time leading dam of seven AAA runners, took two mares to Leo in 1951.

"Leo and Three Bars are the best two sires we ever had," says Wilson. "For a long time I didn't breed to Leo because I didn't have the money. Finally I took Lady Thomas Wilson and another mare up there and it cost

$150 apiece. Lady Leo (the foal from Lady Thomas Wilson and Leo) turned out AAA and a show mare, too. Warren would say, 'This old boy hauled two old crusty mares up here that didn't look like they was worth a dime, and look what he got.' "

Lady Leo is the dam of Win Or Lose, the sire of Sonny Dee Bar, a leading sire and grandsire of AQHA halter and performance champions.

"Leo was a wonderful horse," says Wilson. "He had the heaviest inside back muscle to his leg of any horse I ever saw, and most of them he sired had the same."

Built for explosive getaways that propelled him first under the wire at distances from 200 to 300 yards, the bright sorrel stallion, who stood 14.3 hands and weighed 1,200 pounds, was a burgeoning bundle of strength. A wide blaze, with white front socks and back stockings, added to his appeal.

Bulldog Quarter Horse fanciers loved Leo's powerful physique, but he also had enough refinement for Thoroughbred advocates. Because he was so prepotent for his type, Leo's foals from unregistered or Thoroughbred mares easily qualified for AQHA certification in the days when field inspection was required for registration.

The rear ends of Leo sons and daughters taunted racing adversaries at finish lines and filled the pages of Quarter Horse magazines for decades. Breeders of the fifties and sixties advertised stallions with photographs taken from a three-quarter rear angle—emphasizing their powerful hindquarters. Just the right perspective would capture bulging gaskins and forearms, detonators at the starting gate.

Guy Ray Rutland of Independence, Kansas, bred more race and show ROM than any other horseman. Rutland owned Bar Money, one of the first AQHA champions, but most of his four hundred broodmares carried Leo breeding. Leo is double-bred Joe Reed (Joe Reed is Leo's paternal and maternal grandsire), and Rutland attributed some of his success as a sire to his inbreed pedigree.

"I bred Pacific Bailey's mother back to him," explained Rutland, using Leo's grandson Pacific Bailey as an example. "We got a filly and turned around and bred back to Pacific Bailey again. There was an improvement of conformation with each cross. I think with the right horses you can bring out the strong points with line breeding."

Many horsemen debate the merits of inbreeding, but it is hard to argue with Leo's universal success as a sire and grandsire of racing, halter and performance horses.

Leo daughters have contributed to cutting's top ranks. Flit, by Leo, produced King's Pistol, 1957 World Champion Cutting Horse and the dam's sire of Miss Silver Pistol. Flit also appears in the pedigree of World Champion Ball O'Flash.

Leo Pan, by Leo, is the dam of leading sires Jewels Leo Bars (Freckles) and Son O Sugar. NCHA Futurity Champion Colonel Freckles is by Jewels Leo Bars and out of a Leo great-granddaughter.

Sun Princess, by Leo, is the dam of Zan Sun the 1964 NCHA Futurity Champion, and My Dinah Lea, by Leo, is the dam of 1974 NCHA Futurity Champion Doc's Yuba Lea.

The Leo sons Holey Sox, Okie Leo, Leo's Question and Leo Bingo were all influential cutting sires. Their progeny include War Leo, Mr Gun Smoke and Chickasha Bingo. But Leo San is without a doubt Leo's greatest son in the eyes of the cutting world.

Leo San

Texas oilman Gordon Howell gained a working knowledge of horseflesh in the thirties earning wages as a wrangler on southwestern cattle ranches. He was familiar with bloodlines and particularly liked Joe Reed II horses. As he began accumulating money and broodmares in the mid-fifties, he also scouted for a well-bred stallion.

Like many horsemen of his day, Howell believed a good Quarter Horse should excel in racing, yet possess halter-winning conformation, an easy-going temperament and natural athletic ability. Leo was a template for these qualities. In 1957 Howell purchased seven-year-old Leo San, by Leo out of a Zantanon granddaughter. The next year he bought Peppy Belle, whose dam was a palomino daughter of Gold Rush, the sire of Hollywood Gold.

Hollywood Gold, foaled in 1940, was a popular sire of cowhorses owned by the estate of the great Texas oil and cattle baron Tom Burnett. Burnett horses were raised to fill working ranch remudas and were judged for type and utility rather than pedigree. Breeding records were scant before formation of the American Quarter Horse Association. Belle Burnett's dam, Triangle Lady 17, was registered by inspection. Her sire was Red Buck and her dam is listed as "riding type mare, breeding unknown." The pedigree of the dam of Gold Rush is also unknown, as is the pedigree of Hollywood Gold's dam.

In contrast to Triangle Lady 17, Peppy Belle's sire Pep-Up was a product of the systematic line-breeding program of King Ranch, based on the Old Sorrel.

Peppy Belle's first foal by Leo San, a 1959 sorrel colt named Peppy San,

The Foundation 41

fulfilled Howell's expectations. He was well made, with powerful hindquarters and tremendous heart girth. At maturity he stood 15 hands and weighed 1,250 pounds.

When Matlock Rose, who had ridden 1951 NCHA Reserve World Champion Jessie James, came to work for Howell, he pegged Peppy San as a good prospect for the first NCHA Futurity. Rose and the sorrel colt won the preliminary trial and placed second in the Finals. Howell sold the stallion to C. N. Woodward of Canada shortly after the Futurity, but Rose and Peppy San were to meet again. In 1967 the pair won the NCHA World Championship, and in 1975 Woodward arranged for Peppy San to stand at Rose's Ranch in Aubrey, Texas.

Peppy San was the first World Champion to sire a World Champion— 1975 Open and Non-Pro World Champion Peppys Desire. Peponita, by Peppy San, was 1975 World Champion Stallion, then won the Open Championship in 1977 and 1979. In 1978 Sonita's Last, by Peppy San, was World Champion Stallion. Royal Santana, by Peppy San, won the Non-Pro Reserve World Championship in 1979, and Sanacee is a two-time AQHA World Champion. Peppy San's Canadian Champions include Peppy Isle, Tip It San, Booger San, Chunkys Monkey and Bonita San.

World Champion Gelding Monkey Formula is sired by Chunkys Monkey by Peppy San, and Royal Santana's full sister is Smart Peppy, the dam of NCHA Triple Crown winner and leading sire Smart Little Lena.

Peppy San and Peppy Belle were magic. In 1968, Peppy Belle produced Mr San Peppy, by Leo San. It is doubtful that two full brothers of any breed have been more successful or influential in the performance arena than Peppy San and Mr San Peppy.

Mr San Peppy (see pages 18 to 20) is the 1974 and 1976 World Champion that became the cornerstone of King Ranch's modern breeding program and sired 1982 World Champion Tenino San and 1980 Reserve World Champion Peppy San Badger.

Three Bars

A mediocre racehorse with an unimpressive Thoroughbred pedigree forever changed the look and direction of the Quarter Horse breeding industry.

Three Bars was a 1940 chestnut colt foaled in Kentucky. His sire, Percentage, was a stakes winner, and his dam Myrtle Dee was a sprinter who set a track record in Cincinnati at 5½ furlongs. Both were seventeen-year-olds

Three Bars. AQHA photo.

when Three Bars was foaled, and neither had distinguished themselves with their produce. Myrtle Dee was sold in foal with Three Bars, in a package with two other mares, for $800.

Three Bars was sold for $300, then given away when lameness kept him off the track, by the time he was three years old. Sound enough to run in 1944, he was claimed at Detroit Race Course for $2,000 and hauled to Arizona, where he attracted the attention of Quarter Horse breeder Sid Vail.

Vail had heard about Three Bars' speedy workouts in Tucson and was curious about his potential as a sire of Quarter runners. One look at the well-made colt was enough for Vail. He offered Three Bars' owners $5,000, then agreed to $10,000 with a racing option.

Ten thousand dollars was a whopping sum for any horse in 1945. Paul Waggoner, who had inherited the largest fortune west of the Mississippi, paid $5,500 for Poco Bueno that same year. But Three Bars wasn't any horse to Vail. He was his ideal. From his foxy ears to his flashing feet, Three Bars epitomized the classy, short distance racehorses making headlines in Arizona. Vail was not alone in his opinion of the colt.

"The first time I saw Three Bars, I just fell in love with him and decided

The Foundation

I had to have him some way or another," says legendary Quarter Horse breeder Walter Merrick, who leased Three Bars for a season, in 1951. "When I got him, I just bred everything I had to him, I just liked him that much."

Merrick remembers Three Bars as small for a Thoroughbred—about 15.2 hands. But he was perfectly proportioned, well muscled and weighed about 1,200 pounds.

"Back in that time, people didn't look at a Thoroughbred much for conformation," reflects Merrick. "They went on breeding and endurance. But that's what caught my eye to Three Bars. He was correct and straight and he showed a lot of class. I just liked his looks and conformation."

Cattlemen and cowboys have a keen instinct for symmetry and balance in livestock. While their Kentucky cousins study pedigrees like alchemists in search of gold, cowmen assess flesh and blood with a critical eye. D. Wayne Lukas, the only Thoroughbred trainer to win over $100 million with his runners, eyeballs and evaluates yearlings on conformation before he ever considers pedigree.

Lukas started his career on Quarter Horse tracks and keeps a bronze statue of Easy Jet on his desk—to remind him what a good horse should look like. Easy Jet, many times Quarter Horse running champion and leading sire, was bred by Walter Merrick out of a Thoroughbred daughter of Three Bars.

Not all Quarter Horse breeders liked Three Bars, however. There were purists who wanted to close the Quarter Horse registry to Thoroughbreds and perpetuate the stocky, heavily muscled horses referred to as "bulldogs." Fortunately, the newly formed American Quarter Horse Association inspired the desire for speed and the need for Thoroughbred blood in Quarter Horses.

"A lot of people wanted to keep the Thoroughbred blood out of the Quarter Horse registry," explains Merrick about the mood in the fifties. "But people have realized that those [Quarter-Thoroughbred cross] horses are just more useful and can do things better than a little bulldog can."

In the late thirties and early forties, Merrick built his breeding program around a fleet-footed grey stallion called Midnight, Jr. "He was the best thing around this country at that time," says Merrick. "His colts had tremendous speed, but they didn't run quite far enough. That was the reason I was looking for Thoroughbred blood. I could win lots of races at 220 and 300 yards, but I wanted to go further than that."

Merrick described Midnight, Jr., as a "refined bulldog," the same words Lowell Hankins used to describe King, the influential Quarter Horse stallion owned by his brother Jess. "King was what you'd call a pretty smooth, bulldog-type," Hankins remembers. "He was real refined. Just an average-muscled, bulldog-type Quarter Horse."

The Hankins brothers, Jess, Lowell and J. O., bred Quarter Horses that excelled in all fields, and they all patronized Three Bars. "Three Bars looked like a real stocky-built Thoroughbred," recalls Hankins. "He showed to have a little Thoroughbred in him, but he didn't show that much."

Three Bars proved his siring ability with his first crop, in 1948, when Barred and Glass Bars set track records. By 1954 he was the all-time leading sire of AAA Quarter racing horses, and in 1960 his stud fee was $10,000. But the refined good looks and athletic ability of his foals attracted more than race enthusiasts.

Lightning Bar, a 1951 Three Bars son, earned AAA-rating racing at two, then became an AQHA Arena Champion. He inherited his sire's style and balance and passed these qualities to foals bred at Art Pollard's Lightning A Ranch in Tucson. Many good race horses were sired by Lightning Bar, but his place in cutting history comes through a son that couldn't run—Doc Bar.

Glamour Bars, Lightning Bar's daughter out of a Sugar Bars daughter, made history with her son Impressive, the all-time leading sire of AQHA World Champions. Impressive is by Lucky Bar, a Thoroughbred son of Three Bars.

Although Doc Bar is small in stature compared to the massive Impressive, both stallions were stamped with Three Bars' hallmarks—long, deep hip; short, strong back; deep heart girth; sculpted neck; lovely head and luminous eyes.

The very first three AQHA Supreme Champions were Three Bars sons—Kid Meyers, Fairbars and Bar Money. Cee Bars, a 1950 son of Three Bars, was a AAA runner and stakes sire that also sired cutting horses. Cee Bars Joan, by Cee Bars, was the 1969 NCHA Futurity Champion. Her full sister Cee Holly Joanie was a Futurity finalist, as were the Cee Bars daughters Cee Miss Snapper and Cee Miss Holly.

Sugar Bars was another AAA running Three Bars son that sired champions in all arenas. Bud Warren, Leo's owner, acknowledged Three Bars' standing in the Quarter Horse industry and purchased Sugar Bars to breed to his Leo daughters. The cross was magic.

Jewels Leo Bars, the fountainhead of cutting's "Freckles" line of horses, was sired by Sugar Bars, out of Leo Pan, by Leo. Not only was Freckles a leading performer and sire, but the foals of his sons Freckles Playboy and Colonel Freckles bring top dollars in today's sales and cutting arenas. Son O Sugar, a full brother to Freckles, was also an outstanding sire.

Flit was another Warren-owned Leo daughter who matched well with Sugar Bars, although her first triumph was NCHA World Champion King's Pistol, by King. Flit's Sugar Bars' son, Sugar Leo, sired Sugar Vaquero, the 1973 NCHA World Champion. Flit Bar, out of Flit by Sugar Bars, is the

Sugar Bars. AQHA photo.

paternal grandsire of 1984 and 1985 NCHA World Champion Ball O'Flash.

Other outstanding cutting horses that carry the blood of Sugar Bars include Non-Pro NCHA World Champion Doc's Otoetta; AQHA Champions and full brothers Doc's Sug and Docs Sugs Brudder; 1975 NCHA Futurity Champion Lenaette; and the full sisters Sugarnic, Springinic, Wininic, and Picinic—all champion producers.

Daughters of Three Bars and King were highly valued as broodmares. Their produce consistently graced winner's circles in all events. When the champion King daughter Gay Widow was bred to Three Bars, she produced Gay Bar King, one of cutting's greatest broodmare sires. Although Gay Bar King never distinguished himself in performance, his progeny carried the torch. Gay Bar's Gen and Gay Bars Blues are both three-time NCHA Non-Pro World Champions sired by Gay Bar King. Gay Bar Lady, by Gay Bar King, was an AQHA champion who produced AQHA Reserve World Champion Doc Ware and Super Stakes Reserve Champion Sugs Gay Lady. Other Gay Bar King daughters have produced the leading money earners Doctor What, The Papa Doc, Oak Doll and The Widow Wilson.

Doc Bar

Two time periods divide the history of contest cutting—B.D.B. and A.D.B.— before Doc Bar and after Doc Bar.

In just one decade this little sorrel stallion revolutionized the cutting industry. Modern cutting pedigrees teem with Doc Bar progeny. It is difficult to find cutting horses that do not carry his blood. Ironically, he was never shown under saddle. The race track was Doc Bar's first proving ground, and he was an abysmal failure.

"I remember one race Doc Bar ran," says Art Pollard, the owner of Doc Bar's sire. "The gate opened and he broke and ran about fifty yards and came in last by about ten lengths—way back in the dust. After the race Tom and Jack Finley came and asked me if I would give $1,000 for him, which was about what they had in him—with the stud fee and raising him, and this race. They didn't know what to do with him. He was the cutest little thing. You wanted to put him on a watch fob.

"I said, 'I wouldn't give my pocketknife. He's not my type—the little dumpling-assed thing.' So two fools met—they fool enough to offer him, and I fool enough to refuse him."

Doc Bar, a 1956 foal, was bred and raised to be a racehorse by Tom and Jack Finley of Gilbert, Arizona. The Finley brothers raised do-it-all Quarter Horses that were pretty enough to win ribbons in halter classes, and fast enough to earn bucks on race tracks. Because they liked Clabber, the 1941 World Champion Running Horse that ranched all week and raced on week-

Doc Bar. AQHA photo.

ends, the Finleys purchased Texas Dandy, a stallion by My Texas Dandy, Clabber's sire.

Texas Dandy, teamed with Finley mares, began siring winners in his first crop. Little Egypt, a 1949 Texas Dandy mare, was a track record setter and one of the first AQHA Halter Champions.

Dandy Doll, Doc Bar's dam, was from Texas Dandy's second crop of foals. A moderate success on the race track, Dandy Doll was a good producer for the Finleys. Although Doc Bar was a disappointment, he had five ROM siblings, two that were AAA rated.

At the time the Finleys bred Dandy Doll to Lightning Bar, her three-quarter sister Dandy Duchess, by Texas Dandy, had already established a stakes winning record. Dandy Duchess was bred to Three Bars in 1954 and Dandy Doll went to Lightning Bar, in 1955.

Lightning Bar was full brother to Bardella, a World Champion Running Mare. The big sorrel's race career was cut short by injury, but his celebrated pedigree and bold good looks forecast siring success. The Finleys liked Three Bars, who gave distance and refinement to foals from their stout, sprinting mares. Casbar, by Three Bars out of the Finleys' champion Little Egypt, won two stakes races as a two-year-old the year Doc Bar was born. Both of Dandy Doll's AAA runners were sired by Bar Bob, a Three Bars son. Doc Bar, however, was his mother's son.

"Doc Bar took after Dandy Doll," says Pollard. "She was a little apple-rumped, tight-twisted mare, like so many of the Texas Dandys were. Texas Dandy was a rangy horse, but he sired a lot of very close-coupled Steel Dust types. They could really blast for a couple hundred yards."

"Lightning Bar had the best hip and back leg that I have ever seen before or since," says Pollard. "He was pin eared, long muzzled and pig eyed. He was not forked [in the chest] and he was flat withered. But he was a sight to see. I think in halter he was only beaten one time."

Doc Bar inherited a short back and small stature from his dam, and a pretty head from Three Bars. He also had a special presence and refinement not usually seen in cutting horses of the fifties.

Although Doc Bar chased tails on the track, the Finleys' friend Charley Araujo, of Coalinga, California, thought he might turn heads as a halter horse. His bright chestnut coat and four white socks guaranteed he would be noticed.

Smoothly balanced athletes were winning over bulky, muscle-bound counterparts in California show rings. Araujo, an accomplished showman, collected a modest array of championships with Doc Bar, including the Reserve Championship at the 1962 Pacific Coast Quarter Horse Association show. Then he bred him to his Poco Tivio and Jimmie Reed daughters, hoping to reinforce the athletic ability of the pedigrees and to give some refinement to the foals.

Part of Doc Bar's allure for Araujo and other breeders was his Three Bars pedigree. Three Bars was the hottest horse around. By the sixties his stud fee was $10,000 and out of reach for most mare owners. Only race breeders, who stood a chance to recover the cost, could afford to breed to Three Bars. His foals excelled everywhere they were asked to perform. The first three AQHA Supreme Champions were sired by Three Bars: Kid Meyers, Fairbars and Bar

Money (Supreme Champions must earn a AAA rating on the track and points in performance classes and halter).

Three Bars was extremely prepotent. Not only were his foals race winners, but they had a special refinement that would come to epitomize Quarter Horse type. Short, pretty heads with large eyes and foxy little ears were Three Bars trademarks, along with slender, well-shaped necks attached to muscular bodies.

Charley Araujo was breeding Quarter Horses before the AQHA existed. After its formation he became a respected judge and competitor, as well as a Quarter Horse inspector in California. In 1952 Araujo bought the AQHA Champion Poco Tivio from Don Dodge, who had Poco Tivio's full-sister Poco Lena waiting in the wings.

Dodge had qualified Poco Tivio for NCHA World Champion standings, but Araujo showed him mostly in stock horse classes and bred him to get all-around using horses from his Ben Hur and Jimmie Reed mares and Red Jane C, a full sister to Poco Bueno.

In 1962 Araujo sold Doc Bar to Dr. Stephen Jensen of Paicines, California, who already owned some Araujo-bred Poco Tivio mares. That same year Doc Bar was Grand Champion Stallion at the Cow Palace, and his son Barlet and daughter Janie Bar were Reserve Champion Stallion and Mare.

Fizzabar, out of the Poco Tivio daughter Teresa Tivio, was Doc Bar's first cutting star. Ridden by Don Dodge, Fizzabar became 1968 NCHA World Champion Mare.

In 1969 Doc Bar foals swept second through fourth places in the NCHA Futurity, followed by 1970 and 1971 Futurity Championships for Doc Bar sons Doc O'Leana and Dry Doc. By 1983, twenty-one of the twenty-three NCHA Futurity Finalists had Doc Bar in their pedigrees.

Since Doc Bar had never performed as a cutting horse, many horsemen assumed his foals inherited cow sense from their dams. But many Three Bars sons and daughters were cowhorses.

"I used to hear that it was too bad, the kind of horse that Lightning Bar was, that he wouldn't look at a cow, and it just creamed my milk," says Pollard, who remembers the time an exercise rider entered Lightning Bar in a jackpot roping—and won. A neighbor, Eddie Tappen, filled him in on the details.

"Boy, can that big, young horse rope," Tappen told Pollard. "Remember all the wild cattle you used to see in the wash? Those Lightning Bar hasn't run out of the valley, he broke their necks."

"He was so big and powerful, when the cows hit the end of that nylon, sometimes it was a hell of a wreck," says Pollard. "All this was going on and

I thought Frankie was simply riding him. I had to put a stop to that merry-go-round."

Pollard loved Lightning Bar's sensible and kind disposition. "I have pictures of him working a rope with tack on and dragging a three-year-old kid that is on the ground," says Pollard.

By 1970 every cutter wanted a Doc Bar son or daughter to ride. Leon Harrel rode the Doc Bar daughter Doc's Date Bar in the NCHA Futurity that year. Since that time Harrel has made champions of Cal's Cindy Ann, Doc's Yuba Lee, Nu Niner Bar, Smart Date and Doc's Playmate—all Doc Bar get or grandget.

"Almost all the horses I have ridden have been Doc Bar horses," says Harrel. "If you treated them with kindness and showed them what you wanted, they would be responsive. They were too smart to stand up to a lot of pressure, and they really didn't need it. They didn't want you to be harsh with them at all. Some of the other bloodlines require a little stronger tactics to get the same results."

Buster Welch concurs with Harrel. "Everybody said that you couldn't train them," remembers Welch about the first Doc Bar horses. "They said that they were too chicken-hearted and couldn't take the punishment. People back then were real tough on their horses."

Because Doc Bar progeny were different in appearance and temperament from their contemporaries, yet similar to each other in type and talent, rumors circulated about his pedigree.

"When you look at Doc Bar, that horse has to have some Arabian in him," says a former AQHA president. "That keen head that he had—nobody can verify that, but I suspect there is some Arabian blood that was not documented."

Stephanie Ward thinks the rumors about Doc Bar are ludicrous. "It hardly seems likely that Tom Finley, a past president of the American Quarter Horse Association, would surreptitiously take an Arabian mare to Lightning Bar, and raise a colt that he would then illegally register as a Quarter Horse," says Ward.

Buster Welch has an interesting theory about Doc Bar. "Doc Bar was about seven-eighths Thoroughbred and he looked just like a little Arab horse," says Welch. "I think that through selection they retrogressed him back to an Arab. They have a 1776 village in Pennsylvania, and all the livestock are like they were in that day. They say the chickens were the easiest to get that way because you can retrogress a chicken back to a wild chicken, I believe, in sixteen crosses. Like Doc Bar, unbeknowing, somewhere in the selection of that cross retrogressed back to the Arab."

Rumors and stories are as substantial as air. Doc Bar's success as a sire and grandsire is solid granite. Between 1984 and 1989, Doc Bar was the leading paternal grandsire of NCHA money earners with $51.4 million earned from total purses of $108.4 million. His son Doc O'Lena was second on the list with $8.4 million.

THREE

The Futurity

Cutting came of age in 1962 with the inauguration of the NCHA Futurity. While other arena horse contestants vied for ribbons and small jackpots, cutters rode for big bucks in one prestigious event.

"At the time the Futurity was conceived, it was a period of slow growth," remembers Zack Wood, long-time executive secretary of NCHA. "There was just one kind of cutting event, with open or novice horses. There was really nothing from a breeder-interest standpoint. Most of the open horses were older. So this was a way to involve people in raising better horses. And it developed a purse structure that changed the business completely."

Wood saw the NCHA Futurity grow from 36 entries in 1962 to a $2 million event with nearly 900 entries.

"We had an $18,000 purse that first year," remembers Wood. "The biggest purse that a cutting horse had worked for before that was maybe $6,000. To compete for $18,000 in two days was a pretty big shock to some of those fellows.

"Before the Futurity all the cutting horse finals were total [accumulated] scores. The Futurity was the only finals that stood on its own. So this was a departure, to pay all that money on the one run—the last one."

Because it was limited to three-year-olds that had never been shown, the Futurity offered an equal opportunity for everyone.

"The only honors at that time worth mentioning was the Horse of the Year," explains C. E. "Charlie" Boyd, a host of the first Futurity. "That was a pulling contest—who could afford to pull [their horse] the most.

"We tried to set this up so that the old boy out there in the country, that couldn't afford to pull all the time, could take his horse and have a chance to compete against everybody on a pretty even scale."

The Futurity

NCHA membership included successful ranchers and businessmen who loved cutting horses and wanted to promote their sport. When they put their heads together they made things happen.

"We were trying to figure an incentive for developing a new horse every year," remembers Buster Welch. "Ranches had gone down in their breeding of cowhorses and cutting horses because there wasn't any market for them. There was a market for halter horses. And it looked like they were ruining the horse trying to breed a halter horse. Nobody knew what a halter horse was anyway.

"We were trying to generate enough money to make it worthwhile to breed and train a horse for that one show. The main thing was to do a little bit like Chevrolet—to have them outdated in a year—to where everybody needed a new one."

Creating Legends

The Futurity became a proving ground and showcase for sires and potential sires, as well as three-year-olds. Peppy San and Hollywood Bill, second- and third-place finalists in the first Futurity, became popular sires due in part to their Futurity performances. Peppy San is the sire and grandsire of many champions, including Peppy's Desire, Peponita, Royal Santana and Chunkys Monkey. Hollywood Bill sired Magnolia Moon, the dam of Montana Doc. Montana Doc is the sire of Millie Montana, 1990 NCHA Futurity Champion.

King Glo, Leo San and Hollywood Gold, leading sires of the first Futurity, have contributed greatly to the modern cutting horse. Each succeeding crop of Futurity horses gave breeders a gauge for future success. In the beginning, however, breeding cutting horses was often a hit-or-miss proposition.

"The trouble then, people didn't pay enough attention," explains Welch. "They would just go and buy a lot of cheap mares that had no reason to be cowhorses. They wasted a lot of good stud power. Seemed like when you found a stud that had a great deal of cow, people thought they could just go buy every kind of old, ill-bred mare and breed her to that horse."

One early successful breeder was Gordon Howell of Dallas, who bred Peppy San, then gave the world his full brother Mr San Peppy. Familiar dam lines began reappearing in pedigrees of Futurity Finalists. Miss Ginger Dee, 1964 Futurity Co-Champion, produced two Futurity Finalists. Chickasha Ann, dam of Chickasha Glo and Chickasha Dan, 1963 and 1965 Futurity Champions, produced six Finalists from eleven foals. Her Futurity Champions were sired by King Glo.

The concept of a futurity, where contestants are selected or "nominated" a year or more in advance of the event, originated with horse racing. A purse, composed of nomination fees paid in advance, is one of the drawing cards. Nominating young horses a year or more in advance of an event means gambling that they will train well, stay healthy and sound and be ready on one specific date. Since the market value of promising performers is greatly enhanced by nomination, the risk seems worth taking. Anticipation adds to the allure.

Age of contestants was a special concern for the original Futurity planners. Handling the physical and mental stress of cutting horse competition is a tall order for young horses. The Futurity was supposed to be a debut, not a coup de grace. NCHA members were well aware of the graveyards created by a greedy racing industry. Although cutters were anxious to prove their young horses, they didn't want to destroy them.

"Two-year-olds couldn't stand the strain," Wood explains. "The bone development wasn't there. But they didn't want to wait until they were four, so they settled on the latter part of the three-year-old year."

It was an inspired decision. Coming four-year-olds were primed for a first outing, and the year-end show date spotlighted sires for the upcoming breeding season.

The NCHA Futurity was the first major limited-age event for cutting horses. In 1970 the NCHA Derby, for four-year-olds, was initiated, and in 1981 the NCHA Super Stakes, also for four-year-olds. Although the Super Stakes is a contest limited to the progeny of subscribed stallions, and therefore not open to all horses, the Futurity, Derby and Super Stakes became known as the Triple Crown of cutting. In 1985 the Breeders Cutting, also a progeny contest, was added to the roster of major NCHA limited age events.

Five- and six-year-old classes are now a part of the Derby, Super Stakes and Breeders Cutting, along with corresponding non-pro and amateur divisions. Some of the other large open and non-pro events across the country, include the Bonanza Cutting, the Memphis Futurity, the Augusta Futurity, the Masters Cutting, the Non-Pro, the Pacific Coast Cutting Stakes, the Sunbelt Futurity, the Will Rogers Futurity, the Pacific Coast Derby and Futurity, the Solid Gold Futurity and the NCHA National and World Championships.

The NCHA Futurity was the premiere event of the cutting year. A rich purse attracted competitors, but people also came just to inspect each new crop of horses and to buy, sell and trade. Because so much money rode on this one event, training was continually refined to develop the most polished performers. Heroes emerged both in and under the saddle.

The Futurity

Gene Suiter, NCHA Hall of Fame Rider, began showing Futurity horses in 1967. "I'd always go to Sweetwater [Texas] to get ready for the Futurity," remembers Suiter. "Buster Welch and Shorty Freeman and Leon Harrel and Pat Patterson and James Kenney would all be there. As a matter of fact, I sat right there and watched Doc O'Lena being prepared and trained. That little coliseum would take sixty or seventy percent of the money (at the Futurity). What was really neat about it, they showed everyone how to develop a horse without cruelty.

"I saw some of the great horses developed through the influence of Buster Welch. He was one of the first guys to really show how to develop these horses without any harshness. He's a genius."

Cutters worldwide recognize one Buster. Horseman, rancher, cowboy, World Champion, teacher, mentor, philosopher, historian, innovator—Buster Welch wears all these hats, and more.

Welch was born near Sterling City, Texas, in 1928. His mother died when he was three weeks old, and he was raised by his grandparents on a West Texas stock farm.

At thirteen, with a sixth-grade education, an "uncluttered mind" and a burning desire to learn all he could about ranching, Welch left home on an old bronc named Handsome Harry. Hustling for bed, board and wages on some of the great ranches of the Southwest, Welch cultivated a natural talent for working with horses.

In the early fifties he began earning money training cutting horses for people who wanted them shown in contest arenas. With clients like Gordon Howell, Marion Flynt and S. J. Agnew, and horses like Marion's Girl and Mr San Peppy, Welch soon became a moving force in the cutting industry.

Welch had already won the World Championship, in 1954 and 1956 with Marion's Girl, when he captured the first NCHA Futurity.

1962

Sweetwater, Texas, home of the world's largest annual Rattlesnake Roundup, played host to the first NCHA Futurity on November 23 and 24, 1962.

Forty-seven nominees were honed to thirty-six riders competing for the $18,375 purse. Peppy San, ridden by Matlock Rose, won the semifinals, but the bay gelding Money's Glo, owned by C. E. Boyd, Jr., and ridden by Buster Welch, took the finals.

Boyd grew up riding broncs and breaking horses in Nolan County, not far from Sweetwater. His father was a rancher, but a horse trader at heart, and young Charlie learned how to appreciate good horseflesh by observing his father's transactions. He also came to covet it.

"He had a philosophy, that as soon as a horse got to be worth $100, he'd sell it," remembers Boyd. "We'd go to the pasture, get a damn bronc and start all over again. That's the way I grew up and I swore if I ever got grown with money of my own, I'd get some good horses."

The money came and so did the horses. King Glo, a good-looking bay stallion raised by J. O. Hankins of Rocksprings, Texas, was one of Boyd's first purchases, in the late 1950s. King Glo was followed by his son Money's Glo, a horse as rough and common as King Glo was handsome.

"I had real good luck picking out horses," admits Boyd. "And I didn't necessarily go out and buy the biggest prices. King Glo, at the time, was a record-breaking price. When I bought Money's Glo, nobody but me would have given $100 for the horse. He was just a pure, one-hundred-percent mustang."

Instinct guided Boyd in selecting horses, but King P-234 was his touchstone.

King, foaled in 1932, was sired by Zantanon, "the Mexican Man o' War," and out of Jabalina. Jess Hankins bought him for a sire from Winn DuBose and Byrne James, who were using him as a rodeo roping horse. By the late 1950s, King's reputation as a sire was superseded only by that of his son Poco Bueno.

King Glo, a 1953 black stallion, was out of Hyglo, who equaled the world record for 400 yards in 1946 and was the dam of AAA rated runners. Her dam was Jetty H, by King, also a race producer. King Glo, who never raced, was destined to sire arena champions rather than runners, although he favored his dam's sire—the Thoroughbred Hygro—in appearance.

"He was a good-looking horse," says Boyd. "He showed a lot of that Thoroughbred. He didn't favor King at all, but he had the temperament of a Quarter Horse. At the ranch we would just turn him loose in the yard and mares would come up and he wouldn't do nothing. The fence wasn't but four feet tall—a yard fence. But he never put his foot in the wire or that kind of stuff. He was fantastic. Money's Glo was a lot that way, too."

Boyd's first King Glo foals were yearlings in 1962. Since the stallion was nominated for the $1,000 NCHA Futurity Breeder's Award, Boyd wanted one of his three-year-olds for the event. He bought Money's Glo, who was out of Our Money by Red Star Joe, from George Pardi, the owner of 1958 NCHA World Champion Slats Dawson.

Money's Glo was trained for stock work by Leo Huff, and won the Junior World Roping Horse Championship when he was two. It was Buster Welch, however, who trained the gelding for cutting and rode him in the NCHA Futurity.

This Futurity win was the first of five for Welch, already recognized as a top trainer of cutting horses with 1954 and 1956 NCHA World's Champion Marion's Girl, owned by Marion Flynt.

Money's Glo was also the first horse Welch ever trained using a revolutionary new tool—the round pen. It was a concept that Welch had pondered for some time, but perfected with the bay gelding. Today, round pens are standard for training horses around the world.

"I just wasn't getting that stop on my horses," Welch remembers. "This pony had a lot of stuff right in front of a cow, but I'd have trouble on those ends. I'd read an article about how you couldn't solve a problem until you could diagram it. And I got to thinking a roundup, that I learned to train horses, was a circle.

"I'd sent about eight hundred steers up near Wagonwheel, above the timberline in Colorado. I took some horses with me and there was a big round corral up there where the steers would come for water and salt. I'd cut one out and go to fooling with him, and I got to liking what I was getting done.

"I found that I could just go along five miles if I needed to without breaking a horse's concentration with a cow. And that's where I got that stop on Money's Glo. I stayed up there about two weeks and came back and it wasn't but about two weeks until the Futurity. And I made the most dramatic turnaround right up there in that round pen."

Welch thought King Glo sons and daughters were some of the best cutting horses of that time.

"Money's Glo and Chickasha Glo [1963 NCHA Futurity Champion] were probably as good as were being bred then," says Welch.

"Had King Glo lived and been crossed with some of the modern horses, like Doc Bar mares, I think he would have really contributed a lot."

It is interesting to ponder King Glo's potential if he had lived beyond twelve years of age and bred the number and quality of mares available to today's top stallions. Despite the handicaps, he sired three NCHA Futurity winners.

Boyd agrees with Welch. "At the time we bought King Glo, people weren't as bloodline conscious as they've become through the years," says Boyd. "As I got into it more, I gradually started paying attention to the bloodlines. Originally, I didn't really research King Glo's pedigree, except what everybody knew about King."

With another promising King Glo three-year-old in his barn for the 1963 NCHA Futurity, Boyd sold Money's Glo to Repps Guiter of Abilene, who continued showing him with Welch. The gelding placed in the NCHA Top Ten in 1964 and 1965 and earned over $22,000 in cutting arenas during his lifetime. So highly did the Guiter family think of Money's Glo, when he died, they carried him back to Sweetwater, to be buried next to his sire. A handsome monument marks the graves of King Glo and the first NCHA Futurity Champion.

1963

For C. E. Boyd, Buster Welch and King Glo, 1963 was a repeat performance with a new lead—Chickasha Glo. It was, however, a premiere event for a great producer. Chickasha Ann, dam of Chickasha Glo, is the leading dam of the NCHA Futurity. Six of her eleven foals have been Futurity Finalists and two were Champions.

Welch had a special interest in his second Futurity Champion, Chickasha Glo. Although C. E. Boyd was her owner, Welch had owned and bred her dam Chickasha Ann.

Chickasha Ann is the all-time leading producer of NCHA Futurity Finalists, with sons and daughters that are producing legacies of their own. She was special to Welch in 1959, however, because she was a daughter of Chickasha Mike.

In the late 1940s, while working on the Colorado ranch of Homer Ingham, Welch was introduced to the progeny of Old Mike by Chickasha Bob. Owned by John Zurick, Old Mike had earned a reputation for talent, guts and tenacity by winning a straightaway race, cutting horse contest and tie-down steer roping all in one weekend at the New Mexico State Fair.

Welch especially liked one blaze-faced sorrel colt of Ingham's, out of an Old Mike daughter. The stallion (later named Mike), which was running with a band of Ingham's mares, had been bred by N. T. Baca and owned by Warren Shoemaker.

"Warren Shoemaker," says Welch, "was what I would call the George Washington of the modern-day Quarter Horse breeders. He was the first to set out to breed a modern Quarter Horse with speed, action and cow sense."

Ingham's Old Mike-bred stallion seemed to exemplify all of the Shoemaker qualities. Welch had watched him handle his band of mares and liked the way the sorrel could stop and roll back. He was handy, as were his foals, which were also full of cow.

Partnering on some mares and foals with Midland, Texas, rancher Alan

Cowden, Welch was soon able to recoup his cost on Mike. Welch provided his stallion's services and Cowden provided his ranch mares.

One of Cowden's mares that went to Mike was Maggie, a Billy Clegg granddaughter out of the unregistered mare Grey Eagle. Maggie Cowden foaled a bay filly in 1952 that Welch named Miss Chickasha, in honor of her sire. Mike was registered Chickasha Mike, in honor of his grandsire Chickasha Bob.

In 1954 Maggie produced two fillies by Chickasha Mike. Chickasha Lady, a chestnut, was an early foal, and Chickasha Ann, a sorrel, couldn't wait for the new year and came with the close of 1954. Chickasha Ann was a small mare that resembled her Spanish mustang ancestors more than her sire. Refined rather than heavily muscled, she was nevertheless quick and agile.

Welch never showed Chickasha Ann and doesn't remember even having trained her. Her destination was the broodmare band, along with Chickasha Lady and Miss Chickasha. Progeny of these mares include NCHA champions Chickasha Dan, Annie Glo, Chickasha Gay, Chickasha Ann Doc, Chickasha Anita, Chick An Tari, Tari Chick Gay, Chickasha Marie, Chickasha Bingo and Doc's Hickory.

Chickasha Mike sired other foals, but none as outstanding as the three sisters from Maggie Cowden. Maggie produced four more daughters, including Maria Reed by Asido Reed. Maria Reed is the grandam of Chickasha Marie, NCHA Non-Pro Hall of Fame, and Limited Age Event Champion Pacman Playboy.

Welch sold Chickasha Mike to trainer J. T. Fisher, who won the Reserve NCHA World Championship with him in 1956—second to Welch and Marion's Girl. Chickasha Ann, with the future Futurity champion Chickasha Dan by her side, was sold to one of Welch's clients, Dr. Allen Hamilton of Big Spring, Texas, in 1962.

It was the little sorrel mare Chickasha Glo, owned by C. E. Boyd, that was the harbinger of all the Chickashas to come. She was also the first of six leading cutting horses sired by King Glo out of Chickasha Ann.

Chickasha Glo was her mother's daughter in appearance. While Money's Glo had King Glo's large stature and deep heart girth, Chickasha Glo was small, with a pretty head. Both horses inherited King Glo's intelligence and willing disposition, however, as well as his quickness and speed.

Forty-five entries competed for $12,862 in the 1963 Futurity, held at Sweetwater's Nolan County Coliseum. Jose Uno, ridden by James Kenney, won the preliminary go-round, but Chickasha Glo won the Finals. Cutter's First, the first foal sired by 1962 World Champion Cutter Bill, was Reserve Champion.

Boyd sold Chickasha Glo for $6,500 shortly after the Futurity, to a family who intended to use her as a barrel racing horse. She died before ever producing a foal.

1964

Texas State Fair Coliseum in Dallas served 1964 Futurity contestants. There was a lot of publicity and fanfare for the cutters, who posed their horses around the pool of a Dallas hotel for news photos.

Two horses shared the Futurity spotlight. Miss Ginger Dee and Zan Sun earned identical scores and were named Co-Champions. Bob Byrd of Snyder, Texas, was owner and rider of Miss Ginger Dee. He had also trained her sire, the top World Championship competitor, Mr. Gold 95.

1965

Something special happened in 1965 that served as an impetus to the growth of NCHA competition—an amateur won the Futurity and he won it big.

Dr. Allen Hamilton was an optometrist from Big Spring, Texas, who liked to hang over the corral fence and watch Buster Welch work cattle. Hamilton knew rodeo champion Toots Mansfield and had dabbled in calf roping under Mansfield's tutelage. Then Hamilton saw Welch win a cutting contest on Chickasha Mike, and he forgot all about roping.

It wasn't long before Hamilton, determined to learn how to cut, was mounted on one of Welch's turnback horses. After letting Hamilton get a feel for the action as a turnback rider, Welch put him on a bay Arabian stallion.

"He was a good horse that could really work a cow and he was just as solid as could be," said Welch. "I told Doc to cut a white heifer that I knew would work a horse plumb back to the herd. I went to pushing her, and boy, this little bay stud went to work.

"I'd see Doc's hand nearly on this horse's knee. Then he was pulling the mane. He'd get back up and be nearly behind the saddle. Finally the old heifer stopped and Doc looked up and his glasses were hanging on one ear, and his shirt was torn."

When Hamilton asked how he rated, Welch grinned and said, "Doc, you're not the best rider I ever saw, but you are absolutely the best climber."

From his start on the bay Arabian, Hamilton proceeded to etch his name into the NCHA and AQHA record books. He never forgot Chickasha Mike.

The Futurity

In 1962 Hamilton bought Chickasha Mike's daughter Chickasha Ann from Welch. The sorrel mare was out of Bum Cowden's Maggie, and she had Chickasha Dan, by King Glo, at her side.

With Welch's help, Hamilton learned to stay in the saddle and was soon working with two-year-old Chickasha Dan. "I helped him, but he seventy-five-percent trained that horse himself," says Welch. "He was the best I had seen at that time. And he came on and won it, and won it real handy.

"I sold more horses and had more people interested in cutting after that Futurity. There's a little eye doctor from Big Spring that walks right in there and beats all the horse trainers. That encouraged everybody to become a cutting horse rider."

Chickasha Dan was one of 235 nominees for the $46,958 Futurity, and his winner's share, $7,274, was the largest single check ever awarded for one cutting event. His finals score of 218 points was one point above Reserve Champion Christmas Four ridden by Matlock Rose.

Hamilton had Annie Glo, a full sister to Chickasha Dan, well on her way in training when he sold Chickasha Dan to Casey Burns Cantrell of Nara Visa, New Mexico. Cantrell won the 1967 Reserve Non-Pro World Championship with the bay stallion, and in 1968 Chickasha Dan was named NCHA World Champion, having beaten former World Champions Patty Conger and Senor George, and future World Champion Jose Uno.

Chickasha Dan was the first horse to become both an NCHA Futurity Champion and a World Champion. He held that distinction until Doc's Marmoset won the World Championship in 1981.

Annie Glo, Chickasha Dan's full sister, missed the 1966 Futurity Finals, but she was a leading open competitor for Valerie and Bridget May, earning the 1969 NCHA World Championship Cutting Horse Mare and Hall of Fame awards.

Chickasha Dan became the sire of many good performers and producers including Chickasha Danny, a linebred Chickasha Mike stallion and sire of Chickasha Marie, the mare Carl Crawford rode to a place in the NCHA Non-Pro Hall of Fame.

1966

Registered Quarter Horses have always dominated the Futurity and 1966 was no different, except for the winner. Rey Jay's Pete was an unregistered gelding sired by Rey Jay.

Tom Lee, who stood Rey Jay in Fort Wayne, Indiana, in the early 1960s, bred Rey Jay's Pete out of a buckskin ranch mare, then sold him to Kenneth Peters, also of Fort Wayne.

"When I bought Rey Jay's Pete," recalled Peters, "Tom told me not to tell anybody he was by Rey Jay because he wasn't a Quarter Horse. But I had watched him as a colt, and it turned out that every time we were in the cutting pen, he'd come to the fence and watch. So I took a liking to him."

Peters started Rey Jay's Pete on cattle work, but Buster Welch trained him for cutting and rode him in the Futurity. "Rey Jay's Pete was an outstanding horse," says Welch. "He was really a true cowhorse. He could go with the best of them today."

After the Futurity, Rey Jay's Pete was sold to S. J. Agnew, who successfully competed with him for many years.

1967

"Home sweet home," was the prevailing sentiment in 1967 when the NCHA Futurity was held for the first time in Will Rogers Coliseum. After all, Fort Worth, known as "Cowtown," was the birthplace of NCHA and home of the NCHA offices.

"Dallas wasn't Cowtown," said Marion Flynt, president emeritus of NCHA and a primary developer and supporter of the Futurity. "So we made a deal to come to Fort Worth . . . the ideal town for it."

Page Boy's Tuno, owned and ridden by Leroy Ashcraft, marked 220 points. He was the first cutting horse to ever win over $10,000 in one event. His share of the $85,571 Futurity purse was $12,175.

1968

In 1968 former Futurity Finalists began appearing in the pedigrees of current competitors.

Uno's Princess, a daughter of 1963 Futurity Finalist Jose Uno, won the Futurity Championship with 220 points. Owned by Jess Koy of Eldorado, Texas, Uno's Princess was ridden by James Kenney, who bred, raised and trained her sire, Jose Uno.

"I thought I had a real good chance to win it," remembered Kenney. "She was really a wonderful-looking mare on a cow. I don't think there's ever been a horse that had more expression than she had. She really had a lot of desire to be a good pony."

1969

The Non-Professional division of the NCHA Futurity was inaugurated in 1969, with thirty-six riders competing for $3,802.

"We had started to establish rules for the non-pro class in 1963," explains Zack Wood. "It was slow in coming as far as amount of participation and number of opportunities for riders."

Dr. Allen Hamilton was the winner of the first Non-Pro Futurity aboard Chickasha Bingo. Chickasha Lady, Chickasha Bingo's dam, was a full sister to Chickasha Ann, the dam of 1963 and 1965 Futurity Champions Chickasha Glo and Chickasha Dan. Dr. Hamilton was the first and only rider to win both Open and Non-Pro Futurity Championships until Spencer Harden in 1989.

This was also the first year that the Thoroughbred stallion Three Bars appeared in the pedigree of a Futurity champion. From 1969 through 1990, only three open champions did not have Three Bars, at least once, in their pedigrees.

Champion Cee Bars Joan was by Cee Bars, a AAA-rated racing son of Three Bars. She was owned by the Burnett Estate, who also had her sire. Cee Bars Joan was ridden by Matlock Rose, already renowned for back-to-back world championships, in 1966 and 1967, on Stardust Desire and Peppy San. Rose had also ridden the incomparable Jessie James, 1952 NCHA Reserve World Champion.

Known and respected as a horseman's horseman, Rose saddled broncs, cutters and show horses on some of the world's finest Quarter Horse ranches before establishing his own operation in Aubrey, Texas.

In 1975 Rose won the World Championship for the third time, riding Peppys Desire, a product of his first two World Champions—Peppy San and Stardust Desire. He tied Buster Welch's record for four World Championship wins in 1977, with Peponita, then set a new record with another World Championship win aboard Peponita, in 1979.

Cee Bars was not the only race-bred Three Bars stallion to sire 1969 Futurity Finalists. Doc Bar, a race track washout by Three Bars' son Lightning Bars, was the sire of 1968 NCHA World Champion Mare Fizzabar. This was the first year, however, that Doc Bar foals competed in the Futurity Finals. Doc's Kitty, ridden by Shorty Freeman; Doc Luck Bar, ridden by Buster Welch; and Doc's Leo Lad, ridden by Rose's wife Carol, placed second, third and fourth out of fifteen Finalists.

1970

It was the beginning of a new era for the cutting world. Over six hundred horses were nominated for the 1970 NCHA Futurity. The purse was $112,791. More significantly, from this time forward, cutting pedigrees would blossom with "Docs" and "Lenas."

Doc O'Lena. His mother was a legend. His father was a race track reject. And the dark bay colt was phenomenal from the very first go-round of the 1970 NCHA Futurity.

"Doc O'Lena was just an individual," said his trainer and rider Shorty Freeman. "Whatever you asked him to do he would try his best to do."

Freeman asked and received four times in six days and four rounds of Futurity competition. When Doc O'Lena was named Champion he had beaten all competitors and had become the only horse to sweep both go-rounds, the semifinals and the Finals. His 223-point score was also a Futurity record.

J. M. "Shorty" Freeman began riding cutting horses in the early fifties, after learning the trade chasing cattle on some of the nation's biggest ranches. He was a Finalist in the first NCHA Futurity, as well as thirteen others. Besides the 1970 Futurity win aboard Doc O'Lena, Freeman rode that year's World Champion—King Skeet. Hoppen was Freeman's first World Champion, in 1963, and Lenaette was his second Futurity winner, in 1975.

Doc O'Lena was bred by Dr. Stephen Jensen of Paicines, California. Jensen owned Doc Bar, a typey race-bred stallion that he was crossing on Poco Tivio daughters. Since Poco Lena, Doc O'Lena's dam, was a full sister to Poco Tivio, the Doc Bar–Poco Lena cross was a natural extension of the Jensen breeding program. Doc Bar foals were tremendously successful halter and show ring performers, but they could also challenge a cow.

Poco Lena began her life on the 3D Ranch in Arlington, Texas, part of the huge W. T. Waggoner Estate, which at one time encompassed over 500,000 acres of North Texas. She was sired by Poco Bueno, by King P-234 and out of Sheilwin by Pretty Boy.

Compact and muscular Poco Bueno was all Quarter Horse in type. Because of his aggressive, hard-working style and dedication, the stocky bay was a crowd pleaser whenever he was shown. When Poco Bueno foals began arriving out of Waggoner Ranch–bred mares, manager Pine Johnson had no trouble selling them as weanlings for $1,000.

Johnson started Poco Lena on cattle as a yearling and began showing her at two. The tougher the cattle the better Poco Lena responded. "If you really asked her to put out a lot," remembered Johnson, "instead of coming apart and losing her training, she'd just get more intense and try harder."

While Poco Lena was beginning her career at two, Don Dodge of San Miguel, California, was showing Poco Tivio. In 1952 Dodge won the NCHA Reserve World Championship aboard Snipper W and ranked fifth in the Top Ten standings with Poco Tivio. The following year he purchased Poco Lena.

"Poco Lena was by far better than Poco Tivio," remembers Dodge. "I saw Poco Bueno perform when I was riding Poco Tivio, and he was a real nice kind of horse. But there were none of those that were equal to her.

"She was a good bred mare, but I bought her mainly because she had a lot of moves and she was quick. She was a real stringy mare. And she was good-looking. I showed her at halter in pretty good company. She was Grand Champion several times."

Dodge showed Poco Lena for six years and sold her to B. A. Skipper for $18,000.

"I'm not in the breeding business," explains Dodge. "I never raised one colt in my life. I never believed in it myself. I'm a horse trainer, but I always bought a lot of horses. When I sold Poco Lena it was a pretty good price for the time.

Pine Johnson remembered a show in Tyler, Texas, where twenty-six horses had to contend with one miserable bunch of cattle. "Everybody was having all kinds of trouble," said Johnson. "And Barney Skipper and Poco Lena were the last to work. They went in there and cut two cows and they looked like they were fresh cattle, the way she handled them. She won the cutting. She was just that much above other horses."

Dr. Jensen purchased Poco Lena in 1963 from the B. A. Skipper Estate. Because Freeman had been so successful with Doc's Kitty in the 1969 NCHA Futurity, Jensen offered him an option to buy Poco Lena's first foal, Doc O'Lena, in exchange for training and showing. Freeman was so impressed with the colt, he purchased him as a two-year-old, in partnership with Adrian Berryhill.

Although Doc O'Lena placed third in the 1971 NCHA Derby, he was shown just a few times after that. Freeman purchased Berryhill's interest in the stallion, then sold half to Walter Hellyer of Ontario, Canada. In 1977 Doc O'Lena was syndicated for $2.1 million. It was the first major syndication in the cutting horse world.

Today, at twenty-three, Doc O'Lena is one of the cutting industry's leading sires. He was the first NCHA Futurity Champion to sire a Futurity Champion, and his sons and daughters are producing champions as well.

1971

It was the same producer, but a different cast for the 1971 NCHA Futurity. Dry Doc, the second and last foal by Doc Bar out of Poco Lena, won the Futurity for a Fairhaven, Michigan, partnership, ridden by Buster Welch.

"I had a lot of good horses that year," says Welch. "But Dry Doc was just a super little horse—super to train and easy to show. He was a little athlete."

1972

Midwesterners won the Futurity for the second year in a row when Gun Smoke's Dream took the championship with Dale Wilkinson in the saddle for Mr. and Mrs. Donald Padgett of Gahanna, Ohio.

"It was very satisfying to win on her," says Wilkinson, a leading trainer and judge of Quarter Horses. "We had lived in Ohio all our lives, which made this more rewarding. And it encouraged other people from the Midwest."

No one has ridden more Futurity rounds than non-pro rider Spencer Harden, who saddled his first Finalist in 1968. Pecos Billy, Harden's 1972 Non-Pro Futurity Champion, colicked at the beginning of the trials. The Florida dairy farmer nursed her all week, hoping for a chance in the Open and Non-Pro divisions.

"She got through the Non-Pro Finals in good shape," says Harden. "But she hadn't eaten for a week. The next night in the Open semifinals, she cut her first calf and lost it. I just pulled her up. She'd given all she could give."

1973

Doc's Marmoset, owned and shown to her Futurity Championship by Tom Lyons, was the first of three outstanding horses by Doc Bar out of Susie's Bay, by Poco Tivio. Doc's Solano and Doc's Oak, now leading sires, would follow.

"Back then no one knew what the best Doc Bar cross would be," says Lyons. "I thought the Poco Tivio would be a great cross and it was.

"In those days, the Triple Crown consisted of the Futurity, Derby and the World Championship Finals. Doc's Marmoset was the only one to win all three. She was also World Champion in 1981.

"She has a special place in my heart because of the Futurity. Winning it is still a big granddaddy of them all, as far as I'm concerned."

It seemed that everyone was looking for Doc Bar stallions in the early seventies. Paul Crumpler was no exception. On the recommendation of Shorty Freeman, he purchased Doc Quixote from Leon Harrel for $12,000.

"That was a lot of money for a hobby," says Crumpler, who won the Non-Pro Futurity with the stallion who would later sire 1983 Futurity Champion and Triple Crown winner Docs Okie Quixote.

1974

Doc's Yuba Lea, ridden by Leon Harrel, was the fourth Doc Bar foal to win the Futurity in five years.

"Almost all the horses I have ridden have been Doc Bar horses," says Harrel. "To me, they are a tremendous line of horses. They are the type of horses that if you treat them with kindness, they will be responsive."

Doc's Yuba Lea, out of My Dinah, by Leo, was owned by Chester Dennis of Healdsburg, California, the first Californian to win the Futurity.

Non-Pro Champion Leantoo, by Doc O'Lena, was the first Futurity Champion sired by a Futurity Champion. Tommy Minton of Wilkesboro, North Carolina, purchased the gelding from his breeder, Shorty Freeman, who helped him prepare for the Futurity.

"Leantoo was real quiet," says Minton. "Kind of an old deadhead, really. But in the Finals, he was the best that I can remember him ever being. I couldn't ask for anyone to work any better than he did that night. You could just turn him loose and ask for his life. He wanted to put out everything he could for you."

1975

Doc O'Lena and Shorty Freeman lit the boards again in the 1975 NCHA Futurity. This year, however, Doc O'Lena was the winning sire and the first Futurity Champion to sire an Open Futurity Champion.

This was a particularly satisfying win for Freeman, who bred the champion, Lenaette, and was riding for his son-in-law Terry Riddle. He even broke his own record by scoring 224 points in the Finals—one point above Doc O'Lena's previous record.

Freeman had ridden in five NCHA Futurities since 1962, but the championship eluded him until 1970, when he won the title, and all go-rounds, with Doc O'Lena. Freeman also won the 1970 Derby with Doc's Kitty and the 1970 World Championship with King Skeet.

Good fortune came to Freeman early in 1970, in the guise of a four-year-old mare named Bar Socks Babe. He didn't know it at the time, but destiny had plans for Freeman's Futurity prospect, Doc O'Lena, and Bar Socks Babe.

Freeman covered many miles with King Skeet in 1970. One show took him to Illinois, where he visited fellow horseman and horse trader Cletus Hulling.

"I was always looking for something," says Freeman. "Cletus traded a lot of horses and I picked Bar Socks Babe out of about two hundred mares. She had been ridden but was just barely broke. I bought her for a broodmare."

"This was an impressive mare as far as looks were concerned," remembers Hulling. "I asked $750 for her and Shorty bought her."

Bar Socks Babe, bred by Lowell Jarrett of Silverton, Texas, was a Sugar Bars granddaughter, and Freeman liked that aspect of her pedigree.

"Doc O'Lena crosses better on hotter mares," says Freeman. "That is why I went to the Sugar Bars cross. And it proved out pretty well."

Freeman also liked Dusty Socks, Bar Socks Babe's dam, because she was a Hank H granddaughter. "I rode a lot of Hank H horses back years ago," says Freeman. "They were good performance horses and racehorses too."

Hank H, by King P-234 out of Queen H, was a full brother to stakes winners Squaw H and Booger H, both top-notch quarter racing horses. Hank H's greatest contribution to racing and cutting was through Gold King Bailey and Hanka.

Hanka, by Hank H, is the dam of AQHA Running Champion and sire Tonto Bars Hank. Racing champions descended from Tonto Bars Hank include Hank's Dial Doll, Moon Lark, Gold Coast Express, Lil Bit Shiney, Come Six and Spring Lark.

Tonto Bars Hank progeny are not limited to the race track, however. Missy's Hankie, by Tonto Bars Hank, was an NCHA money earner who produced Doc N Missy, NCHA Silver Award winner and member of the Working Cow Horse Hall of Fame. Doc N Missy is the dam of 1987 NCHA Derby winner Miss N Cash.

Gold King Bailey, the sire of Dusty Socks, is by Hank H out of Beauty

Bailey, by Old Joe Bailey. Beauty Bailey is out of a mare by Yellow Wolf, by Old Joe Bailey. With Queen H, from Hank H, Gold King Bailey has three crosses, in four generations, to Old Joe Bailey.

Gay Ray Rutland, who bred more Register of Merit racehorses than any other breeder from 1945 through 1985, owned Gold King Bailey and bred Dusty Socks.

"I used to tell people that Gold King Bailey had those Bailey brains," said Rutland. "There's a lot of cow back in those Bailey horses. Gold King Bailey's first AAA racehorse was Star Of Texas. I cut a cow away from her calf and drove her up to the house the very first day Star Of Texas ever had a saddle on his back."

While Bar Socks Babe did not make Doc O'Lena's reputation as a sire, she helped. Lenaette was Bar Socks Babe's first Doc O'Lena foal, and she was from his first full crop of foals. Following Lenaette was 1976 NCHA Open Futurity Finalist Bardoc O'Lena; 1977 Non-Pro Futurity Co-Champion Bar O'Lena; 1980 Futurity Finalist Havealena; 1981 Futurity Finalist Lizzielena; 1983 Futurity Finalist Tamborlena; and 1990 NCHA Super Stakes Classic Champion Travelena.

Lenaette was a Finalist in the 1976 NCHA Derby, then retired to the broodmare band of Freckles Playboy, where she produced 1982 NCHA Derby Champion Shesa Playmate; A Lenaette, a 1983 NCHA Derby Finalist; and Freckles Merada, a 1984 NCHA Derby Finalist and sire of 1990 Super Stakes Champion Foxie Merada.

L. M. "Pat" Patterson owned and rode the 1975 Reserve Futurity Champion Sam's Superstar. The legendary and colorful cutter from Tecumseh, Oklahoma, also won the 1972 NCHA World Championship riding Good Judgment, and at the age of seventy-one, in 1987, the NCHA Classic Championship on San Jo Lena.

Patterson is the only World Champion rider with two children who have also earned World Championship titles: Kenny Patterson rode 1987 World Champion Jae Bar Fletch, and his sister Debbie was 1987 Non-Pro World Champion riding Jae Bar Fletch's full sister—Jae Bar Masie. Both Pat and Debbie are NCHA Hall of Fame members.

Spencer Harden made his second trip to the Non-Pro Futurity winner's circle in 1975. This time he was riding Wee Darlin, the only Futurity winner ever sired by a Thoroughbred.

Wee Darlin, by Wee Folk, was out of Rey's Dixie, the first good cutting horse Harden owned. Because she was crippled, Harden didn't want to ship her a long distance, so he bred her to Thoroughbred race sire Wee Folk.

The choice was not without reason. According to Harden's own account, Rey's Dixie was long-backed and a trifle coarse in appearance. He felt the refined Thoroughbred stallion would improve the Quarter mare's foals.

Wee Darlin was everything Harden had hoped for—an exceptionally pretty filly, with balance and refinement. She was also hot-blooded and "broncy," thanks to her Thoroughbred ancestors. Shortly before the Futurity she developed the habit of whirling out from under Harden as he tried to mount her. By the time the pair arrived at Will Rogers Coliseum, the only way Harden could mount Wee Darlin was to load her in the bucking chutes at the end of the arena.

"Once I got on her, I could ride into the arena and be all right," said Harden. "But if I got down, I couldn't get back on her out there."

1976

The NCHA Futurity celebrated its fifteenth anniversary in 1976 with three hundred sixty-nine entries competing for a purse of $200,000.

Colonel Freckles, the 1976 Futurity Champion, was bred by Marion Flynt, started on cattle by Terry Riddle and polished and ridden by Olan Hightower.

"He was sweet minded and an awfully willing horse," says Hightower. "I guess the most trouble I ever had in training him was getting a look to him. About a month before the Futurity I finally got him kind of perked up and using his ears. From there on he just got progressively better. But I rode him a lot more miles than I showed him on cattle. There's very little of Washington County [Texas] that he hasn't seen."

Hightower's methods honed Colonel Freckles to perfection. The sweet-natured sorrel stallion bettered a field that many cutters believe to be the best in the event's history. The Open Finalists included Doc's Becky, Freckles Playboy, Doc's Remedy, Doc's Oak, Doc Athena, Doc's Steady Date, Bardoc O'Lena, Tip It San, Montana Doc, Sittin Pretty and Gold Rush 2.

Marion Flynt of Midland, Texas, accepted awards as breeder of the winner, nominator of the winner and owner of the sire of the winner. In addition, Doc's Becky and Freckles Playboy, both bred and owned by Flynt, shared Reserve Champion honors. Non-Pro Champion Mia Freckles, owned and shown by Kay Floud, but bred by Flynt, was icing on the cake.

Flynt, a host of the first NCHA Futurity, was a longtime supporter of cutting. He served twelve terms as president of NCHA and was awarded the title of president emeritus in 1972. Marion's Girl, two-time World Champion ridden by Buster Welch, was owned by Flynt. Two of cutting's legendary sires—Rey Jay and Jewel's Leo Bars "Freckles," stood at Flynt's Square Top Three Ranch in Midland, Texas.

Kay Floyd, Non-Pro Co-Champion in 1976, was the first woman to win a Futurity championship. Kay managed Flynt's horse operation and had ridden in the Futurity semifinals in 1970 and the Open Finals in 1972, but Mia Freckles carried her to the top.

"She was real solid," says Kay. "You could just accidentally bump her, and if she didn't think that she was supposed to be there, she wouldn't listen. She would do what she thought was right. She was that cow smart."

Dick Gaines won the 1976 Non-Pro Co-Championship on Doc Soc, by Doc Tari. Gaines bought Doc Tari, the 1973 Non-Pro Futurity Reserve Champion, for $2,250 as a weanling, trained him and showed him.

"I intended to cut him until he was a four-year-old and just never got around to it," said Gaines. "I bought him just because he was a Doc Bar. I didn't want a stud."

Doc Sox was one of three foals from Doc Tari's first crop, which included Sally Doc, 1978 NCHA Non-Pro World Champion.

1977

Peppy San Badger, owned by King Ranch, was the first champion to win the Futurity under the five-judge system. He was Buster Welch's fifth Futurity Champion.

"My most important win was the one on Little Peppy," says Welch. "All of them were great, and all of them were thrilling, but none of them meant as much to me as that one."

King Ranch planned to make Peppy San Badger a leading sire in their breeding program and hoped to promote him to outside mares. Less than a decade after his Futurity win, the champion was the leading sire of cutting horse money earners, a spot he still held in 1990.

Co-champions shared the Non-Pro Futurity limelight for the second year in a row in 1977. Paul Crumpler claimed his second Futurity win on Chickasha Ann Doc, and Stuart Gildred made his debut on Bar O'Lena.

Both champions rode daughters of former champions, out of leading producers. Chickasha Ann Doc, out of Chickasha Ann, was half-sister to Futurity winners Chickasha Glo and Chickasha Dan. Bar O'Lena was a full sister to 1975 Futurity Champion Lenaette.

1978

Lynx Melody, owned by Billy Cogdell of Tulia, Texas, and ridden by Larry Reeder, stood 13.3 hands and weighed 750 to 800 pounds. Reeder estimates that the little mare carried 250 pounds, including tack, when he rode her.

"Her size concerned me a little when I first saw her," says Reeder. "But after I rode her, it didn't bother me at all. She was definitely one of the greatest horses I ever rode. She had a heart that was unreal."

By the first of March before the Futurity, Lynx Melody also had a big belly.

"I told Billy that this mare was really getting bellied up," remembers Reeder. "I had her tested and she was in foal. She had a colt about the fifteenth of March. We left him on the mare for two weeks and then put him on a Shetland mare and raised him that way."

Lynx Melody has produced three Futurity Finalists, one of which, Doc's Accident, was foaled three months after his dam won the Futurity.

Randy Chartier, of Fair Haven, Michigan, grew up with horses. Chartier's father owned 1971 Futurity winner Dry Doc. It was Dry Doc's daughter, Miss Dry, that Chartier rode as 1978 Futurity Champion.

"It's elimination, and I happened to be the last one to be eliminated," says Chartier, who had been winning in NCHA competition since the age of twelve. "When I came down to ride in the Futurity, if anyone had told me that I was going to make the Finals, I would have told them they were crazy."

1979

Growing up as Shorty Freeman's son, Bill Freeman was bound to either love horses or hate them. Fortunately for Glenn McKinney, Bill loved horses. Even better, he was crazy about McKinney's colt Docs Diablo.

Freeman had ridden Doc's Prescription, and Docs Diablo was that stallion's first foal.

"The colt was a long two-year-old when I got him," remembers Freeman. "I thought he was fabulous. He was very trainable, and very athletic, and very smart."

Docs Diablo, who won both go-rounds and was second in the semifinals, was undefeated in NCHA competition until his death, as a four-year-old.

The Futurity 73

* * *

Non-Pro Champion Mike Kelly, the 1971 Reserve Non-Pro Champion was competing as a Futurity Finalist for the seventh time. He had trained his horse, Sons Madonna, by himself. Despite pneumonia and sore feet, the game mare captured the Non-Pro class and was a semifinalist in Open competition.

"She probably was the greatest horse that I have ever ridden," said Kelly. "She had an awful lot of try and a big heart."

1980

Nominations enjoyed a brisk increase in 1980. By closing date, a whopping 557 horses were committed for $530,342.

Mis Royal Mahogany, this year's winner, was the seventh Futurity Champion in ten years sired by a Doc Bar son.

This was the first year for a woman to ride the Open Champion, however. Lindy Burch, a familiar face to Futurity competitors, won the Reserve Championship title in 1979 on Diamond Mystery. Larry Reeder trained Mis Royal Mahogany and asked Burch to ride her, two weeks before the 1980 Futurity.

"I always liked Mis Royal," says Burch. "You could create more with her. You could take a bad cow and change it into a good cow. I could always ask that mare."

Mis Royal Mahogany's run was more than great, it was the greatest. Her score of 225.5 is the Futurity record.

Jim Milner had been involved with cutting horses for ten years when he won the Non-Pro Co-Championship on Tari Echo, by Doc Tari. Tari Echo was one good horse of many owned and shown by Milner, who placed in NCHA Open Non-Pro Top Ten standings eleven times between 1972 and 1981, and was Non-Pro World Champion.

1981

Cutting horse competition experienced phenomenal growth in the eighties. Nominations for the 1981 Futurity reached a record high—1,503. There were 638 entries competing for $850,000.

Joe Heim had been trying for a Futurity win since 1977 when he was

Reserve Champion on Doc's Serendipity. He was a Finalist in 1978 and 1980, but 1981 was his year to shine.

Colonel Lil, owned by W. B. Wood of Brenham, Texas, was sent to Heim barely started, seven months before the Futurity.

"We had a very short time to prepare," recalls Heim. "But she rose to the occasion. I recognized her as my best chance for the Futurity, even though she was greener than some of my other horses. She did good things on a cow. She had a lot of flash about her and tried to do the right thing."

1982

It was necessary to extend the 1982 Futurity to eleven days, with a one-day break, to accommodate 872 contestants. The total purse of $1.57 million was a record for any equine arena event.

The first go-round took six days to complete. Bill Freeman and Smart Little Lena won the round with a flashy 222.5-point run, then repeated the score in the second go-round. The pair slipped one point, to 221, in the semifinals, and saving the best for last, they conquered all in the Finals with 225 points.

Hanes Chatham of Aubrey, Texas, raised the Doc O'Lena colt and formed a partnership with Freeman. The two men sold seventeen Smart Little Lena breeding shares, at $5,000 each, before the Futurity.

"I think he was the only Futurity winner to be syndicated before the Futurity," says Freeman. "Of course, right after the Futurity we sold some more shares and they had increased in value to $50,000."

Smart Little Lena was the first horse to win the Futurity, Derby and Super Stakes. He was shown only eight times before being retired, but earned over $700,000.

"Winning the Futurity the first time was the ultimate thrill," says Freeman, who won with Docs Diablo in 1979. "But the second time on a horse that I owned part of was the best. It's a feeling that's indescribable. Of course, the $207,000 that went along with it was great, too."

1983

The 1983 Futurity Champion was born shortly after Joe and Joice Heim moved from California to Texas—a stone's throw from the Oklahoma border. Joice christened the colt Docs Okie Quixote.

The Futurity

Joe trained and rode Docs Okie Quixote in the Futurity, then won the 1984 Derby and Super Stakes with the stallion. He was the second horse in history to win cutting's Triple Crown.

"Things have improved since I began riding in the Futurity," says Heim. "It used to be a hard-packed clay ground and we used to rework cattle every second go-round. Now there is fresh cattle every go-round.

"The first time I made the Finals in 1977 was the first time they used five judges and dropped the high and the low score. I think we began to see a fairer way of evaluating horses."

Non-pros came into a windfall in 1983. This was the first year for the Non-Pro Futurity to stand alone. Riders were not required to enter the Open Futurity, but could elect to ride only as non-pros. The Non-Pro purse jumped from $73,660, in 1982, to nearly $400,000, in 1983.

Cletus Hulling, Jr., of Freeburg, Illinois, won the Non-Pro Championship riding Miss Doc Hollywood. Hulling is the brother of Non-Pro Derby winner Tootie Lyons, who is the wife of NCHA Hall of Fame Rider Tom Lyons. Hulling is also the brother of professional trainer Barbara Schulte, who rode 1988 NCHA Derby winner Freckles Son Ofa Doc.

1984

Doc Per was the only horse in the history of the Futurity to receive a standing ovation from the crowd.

"I think superstars are superstars the first time you ride them," says Ronnie Nettles, Doc Per's trainer and rider. "You have to have a lot of admiration for horses like that because they just want to perform so bad."

Doc Per wanted to perform "so bad" by the time he reached the Futurity semifinals that he tried to cut a cow and got down before Nettles had him out of the herd.

"I had forty head of cattle out in front of me," remembered Nettles, "and he wanted to cut the one right in front of him. I was a little concerned then, and I knew at the Finals I would have to be a little more alert to really keep control until I got him on a cow. I knew once I got him on a cow he would be all right."

Nettles admits that Doc Per was a born showman and that an enthusiastic audience really pumped him up.

1985

Combined purses for the Open and Non-Pro NCHA Futurities reached a record high of $2 million in 1985.

For the second time in Futurity history, a woman saddled the champion. The Gemnist, according to his trainer and rider Kathy Daughn, was a horse that needed a lot of time and plenty of patience. Daughn learned the cutting horse business from trainer Larry Reeder. She also worked for Lindy Burch, the first woman to win the Futurity.

"The Gemnist is what you would call a real hot kind of horse," says Kathy. "He's pretty eccentric, and he wasn't a real easy horse to train. I spent a lot of time with him and worked lots of cattle in lots of conditions.

"I decided that I really wanted to win the Futurity. I knew that this was a horse I could win with, if I could ever get him trained."

1986

Royal Silver King, the 1986 Futurity Champion, was sired by an unproven stallion out of a $900 mare. He was also the first winner since Peppy San Badger that did not carry Three Bars in his pedigree. He did, however, have Top Deck blood. Top Deck, a Thoroughbred, is very influential in the families of Quarter racing horses. In addition to speed, he is infamous for a nasty disposition, which was mellowed by King, Leo and Silver King in Royal Silver King's pedigree.

1987

Drawing last in the first bunch of cattle in the Finals, Leon Harrel was pressed to find a cow that had not been worked. It took a lot of skill and a little luck for Harrel and Steady Date to collect and move a red-and-white paint cow that was hugging the cattle chutes. "I had to go a lot deeper than I planned," says Harrel. "I went back there and declared myself on her and drove her up through the cattle. If I hadn't gotten her cut, it might not have been so great . . . but it worked out perfect."

Smart Date, the first Futurity Champion sired by Smart Little Lena, is out of Trip Date Bar, and a female line that is dear to Harrel's heart. Trip Date Bar is a sister to Doc's Date Bar and Doc's Steady Date, both Futurity Finalists ridden by Harrel.

1988

Veteran Futurity Champion Bill Freeman wasn't sure what kind of horse he had under him when he rode Smart Little Senor into the arena for the first go-round of the NCHA Futurity.

The little bay had shown Freeman plenty of talent throughout the year, but the two months preceding the Futurity were full of setbacks. A cyst on one of his stifles caused Smart Little Senor occasional soreness, a bout with colic caused time out of training, and flu and high fever drained all his remaining energy and resistance.

When the pair got to Fort Worth, Freeman let the Smart Little Lena gelding rest during the Non-Pro Futurity go-rounds and started him back in training before the first Open go-round.

"Really and truly, he surprised me all the way through the show with how strong he was," said Freeman.

Cols Lil Pepper, winner of both go-rounds and the semifinals, set a target in the Finals with 221 points, his lowest score from all four go-rounds. Smart Little Senor, who marked 221 points in the first go-round, matched scores, and the stage was set for a sudden-death work-off—the first in NCHA Futurity history.

Cols Lil Pepper, ridden by rookie Doug Jordan, was first to perform in the workoff. Because of his intensity and style, Cols Lil Pepper had been a crowd favorite throughout the Futurity. When he lost his second cow in the work-off, he received a standing ovation.

Smart Little Senor won the championship with 218 points. It was the third Futurity win for Freeman, who won the event in 1982 aboard Smart Little Lena, Smart Little Senor's sire.

Smart Little Senor's work-off win kept Cols Lil Pep from equaling the Futurity record set by Doc O'Lena in 1970.

Smart Little Senor, out of Senorita Misty by Senor George, was owned by Stewart Sewell of Jacksboro, Texas. An original shareholder in the Smart Little Lena Syndicate, Sewell partnered on a foal-sharing basis with John Meredith of Olney, Texas, who owns Senorita Misty.

Meredith's family owned Kings Michelle, 1962 World Champion Mare, and Bar El Do, the sire of Bar Socks Babe, dam of 1975 NCHA Futurity winner Lenaette. Senorita Misty's sire, Senor George, was 1961 NCHA World Champion Cutting Horse.

Curly Tully and Brady Bowen taught Smart Little Senor cutting basics, but Freeman trained him for the Futurity. Just six weeks before the event, Smart Little Senor was gelded.

"The decision had to be made whether we would give it our best shot," says Sewell. "As a stud he was a little inconsistent. He was going to have to have four good runs and he couldn't have one off day. The goal was to try to win the Futurity."

1989

Two sets of wily black cattle honed a field of twenty-three Futurity Finalists, until two geldings were left gunning for a showdown—Spencer Harden's July Jazz, Reserve Champion of the Non-Pro Futurity, and Commandicate, ridden by defending Futurity Champion Bill Freeman.

The geldings were tied with 221 points. Anticipating a work-off, spectators stayed in their seats while scores were checked.

"I was exhilarated and relieved that I didn't have to go through the pressure," admitted Harden, after learning that a score correction gave July

Spencer Harden as 1990 NCHA Non-Pro Futurity Reserve Champion on All That Jazz, *a son of Jazabell Quixote. Don Shugart photo.*

Jazz 221.5 points and the championship. Even more exhilarating was the fact that by winning both championships, Harden had accomplished something only one other nonprofessional had achieved—Dr. Allen Hamilton in 1965.

"Dynasty" would be an appropriate title for the 1989 NCHA Futurity. July Jazz, an unregistered embryo-transfer foal, represented three generations of Harden-bred money earners.

Winning the Open Futurity meant the fulfillment of a lifetime dream for Harden, who had been close many times, but had never hit the jackpot. Harden was third in the 1973 Futurity riding July Jazz's second dam, Bill's Jazabell. In 1982 he won the Non-Pro Futurity with Jazabell Quixote, dam of July Jazz and Jazalena, Harden's 1988 Non-Pro Futurity Reserve Champion.

"She was the best we ever had," says Harden of Bill's Jazabell. The sorrel mare won the NCHA Reserve Youth Championship for Harden's thirteen-year-old son Mark in 1976, the same year she was named NCHA World Champion Mare.

"The secretaries would call her Wonder Woman when I entered her in shows," remembers Harden. "She was just a gentle, sweet mare to be around and she did so much for my family."

In 1978 Harden bred Bill's Jazabell for the first time. He named her 1979 sorrel Doc Quixote filly Jazabell Quixote. She is the only foal out of Bill's Jazabell, who died the following year.

Jazabell Quixote was a little mare, with much of her dam's flash, including a blaze face and socks. She also inherited Bill's Jazabell's pizazz.

"The fun thing was that Jazabell Quixote was almost identical to her mother," says Harden. "They both worked real bright and intent. They were sticky kinds of mares and real cowy. Bill's Jazabell was just a little freer moving, but Jazabell Quixote was really like riding her mother again.

"I think the mares get the style they have from Royal King. A lot of horses will drop their front ends, but these horses will drop all over. The Royal Kings that I have had always had that drop and look, and a lot of shake and shiver to them."

Jazabell Quixote's first foal was a 1984 bay colt by Doc's Hickory. Hickoryote was a bay like his sire, and sported the blaze of his first, second and third dams, as well as their talent for collecting paychecks. During his cutting career, Hickoryote earned $100,000.

Harden committed Jazabell Quixote to Smart Little Lena for 1984 and 1985 breedings, but almost had a change of heart when he saw her 1985 foal.

"After Jazabell Quixote foaled, they called me and said that I better come and look at the colt before I decided to breed back to Smart Little Lena," remembers Harden.

Jazalena, Jazabell Quixote's second foal, was stunning. A brilliant strawberry roan, she sported a bald face with white under her jaw, stockings above her knees and a chevron on the dock of her tail.

Harden was not impressed with Jazalena's chrome, which disqualified her from registration with the American Quarter Horse Association. Color did not affect her NCHA money-earning capabilities, however. Since her birth, Harden has changed his philosophy about registered horses and is raising embryo-transfer foals.

"I decided to embryo Jazabell Quixote because I wanted to get more than one colt out of her," says Harden. "I don't think papers are that important when you have horses like July Jazz."

In 1987 Harden got five Jazabell Quixote foals—three sired by Sons Doc, one by Doc's Hickory and one by Smart Little Lena. Sons Royal Jazabell, a filly, was the first foal and the one Harden chose to register. Since AQHA regulations permit just one registered foal from a mare per year, July Jazz, by Sons Doc, was unregisterable.

In over thirty years of competition, Harden has ridden some outstanding horses, but he thinks July Jazz may be the best. The sorrel gelding's point-earning penchant for crouching low to the ground developed at an early age and in an unusual way.

"When we weaned this colt and stepped into his stall to put a halter on him, he froze like a rabbit and started lying down," remembers Harden. "If anything scares him, like a cow, he just wants to crouch. He's never been timid. He's a very bold colt. But anything that frightens him, he just wants to crouch down and stare at it."

1990

No guts, no glory. That was the bottom line for 1990 Futurity Champion Millie Montana. The gritty sorrel mare, ridden by Joe Suiter, pinned her ears and defended the line against a red fireball turned kamikaze in the Finals.

"The cow ran right under my mare's neck," remembers Suiter. "About the last two turns it got in my mind that I didn't think we were going to hold it. But she never missed a lick."

Smart Play, a grandson of 1975 Futurity champion Lenaette, was Reserve Champion.

The Futurity

Millie Montana, 1990 NCHA Futurity Champion, ridden by Joe Suiter. Don Shugart photo.

Matt Gaines, 1990 NCHA Non-Pro Futurity Champion. Don Shugart photo.

FOUR

Selecting the Right Horse

A good cutting horse is an American Quarter Horse. Right? Not necessarily. Most of today's best cutting competitors are Quarter Horses because over the past fifty years the Quarter Horse industry has developed bloodlines that consistently produce top performers.

The Quarter Horse developed as a horse type suited for the rigors of ranch and cattle work. There are many romantic tales about quarter-mile racers of noble heritage, but the truth is that, beyond one or two generations, the pedigrees of most foundation Quarter Horses are lost to posterity.

Southwestern ranchers of the late nineteenth century bred horses to meet the needs of environment and their work. Stamina, soundness and quickness were all cowhorse prerequisites.

Demand for horses often exceeded supply, and large ranches sometimes mustered native mares, descendants of Spanish-bred mustangs, into their broodmare bands. Thoroughbred stallions were popular sires of cowhorses, but their blood was often tempered with that of Belgian or Percheron draft horses. Morgans, Arabians and Saddlebreds sired many cowboys' mounts as well.

Pedigree, whatever the breed, does not guarantee a cutting horse. You are most likely to find a cutter with horses like Doc Bar, Leo San, Jewels Leo Bars or Royal King in his lineage. But any horse that is built to easily squat and turn on his rear end has potential. If he can be taught to look at and follow a cow, you may have a winner.

Selecting the Right Horse

Popular Breeds

THE AMERICAN QUARTER HORSE

When young horses joined ranch remudas at the turn of the century, they were trained, tried and culled by cowboys. Patterns emerged, and the offspring of some stallions were preferred over others for ranch work.

By the late 1930s, a distinct type of horse had become prevalent in work stock throughout the Southwest. They were notorious for quick blasts of speed at short distances, and because they were often matched for money on straightaways, they were called Quarter Horses, after the colonial American sprinters of English and Spanish ancestry.

Three breed associations were formed in the early 1940s to establish specifications and breeding registers for the Quarter-type horse: the American Quarter Horse Association, the National Quarter Horse Association and the American Quarter Racing Association. In 1949 the three associations merged into the American Quarter Horse Association.

In the beginning, Quarter Horses could be distinguished from other breeds by their size, conformation and temperament. They were medium in height, stocky and muscular, and possessed easygoing, tractable dispositions. The stout "bulldog" Quarter Horse soon lost favor, however, to a more refined and statuesque version, with lighter bone and longer legs, but still enough muscle and strength behind for "get away" power.

Today's Quarter Horses have evolved into three specialized groups with many common ancestors. The racing Quarter Horse is virtually a sprinting Thoroughbred with some ranch horse blood, usually in the third or fourth generations. Show and halter Quarter Horses are essentially the old "bulldog" with more refinement, smaller bones and longer legs. There is a concern among some breeders that the halter prototype is an inefficient model, impressive in bulk and stature but useless in action.

Happily, the stock-type Quarter Horse still exists. His heritage is mixed with ranch horses and racehorses, and much that is unknown. But somewhere in his pedigree he will probably carry Old Sorrel, King, Poco Bueno, Leo or Doc Bar.

While racehorses are bred primarily for speed, and halter horses for bulk, cutting horses are bred for many qualities of equal importance—quickness, athletic ability, soundness, intelligence and a willing nature.

It is the cutting-bred Quarter Horse that, more than any other, merits the title "most versatile."

THE APPALOOSA

Appaloosa horses appeal to today's owners for the same reasons they were valued by their champions, the Nez Percé Indians.

Spanish conquistadors introduced Andalusian stock, which included spotted horses, to North America, and by the nineteenth century Indian tribes were using horses for hunting and warfare. The Nez Percé Indians of the Northwest became master horsemen, selectively breeding for desirable qualities, including courage, endurance and speckled coats.

Buffalo meat and hide were a staple in western Indian societies, and buffalo hunting required special skills of horses and riders. While a hunter's hands were occupied with bow and arrow, his horse had to run with a fleeing buffalo, staying close enough to share dust, and long enough for the rider to deliver as many as thirty arrows to drop the beast.

Besides their aptitude for buffalo hunting, Appaloosas were also treasured war-horses. Swift enough to outrun the enemy, the brilliantly colored horses came with ready-made "war paint." Indian "ponies" were especially vexatious to the U.S. Army. When General Custer reported that mounted Indians were too quick to catch with cavalry mounts, the word came from Washington to kill Indian horses.

In addition to aesthetic appeal, the Nez Percé prized spotted coats for natural camouflage. Although flashy at close range, Appaloosa spots blended into the shadows and highlights of distant backgrounds.

White settlers referred to the colorful Indian mounts as "Palouse horses" because the Indians were numerous along the Palouse River in northern Idaho. Thus the name Appaloosa.

After the Nez Percé were relegated to reservations, Percheron and Belgian stallions were sent by the government to be bred to the Indian mares. Gradually the magnificent "Palouse" was evolving into a plow horse.

In 1938 a small group of horsemen joined forces to preserve the spotted horse of the American West, and the Appaloosa Horse Club was established. Today there are over 500,000 registered Appaloosa horses and 20,000 ApHC members.

Athletic ability, endurance and intelligence are hallmarks of the Appaloosa breed. In addition, because the Appaloosa registry is still open to Quarter Horses, Thoroughbreds and Arabians, and because the Appaloosa coat pattern is readily inherited, breeders can specialize with prominent outcross bloodlines from other breeds.

A good example of this successful approach to breeding is Ima Little Lena, sired by NCHA Triple Crown winner Smart Little Lena, a registered Quarter Horse, and out of Wa-Jo's Freckles, a registered Appaloosa. Ima Little

Lena, with the spotted coat and mottled skin of his forebears, is a natural ambassador for the Appaloosa breed and was a leading NCHA money earner in 1988.

Joe Ellard of Dallas, Texas, has a barnful of top-dollar registered Quarter Horse cutting champions and two Appaloosa mares, who are producing cutting champions. "It's fun to have an Appaloosa," says Ellard. "Of all the colts I breed . . . it's the Appaloosa I'm looking forward to most, to see what it does. Does it have spots? Is it colored? That's what excites Appaloosa people."

Although Appaloosas appear sporadically in NCHA competition, spotted coats have been scarce, and the ApHC would like to reverse that pattern. The American Appaloosa Cutting Horse Association, founded in 1985, is working to improve the quality of shows and purses for Appaloosas, with the goal of broadening the market for well-bred Appaloosa cutting horses.

THE PAINT HORSE

Spotted horses have captured man's imagination and admiration for over 50,000 years. Drawings of black and white horses decorate the walls of prehistoric caverns in France and Spain. Virgil wrote about particolored mounts, and Homer tells of bay and white cavalry horses. One thousand years ago, Bedouin breeders used over thirty descriptive terms to distinguish the pied markings of their pureblood Arabian steeds.

Sixteenth-century Spanish conquistadors brought spotted horses to the New World, where they proliferated on the plains of North America. Painted horses cut cattle, pulled wagons and matched the speediest sprinters. Many of the best shared ancestors with early "Steel Dust" Quarter Horses.

In 1950 the American Quarter Horse Association adopted a rule that banned horses with "excessive white markings" from their breeding registry, including foals born with AQHA registered parents. Fortunately, the rule was not retroactive. If it had been, some of the early Quarter Horse foundation stock would have been disqualified from registration.

There are as many controversies over the AQHA rule against excessive white markings as there are rumors about its origin. In spite of the discord, breeders of "Quarter-type" horses with flashy spots persevered. The American Paint Horse Association, founded in 1965, recognizes and registers stock horse–type individuals from American Paint Horse, American Quarter Horse and Thoroughbred pedigrees, including crop-outs—horses with Paint markings whose parents are registered Quarter Horses or Thoroughbreds.

Although most cutting horse breeders prefer registerable foals from Quarter Horse parents, crop-outs are still eligible for $15 million in annual

NCHA purses. Well-bred Paint cutting horses also bring as much money in the sale ring as registered Quarter Horses. Dolly Doc Doll, a 1984 bay Tobiano mare sired by Doc Doll (APHA), was one of the top ten high selling horses in the 1989 Star Select Cutting Horse Sale.

Jazalena, a 1985 crop-out filly by Smart Little Lena out of NCHA Non-Pro Futurity Champion Jazabell Quixote, could not be registered with AQHA because of her white markings. But Jazalena's owner, Spencer Harden of Millsap, Texas, registered with APHA and showed her in NCHA competition. Jazalena was the leading non-pro money earner in 1989.

Jazalena was not the only Paint to place in NCHA's 1989 upper echelon. Lynda Lynx, a brown overo daughter of Doc's Lynx, placed third in Non-Pro World Championship standings. Jason Cox tied for Reserve Youth World Champion riding Miss Scenic Tagbar, two-time APHA World Champion Cutting Mare.

Two of NCHA's great past performers are a Paint mother and her son. 1986 Super Stakes Champion Delta Flyer is out of 1973 NCHA World Champion Cutting Mare Delta.

Smoke's Peppy San, a champion cutting horse stallion, is a crop-out son of Pep's Holly, a full sister to AQHA World Champion Cutting Horse Sanacee. Although Bert Dedmon, Smoke's Peppy San's owner, admits most people breed mares to his stallion because they want a Paint, he breeds his mares because he wants good cutting horses. "I don't care what color the horse is," says Dedmon. "He can be purple with pink polka dots, and if he can cut a cow, that's all I care about."

THE ARABIAN

There are as many myths and misconceptions about cutting horses and cutting horse competition among Arabian owners as there are about Arabians and their owners among Quarter Horse people. What most cutting horse enthusiasts don't know is that Arabians make great cutting horses. And what most Arabian owners don't know is that Arabians make great cutting horses.

Arabians are an ancient breed tracing thousands of years into the deserts of the Middle East and Africa. Arabian pedigrees were carefully cultivated and maintained by marauding Bedouins who prized the swift mounts as warhorses. Perhaps because of centuries devoted to perpetuating the breed, Arabians are very prepotent for temperament and type, and readily impart their hallmarks of beauty, courage, intelligence and stamina.

Quarter Horses that dominate the cutting arena today share Arabian ancestors with all light breeds of horses. Cattle ranchers at the turn of the century often used Arabian stallions to breed to some of the coarse-looking

Selecting the Right Horse

ranch stock with draft horse lineage for refinement in the foals. But Quarter Horses sometimes carry Arabian blood up closer in pedigree than most horsemen suspect.

The Jockey Club, the official registry for Thoroughbreds, accepted Arabian registration until 1943, when they closed their books. Consequently, some foals by or out of Arabians double-registered with the Jockey Club were accepted for registration by the American Quarter Horse Association.

Punk Carter of Celina, Texas, is a professional cutting horse trainer who competes successfully in NCHA competition. Naw Walid, winner of the 1987 Arabian Horse Foundation Open Cutting, was Carter's first champion in Arabian competition. In 1959, however, he rode the AQHA World Champion Junior Cutting Horse, Hollywood Sana. Hollywood Sana was by Hollywood George and out of an unregistered Arabian mare.

In the early fifties, AQHA registration could be issued by inspection.

"The AQHA inspectors came to look at her," Carter recalls of Hollywood Sana, "and they wanted to see her work. I was about thirteen, and back then everyone rode without holding on to the saddle horn. About two good turns and she dumped me. The inspector laughed and said if she could turn that good, they better give her a number.

"The first cutting I ever took her to, I tied with Cutter Bill. I thought that was the greatest thing I had ever done. The next year he was NCHA World Champion."

Jim Reno, past president of the National Cutting Horse Association, began his career as a cutting horse trainer by riding Arabians in the fifties and sixties. Today, Reno's son Jimmy is earning money with Arabians in NCHA and Arabian competition.

Jimmy Reno, as well as other cutting horse trainers who have ridden Arabians, appreciate their quick minds and sensitive spirits, which they also often compare to Doc Bar–bred Quarter Horses. Arabians have the credentials, yet few owners have concentrated on breeding or showing Arabian cutting horses.

In the fifties, two geldings so dominated the Arabian cutting shows that they scared off their rivals and had to perform in open competition against Quarter Horses. El Hadi and Arraff were probably seen and admired by more Quarter Horse riders than Arabian owners. Arraff, the son of an imported English stallion, was Reserve Champion against NCHA Champion Miss Texas at the first Chicago International Show, and defeated World Champion Slats Dawson.

Forty years have passed since Arraff first cut a cow. It has been a slow start, but momentum is building. Recent renewed interest in cutting has increased membership in the International Arabian Cutting Horse Association and has added money to Arabian cutting purses. Arabian cutting horse owners are now recruiting Quarter Horse trainers and aiming long range for NCHA competition and purses.

"It's kind of funny, but when I started showing Arabians, people would laugh at me," says Jimmy Reno, who consistently scores high on Arabians in NCHA shows. "They don't laugh at me anymore."

Other Breeds

Pedigree has never been a prerequisite for NCHA competition. Many of the first horses awarded the NCHA Certificate of Ability were of mixed blood or unknown parentage. The 1966 NCHA Futurity Champion Rey Jay's Pete was out of an unregistered mare. July Jazz, 1989 NCHA Futurity winner, was denied Quarter Horse registration because he was an embryo-transfer foal with a registered sibling born the same year.

Thoroughbreds are generally considered too large and hot-blooded for cow work, although when crossed with Quarter Horses the results are often spectacular.

Spencer Harden won the 1975 NCHA Futurity on Wee Darlin, who was sired by the Thoroughbred Wee Folk. Although Harden admits the mare was flighty, she was an outstanding performer, and has produced several money earners. Squeak Toy, 1988 NCHA Non-Pro Derby Champion, is also out of a Thoroughbred race mare.

Two-time World Champion Cutting Horse Marion's Girl, that cutting legend Buster Welch says is the greatest horse he ever rode, was out of Joan Scharbauer, by the Thoroughbred Tallwood. Joan Scharbauer's dam was an unregistered ranch mare sired by a stallion called Old John.

Hollywood Sana, who outscored World Champion Cutter Bill, was sired by a Quarter Horse and out of an Arabian mare.

Perhaps the most unusual cutting horse pedigree belonged to I'd Rather Walk, a half-Arabian, half–Shetland Pony gelding, who was also a registered Paint. John Carter, who trained and rode many cutting legends, owned I'd Rather Walk for nearly thirty years. The black-and-white pony won a multitude of cutting awards and taught many aspiring cutters the basics, including John's sons Punk and Roy, both successful cutting horse trainers.

Other Selection Factors

AGE

For a beginner, the best horse, no matter the breeding, is a "seasoned" horse with some mileage. Most cutting horses begin their training as two-year-olds and require at least one year of training before they are shown. Showing is just the beginning of a cutting horse's education, however. It takes another year or two of riding before a cutting horse is confident enough to be considered "solid."

A solid horse is not easily rattled by unpredictable behavior of cattle or riders. He has entered enough herds to be familiar with the procedures of cutting, and he handles pressure with confidence and self-assurance. A good example of this type of horse is Mia Freckles, Kay Floyd's 1976 NCHA Non-Pro Futurity Champion.

A step above solid is the seasoned horse. He has full measure of the cattle and the rider, and confidence in his own ability. A seasoned horse may even ignore spurring from an inexperienced rider, in order to do his job right.

There are exceptions. Occasionally, a young horse will "fit" a beginner, but the rider with a young horse must spend a considerable amount of time in the saddle, as well as money for training and schooling.

On the other hand, an older, seasoned horse, five to six years of age, usually requires a minimum of riding or "tuning" by a professional. He can be kept at home or at a stable and taken to shows with little or no preparation.

A well-cared-for cutting horse, kept in condition, may perform into his twenties. Two-time NCHA World Champion Ball O'Flash began his career at eleven. Nineteen-year-old Royal Santana, a World Champion Gelding, earned his twelve-year-old rider a championship trophy and scholarship money in the 1990 NCHA Youth Scholarship Cutting.

When Bryant Dyer of Greenwell, Louisiana, won the 1986 NCHA Youth World Championship he was eighteen years old, and his gelding, Wimpy's Bran, was twenty.

"We were kind of scared to buy him because of his age," says Bryant. "His age is old, but he's not an old horse. That's what is so great about him."

Mary Lee Dixon sold Wimpy's Bran to the Dyer family and remembers their concern. "They were worried about resale value," says Dixon. "Of course, you couldn't make them sell him now for anything in the world."

SEX

Stallions are out of the question for anyone but experienced horsemen. Even the best-mannered stallion can be dangerously unpredictable in the hands of a novice. Some horses, but especially stallions, take advantage of inexperienced handlers and riders whenever they find the opportunity. They also sense fear in humans and quickly assert dominance.

Even professional trainers often geld good stallion prospects when they perform inconsistently. Rockys Playboy won the 1990 NCHA Derby just four weeks after he was gelded. His owner and rider, Terry Riddle, knew that castration was the only way to make him a dependable performer.

1988 NCHA Futurity Champion Smart Little Senor was gelded six weeks before the Futurity.

"It was for the betterment of the horse," explained Bill Freeman, the colt's trainer. "He always had talent, but it was the consistency problem that I had been fighting. He might have two good days, and then one bad one. Almost immediately after we cut him, I saw drastic changes in the horse."

Three-time World Champion Jazzote was kept a stallion until he was a four-year-old. "I took him to a show in Augusta," remembers Dennis Funderburgh, Jazzote's owner at the time. "He had been just as nice as he could be, but when he got down there, he never could even see a cow. On the way back to Texas, I told my wife I was going to geld him the minute we got home. She said that I'd better think about that before I did it. I said that I had—all the way from Georgia."

Some horse owners do not like to ride mares because of their heat cycles, which occur every three to four weeks, from February through September. This can be a nuisance for owners with mares that will flirt, or "show" in heat to stallions, or even geldings and other mares.

Generally, however, mares make excellent mounts. Aside from frequent urination during heat cycles, their hormones have little effect on performance. Some horsemen believe that mares are more alert, sensitive and tuned in to their riders than geldings and this more than offsets any inconvenience because of heat periods.

Many old-time horsemen will put copper tubing in a mare's water bucket, in the belief that this will keep her from cycling or showing in heat. It is also a common practice to rub Vicks VapoRub in a stallion's nostrils to mask the scent of mares in heat.

Owners of well-bred mares have the option of breeding them and raising foals. The mare will be out of action for at least a year, unless embryo transfer procedure is used. There are exceptions. Lynx Melody won the 1978 NCHA Futurity while carrying a foal, which was christened Doc's Accident.

Geldings, with the exception of some "proud cut" individuals who still exhibit stallion characteristics, make very dependable mounts and are excellent for beginners.

Selecting the Right Horse

SIZE

Cutters prefer small to medium-sized horses, from 14 to 15 hands, which are well balanced with a proportionate ratio of muscle and bone. Few riders like a horse over 15.2 hands, but if a cutting horse has all the right instincts, a trainer never discounts it for being too small. Little horses are generally quicker than bigger, bulkier ones. They are also usually less threatening to a cow. Because they are better able to get down to the cow's level, the smart ones can more easily "draw" or move the cow. They also may look more impressive when they drop down because they are closer to the ground.

Lynx Melody stood 13.3 hands and weighed 750 pounds the year she won the Futurity. Her rider, Larry Reeder, estimated that the little mare carried 250 pounds, including tack, when he rode her.

Hickorys Prescription, the 1990 NCHA Derby Reserve Champion, tops the measuring stick at 13.2 hands.

On the other end of the scale, Lee Garner, a 215-pound former linebacker at Mississippi, took the NCHA's 1990 World Champion Non-Pro title on Baldy Freckles, a gelding that tips the scales at 1,300 pounds.

Another star of recent years, Gangalena, was big enough to carry Skip Hobbs of Germantown, Tennessee, who stands 6'8", to the Non-Pro title at the 1990 NCHA Super Stakes.

CONFORMATION

Good conformation is the foundation of any successful performance horse. The structurally correct horse is most likely to possess natural athletic ability, being able to move freely with minimum strain to joints, tendons and ligaments.

Although anatomical faults can be overcome with sheer determination on the part of the horse, the importance of a good chassis should not be overlooked.

One of the keys to good conformation is balance. Every part of a horse should look as if it fits. A balanced horse pleases the eye. On the first viewing, no single aspect of the horse's appearance draws attention.

Because of the physical demands of cutting—slides, pivots and hard stops—adequate muscling is important. While muscle tone can be improved with conditioning, overall muscle mass is a matter of genetic makeup and cannot be altered.

Muscling should be in proportion to bone and frame. A light frame does not require as much muscling for movement as a heavy frame. Heavily muscled horses require more maturity, more care in conditioning and more bone in order to stay around.

This Peppy San Badger daughter is built for cutting.

Legs should be "clean" and free of bumps, swellings and blemishes, and the horse should exhibit a free, easy and relaxed stride. The horse should stand evenly and squarely on all four feet, with toes pointed straight ahead, as opposed to toeing in or out.

Pasterns should slope at about 45 degrees—an angle that should correlate to the angle of the shoulder. Knees should be straight, but are better slightly over than back when viewed from the side. Viewed from the front, legs should be straight from shoulder to hoof.

You do not see good cutting horses with short, upright necks. Because it is important for a cutting horse to be able to greet a cow at eye level, it is preferable for a horse to have a fairly straight neck, set relatively low, in relation to the body. Stargazers do not make good cutting horses.

It is preferable to have the length of back and hip in proportion to the length of neck. If a horse is balanced and has a nice long, well-muscled hip—essential in cutting—then it will also have a good neck. If the back is short in relation to hip and neck, then a horse is short-coupled. This is okay, but many cutters like a horse with a longer, more supple back.

Generally, a cutting horse's center of gravity is lower to the ground than other performance horses, and it is acceptable for a cutter to be longer than tall, proportionately.

Selecting the Right Horse

Most cutters will say that they like a horse whose hocks are low to the ground, which is the same as saying the legs may be shorter in proportion to the length. Also, good muscling on the inside and outside of the gaskins gives the illusion of the hocks being nearer to the ground than a lightly muscled horse.

Slightly turned-in hocks, or cow hocks, are acceptable. And some riders say that horses that are slightly sickled-hocked are able to stop and slide better than their well-turned-out brethren.

There are two schools of thought on the head of a horse. Some people think that pretty is as pretty does. Others say you don't ride the head so it doesn't matter.

Chuck Drummond, who owns 1990 Super Stakes Champion Foxie Merada, likes good-looking horses. "She has big eyes," he says of Foxie Merada. "I like her big eyes, her neat throatlatch, and the little head and little ears. It's more or less personal preference, I guess. But it shouldn't cost you more to show a pretty mare that's good than a mare that's ugly and good."

Smart Play looks great in front of a cow. Don Shugart photo.

Terry Riddle rode Foxie Merada for Drummond. He also rode and gelded 1990 Reserve Futurity Champion Smart Play.

"He was so ugly that I didn't see any need to leave him a stud," says Riddle. "He was the ugly duckling in the yearling pen that year. But he looked a lot prettier when I put him behind a cow."

If a horse is balanced in all other respects, the head will fit the body and be pleasing. Big eyes, tiny muscles and foxy ears are attractive, but there are plenty of good horses with plain heads and lots of cow sense.

DISPOSITION

Because cutting horses are the only equine athletes required to perform on their own initiative, they must be intelligent, willing partners in the cutting game. Cutters and their horses often form strong bonds of trust.

Show ring horses learn by rote, relying on the rider for commands. A cutting horse must also follow commands, but once the rider cuts a cow from the herd the horse is on its own. A difference of opinion exists among cutters as to whether a horse reacts to cattle because of instinct or learned experience. Whatever the origin of "cow sense," a savvy horse will improve with each exposure to cattle, computing every experience into a memory bank for future reference.

The extreme mental and physical demands of cutting draw on special reserves, but good cutting horses love the challenge of competition and are generous in giving. A horse's driving desire to excel, combined with a willing nature, is referred to as "heart." A horse with great heart can overcome many limitations.

Heart does not always guarantee a personable disposition. But it is nicer to be around a horse that likes people. Kay Floyd, 1988 Non-Pro World Champion, feels that way about her mare Playboys Madera.

"She's really rotten," Floyd explains about cutting's richest mare. "She's in your hip pocket all the time. I feed her carrots and she drinks Gatorade out of the bottle. She's really curious, and whatever you've got she wants. I've always been real attached to my horses, but since Madera, well—she's one of those you dream about."

Lover or loner, a cutting horse must be steady and dependable. Calmness and control in the herd are as much a part of cutting as flash and action in front of a cow. A horse that can combine control and action is ahead of the game.

The great Peppy San Badger (Little Peppy) was a master at combining control and action. "He was so strong and yet controlled that he never had to slam himself around," explains his rider and trainer Buster Welch. "He reminded me of the golfer's prayer: Lord, grant me the strength to hit the ball easy. He was a quiet horse. He never fretted, yet he always seemed to have the energy for whatever was needed."

Although they require lots of patience, most trainers make allowances for "spooky" horses, especially young ones. Open and Non-Pro World Champion Jazzote is still terrified of mules and horse-drawn vehicles. Spencer Harden stuffed cotton into the ears of 1989 leading money earner Jazalena so she would not spook and shy from noises in the show arena.

"I think a lot of good horses border on the point of being too wild," says NCHA Hall of Fame Rider John Paxton. "They are almost hyperactive. To make horses great, you have to have the ability to get [that energy] under control. Then you can ask the horse for a little extra."

Smart Whittle Wena, winner of the 1990 NHCA Non-Pro Classic, had lots of athletic ability when Julie Roddy purchased her as a two-year-old. But she was terrified of cattle.

"She was so bad that she used to tie up when I'd walk in with a herd of cattle," said Roddy. "I had a lot of trouble getting her to break away from the cow I was cutting because she was so scared of the cattle behind her.

"She's afraid of everything. Dirt. If the dirt changes color, she's scared. She's real afraid of tractors that have headlights—she thinks they're eyes."

Roddy is an accomplished non-pro who trains her own horses. With patience, she has helped Smart Whittle Wena overcome her fears. Generally, however, timid amateurs and timid horses are not a good combination. Horses that are easily intimidated need the assurance that only an experienced rider can transmit.

1990 NCHA National Finals Champion Especials Lady is another high-strung horse that is dynamite in a cutting arena. "Anything you do, you've got to be awful careful," explains her owner, Harold Kuehling, who even saddles the mare for her rider, Bob Bouget. "Anything can scare her to death—anything but a cow."

Most intelligent horses will try to bluff their riders occasionally, especially amateur riders. Don't take it personally. If you are as smart as the horse, you will see a pattern in his errant behavior. Get professional help if you need it.

Sandy Bonelli bred, raised and trained 1989 Non-Pro Futurity Champion Bella Coquette. Although Bonelli has successfully trained and shown many champions, she knew when to ask for help. She had a professional work with Bella Coquette in the early stages of her training.

"I had a little trouble with her bucking, and it scared me real bad," Bonelli explained about her problem with the mare. "I'm not a bronc rider, and it was really hindering my training because she had me bluffed and I was scared of her. Now it's under control to where I can at least pull her up if she starts."

Sometimes there may be a personality conflict between a horse and rider that hinders performance. This is not unusual and happens with pros and non-pros. When a cutter says that a horse fits, he means that the two of them work together well, and that the horse fits his personality and style.

FAULTS AND VICES

It is better to buy a horse without any serious vices than to try to correct those which are already ingrained. Sometimes a horse will be offered at a bargain price because it has "a little problem." Most small problems become larger for beginners, so it is best to avoid them altogether.

Although you should ride a horse you are considering, it is wise to rely on an adviser for an assessment of a horse's good and bad points. There are other things you can and should check, before buying, even if the horse passes the performance test:

- Some horses develop the habit of cribbing (chewing on wood) or windsucking (sinking their teeth into wood and sucking air into their windpipes). Sometimes a windsucker will be fitted with a special strap around its throatlatch to discourage the habit. This is an annoying, destructive and obsessive habit that is rarely cured. In addition, one cribber in a barn can inspire others. Some stables will not accept a cribber as a boarder.
- Pawing is another destructive and obsessive habit. Pawing horses dig holes in stalls, shred trailer mats, tear their shoes off and split their hooves.
- Weavers, horses that shift their weight from one front foot to the other while nodding their heads in rhythm, are not as destructive as cribbers and pawing horses, but the habit is an escape and indicates a long-term discontentment with environment. If the horse were human, he would be in therapy. Thoughts of rehabilitation are impractical.

UNSOUNDNESS

Never purchase a horse without a veterinary examination. This should be done at your expense and may include X rays, and transportation, as well as the regular exam. It is absolutely essential for a performance horse or a breeding animal.

Insist on selecting your own veterinarian. If the owner refuses to allow the horse to be examined, do not buy the horse.

Make sure you have a record of the horse's current vaccinations and worming schedule for the exam. The veterinarian will check the horse's eyes, ears, mouth, teeth, throat, skin, hair coat, heart, lungs, sex organs, legs and feet. In addition, he will watch the horse as he is walked and trotted away from him and back again. Ask the veterinarian to confirm the horse's age by examining his teeth.

Before You Buy

Always insist on watching the owner put a halter on the horse and lead it from the stall to make sure the horse can be easily caught and haltered. Let the horse stand tied for half an hour in a busy area to make sure it is broken to tie.

Ask the owner to load the horse in a trailer to be sure he loads easily and stands quietly. Then take a short ride. Some horses will load well but go berserk when the trailer is in motion. You will be able to hear it knocking around if this happens. Climbers, as these horses are called, are difficult to haul with other horses or in a trailer with a partition.

Ask to see the horse saddled and bridled. Watch for horses that are head-shy and refuse the bridle or that kick or bite when the saddle is cinched. Pick up the horse's foot and hold it up for a minute or two to make sure you won't have to throw and tie him to clean his feet. Bad habits can make routine care and maintenance a headache.

Watch the horse eat grain. If he drools or drops his food, there could be a problem with his mouth or tongue. Besides hindering chewing, irregular teeth can cause difficulties when a horse is bitted.

Lead the horse around, inside the barn and out. Does he shy and jump into you? A hot horse that is always looking for boogers or is easily spooked may be more than you want to handle if you are a beginner. This type of horse is usually better with an experienced handler who knows what to expect. The confidence of a familiar caretaker or rider tends to calm a flighty horse. A beginner usually makes this type of horse doubly apprehensive, and he becomes an accident waiting to happen.

HOW MUCH TO SPEND?

Before you begin to even look at horses to buy, get a good feel for the market. Talk with owners, breeders and trainers and find out what the price range is for horses in the age bracket you have selected. Then figure out the range for pedigrees and performance levels. It will help to check results of recent cutting horse sales, which are usually listed in cutting publications such as *Cuttin'*

Hoss Chatter or *The Quarter Horse News*. The sale company will also provide you with a list upon request.

If you don't plan to breed, pedigree is not as weighty a matter as if you do. There are plenty of good, solid cutting horse performers with less than fashionable or "hot" pedigrees. You will, however, want to consider resale value. The better the pedigree, the easier it usually is to sell the horse, and the higher the price.

Beware of bargains. Although cutting has its share of Cinderella stories, most of them came about through the efforts of experienced professionals. Two-time World Champion Ball O'Flash was purchased for $250 at an auction frequented by horsemeat buyers. But Leroy Ashcraft, who raised and trained 1964 Reserve World Champion Mare Jill's Lady, was the one who brought the gelding to the limelight.

Expect to pay anywhere from $1,500 on up for a cutting horse, depending on age, experience, sex and pedigree.

Another practical option for a beginner is to rent or lease a cutting horse. Many trainers will provide a horse with lessons or may know of an owner who has little time to ride and would consider a lease with a supervised beginner. This option also allows a beginner to try different horses, and advance in experience, before putting money into his own.

If you buy a horse from a trainer, make sure someone you trust also rides the horse. Although in the minority, there are a few trainers who will misrepresent horses and use distracting cover-ups to conceal performance problems. An experienced rider should be able to spot them.

If you are considering a horse with a show record, talk with people who have seen the horse perform. This will give you an objective picture of the horse's style and ability. Be sure to check his earnings record with NCHA and AQHA.

A SECOND OPINION

It is a good idea to get an expert's unbiased opinion before you purchase a cutting horse of any age. The younger the horse and the more limited its show record, the more important it is to have at least one other experienced cutting horse rider look at it and ride it—on more than one occasion, if possible.

If the horse is registered, check with the breed registry for names of the breeder and previous owners and contact them for input and information. Call the trainer and ask about his experiences with the horse.

If the horse is not registered or if you are considering purchasing from the breeder or trainer, ask for references. There is not much difference between

Selecting the Right Horse

buying a horse and hiring an employee. Résumé and references are critical. The cost of most horses is minimal compared to the cost of caring for it over the long haul.

Once you have selected a horse, your next consideration must be the tack you will need for cutting and what kind of attire you will wear when you compete.

Tack

THE SADDLE

The main purpose of a saddle is to align the rider with the horse's center of balance and to make it easy and comfortable for the rider to keep his seat.

Jockeys ride crouched in the stirrups of very small, light saddles while leaning over the withers and neck of horses that carry most of their weight on a front end that is propelled forward at maximum speed. Stock horses, unlike racehorses, work from their hindquarters and low to the ground; there-

Cutting saddles have relatively flat seats and long, narrow horns.

fore Western saddles are designed to center the rider over the back, behind the withers.

Many people assume that there are two kinds of saddles—English and Western—and that any Western saddle will do for cutting. There are, however, specially designed saddles for cutting. So if you plan to cut, you should buy a cutting saddle.

Cutting saddles have relatively flat seats and low cantles that permit a rider to flow with quick movements of the horse. They are lightweight and have fenders that allow easy backward and forward motion of the legs and a feel for the horse under the leather.

In the fifties, cutters rode deep in the saddle with both hands in the air above the saddle horn. Pine Johnson, who rode Poco Bueno, changed that style when the famous stallion turned hard during a performance and left Johnson with nothing but air between his knees. From then on Johnson rode with one hand braced on the saddle horn, and the cutting industry followed suit.

Today cutting saddles are made with long, narrow saddle horns that allow a rider to brace and pull with the movements of the horse. Before you buy a saddle, it is best to get professional advice about the seat size. A sixteen-inch seat is average, but you should try several different sizes. Also try a smooth seat and a roughout to see which you prefer. Most saddles come with some amount of padding. The important thing is to buy a saddle that feels comfortable. The less riding experience you have, the more saddles you should try before you decide. Don't overlook used saddles. If they are name brands and have been well cared for, used saddles cost less and are already broken in for riding. In addition, you can probably arrange for a demonstration ride on a horse. New saddles, however, usually stay on saddle stands, although you can sit in them in the stands.

Cinches, or girths, are usually made of woven-web mohair or synthetic ducking, padded with fleece. You want to be able to move your heels in front of and behind the cinch, so make sure the cinch is not too wide for these maneuvers.

Cutting saddles should have back cinches. The back cinch holds the back of the saddle in place during jolting moves. It is never drawn tight and usually hangs loose an inch or so beneath the belly. Always unfasten the back cinch before the front cinch when unsaddling. Conversely, when saddling always fasten it after the front cinch is in place. Some horses will bolt if a saddle slips underneath them. A loose front cinch is much easier to disengage than the back cinch, which is buckled.

Some riders use a breast harness, or collar, which is attached to the

Selecting the Right Horse

saddle at the sides and also to the cinch under the belly. Should the cinch become loose, the breast harness will prevent the saddle from slipping back on the horse. The breast collar should not be snug but should allow room for movement. NCHA rules prohibit breast collars that pass over the horse's neck. This eliminates martingales, which are considered training devices because they exert pressure on the bit. Tie-downs (straps attached to a noseband at one end and breast harness or cinch at the other) are also not allowed in the show arena.

THE STIRRUPS

Stirrups for cutting should be open ended and not more than two inches wide. While pleasure saddles have wider, heavier stirrups for the rider to rest the ball of the foot, cutters shove their feet through to the arch, where the heel stops the boot. The oxbow-shaped stirrup, which does not have a platform

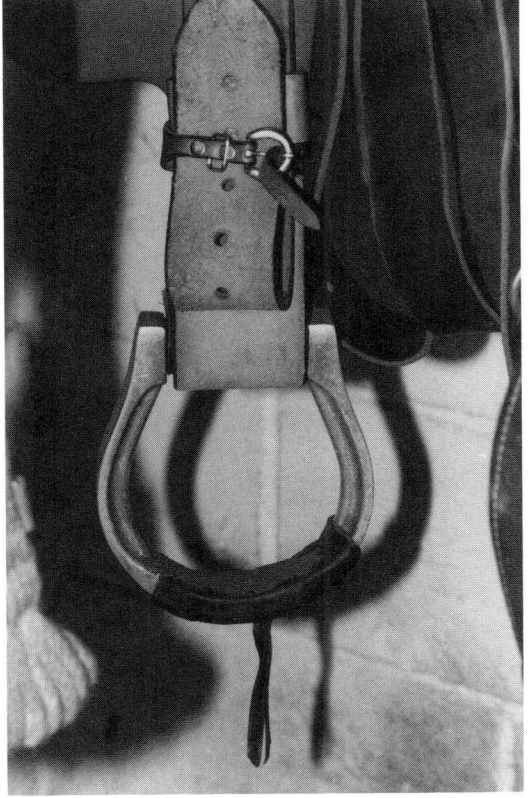

An oxbow stirrup.

or a flat bottom, is popular with cutters. These stirrups keep the foot in place but can be dangerous for the very same reason. Beginners should take care not to get a foot hung in the stirrup when mounting or dismounting.

Stirrup length should be adjusted to allow a slight bend in the knees. If the stirrups are too short, the rider will push back to the cantle when he straightens his legs on turns. If they are too long, he may lose them when stretching for a foothold.

SADDLE PADS

One saddle pad of medium thickness is usually sufficient under a cutting saddle. Fleece pads are lightweight, easy to wash and dry quickly. Woven pads, especially wool, are more durable because they keep their shape longer than fleece. Some pads combine fleece on the bottom with a woven cover. Colorful Navajo rugs, over light fleece pads, are popular for the show arena.

THE BRIDLE

Sometimes it is possible to buy the bridle and bit when you buy the trained horse. This is an advantage because the horse will be accustomed to the rig. If it is not possible to do this, find out what the horse usually wears and try to duplicate it as nearly as possible. Keep in mind, however, that NCHA rules do not allow the use of bridles with nosebands or bosals, and hackamores must be of rope or braided rawhide with no metal portions.

Headstalls are mainly a matter of personal preference, but it is not wise to change a bit on a horse that is working well. Depending on the stage of training, a horse may use one of a variety of bits. If he has just been started in training, he may be fitted with a hackamore or "sidepull" bridle. Such a bridle does not use a bit for control, but rather the pressure of a noseband and reins. If a hackamore is used in the show arena, the judge is allowed to check to make sure that two fingers may be passed freely between the hackamore and muzzle.

Snaffle bits are used with young horses. A snaffle bit consists of a mouthpiece, either straight, twisted or broken, attached to rings at the checks, so that pressure comes from direct pull of each rein. Most cutting horses are out of the snaffle bit and into a curb bit by the time they compete in the show arena. But Cols Lil Pepper, the horse that captured the hearts of fans in the 1988 NCHA Futurity, was ridden with a snaffle. His trainer, Doug Jordan, uses snaffle bits because he wants his horses to feel relaxed and comfortable.

Curb bits are any bits that require a curb chain and have shanks to which the reins are attached. They may have a broken mouthpiece or a solid bar. The bar may be straight but is usually curved to some degree and has a port

Selecting the Right Horse

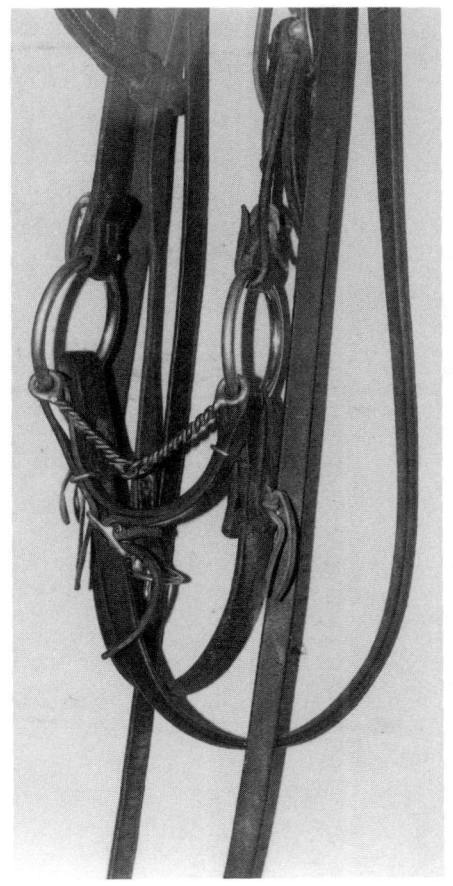
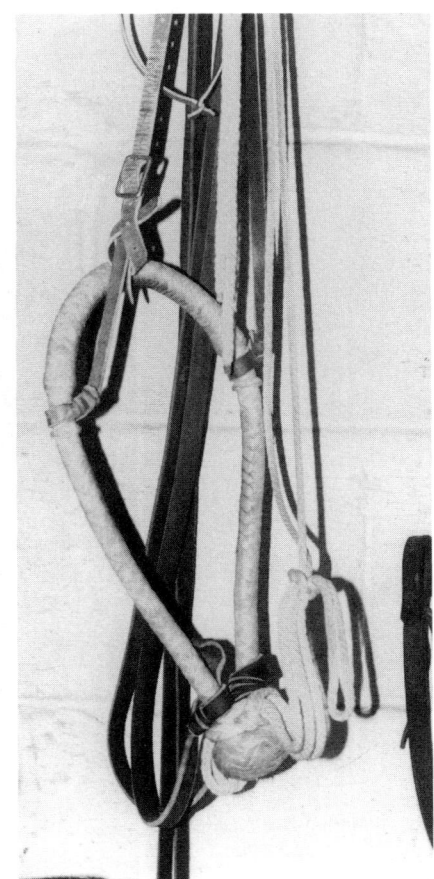

A snaffle bit with a twisted mouthpiece and curb strap to prevent the bit from slipping at sides of the mouth.

A plaited rawhide hackamore bridle (bosal).

in the center that may vary in width and height. Shanks vary in length from a few inches to six inches or more. A chin strap or chain is attached to the sides of the bit, above the shanks, and rests behind and under the chin. This chain produces a viselike effect in conjunction with the mouthpiece, when the reins are pulled back. An Argentine snaffle bit is used with a curb chain and has a snaffle mouthpiece and hinged shanks.

Many horses are ruined through the misuse of bits. In good hands, they are invaluable training aids. In the wrong hands, they produce the cruelest abuse. No one should ride a horse without learning the correct way to use his hands and bits.

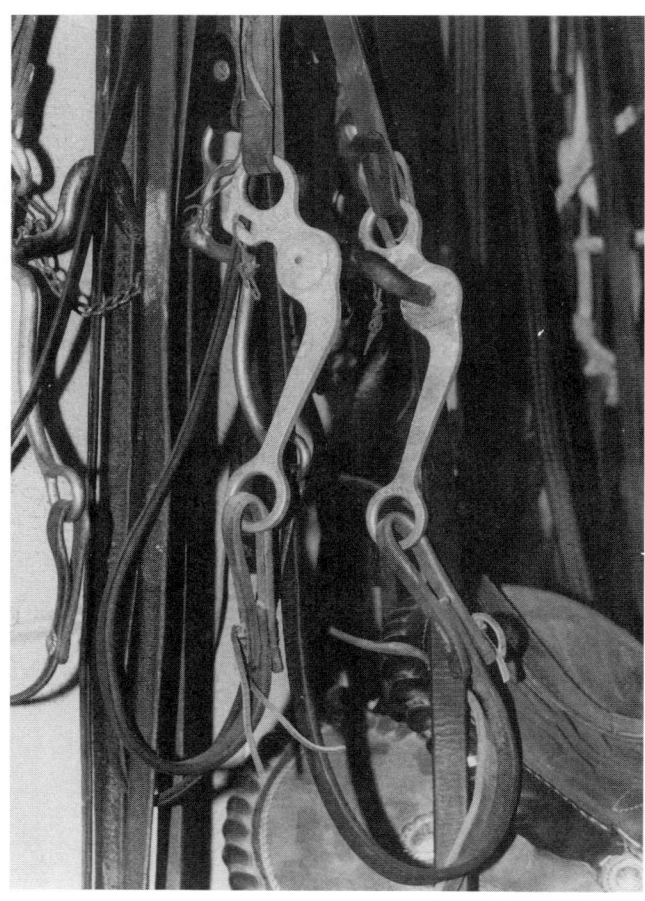

An *aluminum grazing bit (curb) with medium shanks.*

Theoretically a horse is driven forward, with leg and seat cues, into the bit. Most beginners use front and back aids independently and precipitate problems that are difficult to remedy. Bits should be used in a give-and-take manner—the horse meets resistance and is rewarded by a release of pressure if he stops or maintains the required gait. Bits should not be instruments of abuse or even of restraint.

Reins should be long enough to easily touch the ground when dropped. Usually they are between six or seven feet long and between ½ and ⅝ inch wide. Ideally, reins should be heavy enough to hang well and feel comfortable in your hand. New reins may feel stiff at first, but with use they will become more pliable. Neat's-foot oil is good for softening new headstalls and reins.

SPLINT BOOTS

It is a good idea to use splint boots on the front legs of a cutting horse during practice or in the show pen. The boots, which fit around the cannons and fetlocks and fasten with buckles or Velcro, are made of leather or synthetic material. Splint boots protect the cannons from strikes made by the opposite foot, or back feet, during athletic maneuvers.

Skid boots, over the fetlocks of the back legs, prevent the fetlocks from being burned, or rubbed raw, by hard, deep stops. Once a horse is burned, he will be reluctant to stop as hard as he is capable of stopping. For this reason skid boots should be used.

Grooming and Conditioning Your Horse

Bubba Cascio takes credit for today's style of natural manes and tails in the cutting arena. Cascio owned and rode Royal Jazzy, a leading performer in the early sixties. At that time the preferred style was short tails and roached manes. But Cascio thought Royal Jazzy's flowing mane and tail added a lot to her eye appeal, and he let them grow.

Some of today's performers have tails that brush the ground and therefore are kept in braids or mudknots outside the show ring. A small braid, often fastened with a bright ribbon, pulls mane hair away from the bridle path. The forelock is left natural and can be pulled under a browband if it is long enough to obstruct vision.

Hair on fetlocks and in the ears is usually clipped for shows, and so are whiskers on the muzzle. Stray tail hairs are plucked or shaved to give the dock a smooth, neat appearance.

Some cutters rub a small amount of mineral oil into the muzzle and around the eyes and ears to bring out black skin beneath the hair. Pond's cold cream is very good for this and is not as heavy as mineral oil.

Summer hair coats are easier to care for than winter ones, which take longer to dry after the horse is worked or bathed. Winter blanketing will keep the coat thinner and make it lie close to the body. It will also keep dust from clinging to the hairs with static electricity. But blankets must be kept on your horse except when he is ridden, and a great deal of care must be taken to dry him thoroughly before reblanketing. A hood will also be needed to prevent excess hair growth on the neck and face.

Feet should be kept clean and dry and trimmed every four to eight weeks, depending on rate of growth and wear. A good hoof dressing applied daily will help prevent dry, cracked hoofs. If shoes are worn, they should be reset when the feet are trimmed and replaced as necessary. Choose a farrier with the same care you would a veterinarian or trainer.

Horses should receive an adequate ration of both good quality hay and grain. Portions are calculated according to size, use and condition of the horse. Annual vaccinations should be up to date and a bimonthly worming program followed religiously. If you are not sure about feeding or preventative health measures, consult a veterinarian.

If you travel across state lines for shows, your horse will need a health certificate signed by a veterinarian and a Coggins test to prove he does not carry equine infectious anemia. You may want to vaccinate your horse for distemper and influenza, especially if he is young. Consult your veterinarian about this.

All horses need conditioning, but especially those that perform only once a week or infrequently. Cutting is stressful to muscles, joints and ligaments, and the best way to prevent soreness and injury is to make sure your horse is adequately exercised at least three times a week.

Often horses cheat on their performances because they are sore and it hurts to turn or stop hard. Stiff muscles and joints may not produce overt lameness, but they definitely affect a horse's performance and attitude.

Tuning and practice are not the only forms of exercise your horse requires. He should be trotted and loped at regular intervals. Pleasure riding is good exercise and a break from arena work. Just make sure that he gets a workout.

Riding Attire

Rules for NCHA competition specify that participants must wear western attire, including a hat. Men must wear long-sleeved shirts with collars and buttons or snaps completely down the front. Women must also wear long sleeves and a collar, but buttons are not required. A sweater or jacket may be worn over an appropriate shirt.

Jeans are standard attire for men and women. Blue, black or gray are the most popular colors, although you may see some cutters wearing flashier colors. Stone-washed or faded jeans are unacceptable. Dark, starched jeans are the norm.

Although chaps and spurs are not required, most riders wear spurs as a riding aid, and Finalists at major shows wear chaps. While spurs are allowed, spurring the shoulder is not permitted and will be penalized. Spurs may not be used forward of the cinch, and a judge may stop any run if he thinks the rider is training or abusing the horse.

Selecting the Right Horse

Chaps are leather leggings that can be useful for maintaining contact with the saddle. At one time they were essential to the wardrobe of any cowboy who gathered cattle in brush because they protected his legs from gouges, tears and thorns. Such cowboys often used covered stirrups to help push through the brush.

Chaps come in two styles: batwing, which are wide and flared at the bottom, covering boots and stirrups, and shotgun, which are straight and narrow. Chaps are attached with a belted waistband and buckles or zippers.

Boots are a matter of personal preference. Some riders like ropers, which have a low, flat heel. But many cutters prefer high-heeled boots, which make it easier to keep their feet in the stirrups.

The choice of hat also reflects personal taste, but cutters usually wear similar styles with slight variations. Most hat manufacturers have a cutting model, so ask for that if you are buying a new hat. Natural-colored straw hats are appropriate and most comfortable for warm weather, while wool and beaver are worn in winter. Beige, silver-belly or black are most commonly worn.

FIVE

The Basics of Cutting

Learning to ride a cutting horse requires at least a basic knowledge of horsemanship. Although most horse owners profess familiarity and proficiency with riding skills, many have acquired experience through trial and error. Hours in the saddle have given them a sense of balance, but a poor understanding of the physical and mental aspects of horsemanship.

I once owned a tack shop on the outskirts of a southwestern metropolitan area. Many of my clients were pleasure horse owners and aspiring barrel racers and rodeo riders. The most important items on their shopping agendas were bits. They would start with the bit recommended by the horse's former owner, then work through the inventory, bit by bit, literally.

If the road to hell is paved with good intentions, the road to a horse's hell is paved with discarded bits. A bit is only as good as the hands, legs and seat of the person holding the reins. Riding logic is not a complex concept to grasp, yet many riders never do.

Horses learn from consistently repeated behavior. Some are quick studies, while others require patient perseverance. They are all creatures of habit, however, whose security is tethered to the familiar. Ninety-nine percent of the time, when a beginner has trouble with a horse, it is the rider's fault. Yet most beginners have trouble accepting their own incompetence when it comes to horses. If a horse bolts or jigs, they buy another bit. If the bit is severe and causes the horse to throw his head up, they purchase a tie-down so he cannot escape the pressure and pain.

If you are a beginner, do yourself and your horse a favor and learn how to ride. Before you ride any horse, young or old, talk to the owner and learn the horse's routine, including the tack that is used, and stick with it in the beginning.

If you want to change some things later, do so gradually. Horses cannot be rushed in a learning situation. An accomplished rider or trainer can produce miraculous results in one or two saddlings, but the results are not ingrained and can be just as quickly undone.

How a Horse Moves

Understanding the locomotion of a horse is a good starting point for beginning riders. Before ever stepping into a stirrup, a beginner should know that a horse begins all forward, lateral, and backward movement with his hindquarters. Many riders mistakenly think of impulsion only as a direct result of a kick to the ribs. Beyond that, they assume all control is in the hands and front end.

Real control and impulsion come from the seat and legs. The horse is essentially ridden into the bridle or bit. Most horses seem to know when they carry a novice because they do not feel the secure seat and legs of an experienced rider.

Riding just the front end of a horse works if you are a jockey and only interested in moving forward. For real control, however, you must learn to work with the driving end of a horse.

BALANCE

Balance, whether riding a horse, bicycle or surfboard, is a feeling that cannot be communicated, but must be experienced. Since it is especially important to a cutting horse rider, it is a good focal point for a beginner.

Because cutting horses move closer to the ground with short, explosive bursts of power from the rear, it is important for a rider to remember to keep a deep seat. Many trainers remind non-pros to sit on their pockets. In this way, they are ready to move with the horse. If they are too far forward in the saddle, they will be thrown up against the horn when the horse moves quickly.

Learning to sit correctly involves more than actual placement in the saddle. That can be accomplished just as well if the saddle is still on its rack. A rider should be as fluid in rhythm and balance as a skater gliding across ice. So much of the finesse of riding is in the feel of the horse's motion. Horse and rider should be moving together toward the same goal—a fence, a field or a cow.

One of the best ways to learn balance and gain security is to ride bareback. A rider is much more conscious of the sharp withers of the horse than the

Punk Carter pursues a baldy as his horse explodes out of the ground.

Jan Hurley, a beginning rider and student of Punk Carter, shows good form, sitting on her pockets for a stop.

Jan's seat is good and her back is relaxed as she moves in balance with the horse.

The Basics of Cutting 111

saddle horn, and will learn to adjust and sit down with the center of gravity of the horse.

The round pen, or small arena, is a good place to begin bareback riding. The key is relaxation. It really is fun and a great way to feel the motion of a horse. Once you are relaxed and walking, close your eyes and concentrate on moving in rhythm with the horse. Rhythm is an integral part of balance. If you have two left feet when it comes to dancing, you will have to work especially hard to acquire balance in riding.

As you become comfortable with your balance at the walk, move to a trot and then a lope. Bareback riding also helps to acquaint you with the leg aids, which are necessary at the faster gaits. Since there is no saddle leather, it is easier to apply leg pressure and gauge your horse's response.

Depending on how they have been trained and who has been riding them, some horses respond to a subtle nudge of the leg, while others need a shove. Tension and urgency also dictate degree and timing of the response. Every horse will be a little different, so be prepared to adapt.

The Aids

LEGS

A horse is started forward with leg and seat pressure, sometimes implemented with spurs. The position of the legs determines whether the horse moves straight ahead or to the right or left.

Cutting, as much as any equine sport, utilizes the rider's leg pressure. While it is true that the rider relinquishes control of the reins after cutting a cow, he is still very much in control with his legs. He can increase the speed of forward motion or turns, and he can move a horse into a cow or turn it away—all with leg pressure.

The principle is simple and it becomes second nature with experienced riders. To move or turn a horse to the right, apply pressure with the left calf, or heel, slightly behind the girth, and keep the right leg steady at the girth.

Sometimes it helps to think of the right leg as a post around which you turn the horse. Pushing with the left leg behind the girth causes the horse to resist the pressure (some people think the horse is moving away from the pressure) and swing his haunches to the left. If you've ever stood on the ground and tried to push a horse's rump away from you, you will understand the principle. Horses resist and push against steady pressure.

If a cutter is standing parallel to a calf and his horse wants to turn in toward the animal, the rider simply moves the horse's rear end toward the

Jan, an artist from Pilot Point, Texas, cues her horse to follow the cow.

Head-to-head with a cow, Jan keeps her legs relaxed and her heels away from the horse's sides.

The Basics of Cutting

Kathy Burkett had only ridden "rent" horses a few times in her life before starting cutting lessons. This is just her third time on a cutting horse.

cow with the inside leg (leg nearest the cow) and holds the shoulders steady with the outside leg.

The same techniques work when the horse is in motion. For a turn to the right, the rider cues the horse with the left leg and reinforces the direction and degree of turn with the reins. As the rider cues a moving horse with the left leg, for a right turn, and looks in the direction of the turn, his weight will also shift, without any conscious effort, into the turn.

The same principles apply in the cutting arena when the horse is working on a loose rein. If the rider watches the cow, he will move easily with the horse when the horse moves.

Remember that leg pressure works on the principle of stimulus and response. When the horse responds to the cue, remove the pressure.

SEAT

The cutter's seat is relaxed. In fact, the rider's posture in the saddle is often referred to as the "cutter's slouch." Beginners are told to think about sitting on the rear pockets of their jeans. This puts the hips underneath the torso and gives proper balance for quick, hard movements of the horse.

114   CUTTING

Ellen Leonard shows English pleasure horses and hunters and jumpers. This is only her second time on a cutting horse.

Ellen is too far forward in the saddle—a very common problem for English riders the first few times on a cutter.

The Basics of Cutting

Ellen is already getting a feel for sitting deep in the saddle for a stop or turn.

If hips and seat are forward, the rider will be thrown against the horn when the horse suddenly stops and turns. It is a common problem for former barrel racers, jumpers or English pleasure riders to sit too far foward on a cutting horse and be ahead of the action.

When a rider sits in the saddle without putting his feet in the stirrups, his legs should hang slightly bent at the knees. A good way to be sure you have the correct stirrup length is to sit on the horse with your feet in the stirrups. If you can look down, without bending over, past your knee and see about one inch of your toe, the stirrups are the right length.

A cutter rides with his heels pushed to the platform of the stirrups, with toes pointed slightly out, a position that allows freedom of movement for the legs. Toes should not be so far out that the heels are close to the horse's side. Otherwise, the horse will be accidentally jabbed with the spurs when he stops and turns.

Even though cutting requires a deep seat, if a rider sits with feet shoved forward and thighs parallel to the ground, as if sitting in a chair, he will be thrown forward when the horse jumps out of a turn. Instead, the rider's thighs should gently curve with the horse's ribs and with the knees gently flexed. Everything should feel relaxed. Since a rider's tension and awkwardness inhibit free movement of the horse, the rider must flow with the action.

Ready for a turn, Jan is centered over the horse . . .

. . . Jan rides her horse out of the turn.

The Basics of Cutting

Cutting, more than any horse sport, demands that the rider play a passive role when the horse is working. Although leg pressure may be used, it is contact and release, not a grip. Relax and sit down—that advice is repeatedly given to amateurs and non-pros during a performance, and it's the best advice.

HANDS

Since the rules of cutting competition require that a horse work on a loose rein, a rider picks up the reins only when he is cutting a cow from the herd or when he is quitting a cow. The cutter's free hand is always on the saddle horn.

Entering a herd and driving the cattle, the rider picks up the reins as a signal for the horse to step forward. The movement of the hand is vertical and does not create bit pressure. It is, however, an acknowledgment that the rider has contact with the bit and is in control.

When the rider has separated the cow he intends to work, he drops the rein hand to the neck of the horse, in front of the saddle horn, and keeps it there until he quits that cow.

Beginners sometimes have trouble remembering to keep the rein hand down on the neck. It may help to grab some mane hair as a reminder and an anchor.

Punk Carter lifts his reins to drive the horse forward.

Reins are lowered to drop the horse into action.

Kathy watches the cow. She looks good but her rein hand should be down.

As her horse pushes out of the turn, Jan watches the cow and keeps a relaxed grip on the saddle horn.

The Basics of Cutting

Out of necessity, non-pro June Roberts rides her World Champion Gelding, Monkeys Formula, with both hands on the horn. The gelding's hard, fast moves can take a rider by surprise.

Horns on cutting saddles are long and narrow to permit the grip that helps modern cutters brace for quick turns. Early-day competitors, who rode with hands free, sometimes parted company with their horses during explosive maneuvers.

The horn should be gripped loosely so that the wrist and arm are relaxed. When the horse drops low in front to counter a cow, the rider braces against the stirrups and horn to maintain balance with the horse. The action is a flexing of the arm and hand rather than a stiffening. A constant death-grip will create tension in the rider's body and may interfere with the performance of the horse.

The Gaits

THE WALK

In some western pleasure classes it is not unusual to see horses with necks stretched and noses nearly touching the ground—in an exaggerated imitation of a relaxed walk. Since it is unnatural and forced, tension is inherent. Cutting horses, however, are trained to walk with a calm, unhurried, relaxed stride. Because cattle are volatile, cutting horses must be masters of the low profile when approaching and entering a herd.

Balance is the key in all cutting action, even at the walk. Length of stride is a matter of preference and circumstance. Some riders move one step at a time, especially if they want to stall for time. Others, like five-time NCHA Futurity Champion Buster Welch, move through a herd like a hot knife through butter. Whatever the technique, the key to the walk is a natural and relaxed posture.

THE TROT

Much of a cutting horse's work is performed at the trot, even though some riders and trainers spend very little time practicing at this gait. It is wise for a beginner to become adept and comfortable at a sitting trot. Not only is it good for balance and coordination, it is also an excellent conditioning exercise for horse and rider. Trotting bareback also strengthens the muscles in a rider's thighs.

Handle Bar Hanna rates a running cow.

At a fast pace the mare is still hooked on the cow.

THE LOPE

A cutter probably spends more hours at the lope than any other gait. He lopes to prepare his horse for a performance. Loping gets the heart pumping, the blood flowing, and warms the muscles. It also helps relax a horse mentally and physically.

Although most cutting performances consist of short, explosive moves, stamina is required to string those moves together for twenty- or thirty-second intervals. Loping is an aerobic exercise that can prepare a horse for the rigorous demands of cutting.

Stopping and Backing

Backing is one thing that a cutting horse has to do that is completely unnatural to him. The movement has to be taught and then performed very carefully. As a basic training and tuning maneuver, backing is useful for reminding a horse to stay balanced over his hocks and to be ready for quick action. Often, a trainer will stop a horse, then back him a step or two in preparation for a 180-degree turn with a cow.

Dry work—Carter backs Bandito Maid. Notice the loose reins.

Bandito Maid steps back up with hind legs collected under her body.

Carter likes to use a hackamore, even with five-year-olds like Solid Gold Doc.

A trained cutting horse should stop with leg and seat pressure. In executing or aiding a stop, a rider sits down deeply into the saddle, applying pressure with his hips and seat. Not only does this signal a stop, it helps the horse execute the stop and puts the rider in a position to ride through the stop and into a turn if necessary. Since the power in a stop comes from the rear, a rider prepares for the action by sitting down, rather than leaning backward. If a rider leans back into a stop, the power of a quick stop will jar him off balance. If the horse turns after the stop, the rider is behind the motion.

When a rider sits down and into a stop, he is ready for a turn. If the horse continues out of a turn with fast forward motion, the rider can rotate his hips slightly forward to go with the action or push back down for another stop or turn.

Cattle

BREEDS

Serious cutters study cattle. Although many non-pro riders rely on their helpers for advice, they still watch the cattle to get a feel for the action.

Major NCHA cutting events follow strict guidelines for cattle selection and contract for specific herds months in advance of an event. The cattle, all heifers, are uniform in size and predominately crossbred English or English bred. Smaller cutting events use a variety of cattle, both heifers and steers, between the ages of four months and two years of age. Heifers are females that are too young to have produced a calf. Steers are castrated males. Cows are females that have produced calves. Although cutters refer to their quarry as cows, cows are not always used in cutting competition. Because each breed of cattle differs in temperament as well as in appearance, trainers develop preferences. For beginners, however, mild-mannered English-breds are the best teachers.

The two most popular English breeds are the Hereford and the Angus. The Hereford is reddish-brown with a white face, legs and belly. The Angus is solid black or red. A Hereford-Angus crossbred is called a black baldy because it is black with a white face. These cattle are usually gentle and easy to drive. Because they are not as quick as their exotic cousins, they are easier to follow and control. A beginner is much safer cutting English-bred cattle than Brahmas.

Brahman cattle and Brahman crossbreds are distinguished by their large drooping ears and a hump at the crest of their necks. Often referred to as exotics or eared cattle, Brahmans tend to be flighty and more difficult to handle than English-breds. Yet some cutters prefer them because they are quick, agile and challenging. But they can also be difficult to drive from the herd and cut cleanly.

TRAITS AND TEMPERAMENT

Riders like to watch herds being settled to get a feel for the group as a whole. If the cows bunch closely together, cutters say they are sticky. These cattle may be hard to separate and drive from the herd, but they will be easier to drive collectively. If the herd is restless, extra care must be taken not to excite them when driving, or they may scatter in every direction. Observing cattle as they are settled also gives riders the opportunity to watch for animals they want to avoid cutting and to spot those that might make good prospects.

Cattle are judged by appearance the same way horses are evaluated for conformation. Experienced cutters and cattlemen avoid individuals that stand out because of poor condition or inferior quality. A "sorry-looking" calf may also be dull-witted and lifeless.

Cutters look for cattle that are healthy, bright-eyed and curious. Good cows react to riders with curiosity, but do not panic and bolt without provocation. Fearless cows are called alligators and are to be avoided. Numb or unresponsive cattle are also undesirable. It is difficult for a horse to become hooked with either alligators or numb cows. Alligators will run over a horse, and numb or sour cattle just don't care enough to play the game. To be able to score well, a rider must cut a cow that will acknowledge his horse and try to find a way past it, to the herd.

A good cow does not overreact to a horse and rider. She is savvy enough to respect her competition, but game enough to look for a way around. This type of cow will look at a horse before she moves. A bad cow, on the other hand, will shy away from a rider without actually looking at it. If cut, this type of cow is likely to run back and forth across the arena, or bolt out past the turnback riders.

Fortunately, a rider can learn a lot about the cattle he will cut by watching how they react to the settlers. If he is working late in the herd, he can also watch to see what the earlier riders pick. By the time he rides into the herd, a rider should have a feel for the herd. Since most cows are followers rather than leaders, it is possible to drive and shape them in specific flow patterns with the aid of herd holders. This gives a rider the option of cutting a cow he has selected before entering the herd or simply "cutting for shape" by taking the cow which is left standing in the center of the arena.

If a rider enters the herd from the back fence and begins driving toward

The Basics of Cutting

the center of the arena, the herd holders move in and help shape the flow by riding forward. Some of the cattle will begin to peel off to the sides and return to the fence. The cows moving in front of the rider will probably be following a lead cow that is still moving forward.

The rider should be aware of the lead cow and use her to his advantage. It is not necessary, or even desirable, for her to be immediately in front of the rider. Many other cows may separate them. The idea is to keep the cattle moving forward until there are a sufficient number to select from near the center of the arena. If the process has been smooth and the cattle have not been frightened, the cutter will be able to commit to a stationary cow that has been separated from the herd. If the cattle are sticky, however, the rider may have to cut on the run.

HORSES AND CATTLE

Since horses are herd animals, it is natural for them to respond to the herding instinct when working with cattle. Some horses have stronger herding instincts than others. Even when the instinct is strong, if a horse does not have the desire, he will not make a good cutting horse.

Although few domestic horses live in social units, as they would in a natural state, they still retain herding instincts. This is especially apparent with mares and foals. Mothers instinctively drive their curious foals away from potential danger. They may also drive away other horses.

Driving posture in the wild is the same as in a cutting arena. Horses have an innate sense of distance and timing in relation to animate creatures, whether human, horse or cow, and will drive by moving parallel to another animal, yet behind enough so the nose is on a line with the driven animal's neck or shoulder.

Other herding, or driving, postures include swanning the neck and head toward the quarry, pinning the ears back against the neck in a threatening gesture, nosing and nipping. Nipping is penalized in competition, but all of the other postures are commonly seen.

It is always desirable for a horse to prick its ears forward when working a calf. A horse that works with ears forward is alert and intent on business. But some great horses, like 1990 NCHA Non-Pro Futurity Reserve Champion All That Jazz, work with ears pinned in a menacing demeanor.

"She's probably the grittiest little horse I've ever ridden," says Spencer Harden of All That Jazz. "She's very pleasant until you drop your hand, then the ears go back. I was Reserve Non-Pro Champion on her grandmother and she was that way, too."

NCHA Futurity Champion Millie Montana also pins her ears in action.

Buster Welch and Clays Little Peppy show how to drive cattle without any fences.

"She's cranky on a cow," said her rider, Joe Suiter. "But she shows a lot of expression that way."

Occasionally intensity turns to temper. It is not uncommon to see a horse, in the heat of competition, particularly a stallion, nip a cow that slips past. Aside from herding instinct, many horses share competitive and playful natures that blossom in the cutting arena. Smart Play, 1990 NCHA Futurity Reserve Champion, lost his footing and fell completely to the ground while working a cow during first go-rounds of Futurity competition. But the game gelding was so intent, he kept the cow in line and bounced back to his feet to finish his business.

Miss Silver Pistol, the 1985 NCHA Non-Pro Futurity Champion, stunned spectators, during Futurity go-rounds, when she dropped to her knees and challenged a calf eyeball to eyeball. According to her owner Wes Shahan, this was not a first-time occurrence for the feisty grey mare. Although this is an unusual posture for a saddled horse, it is quite a common sight when pastured foals joust and play.

Cutting horses also draw on inner resources when driving and working cattle. A horse's keen sense of timing can be appreciated by anyone who has tried to catch a horse that didn't want to be caught. I own a sly mare who didn't want to be taken from her lush thirty-acre pasture to have her feet

The Basics of Cutting 127

Solid Gold Doc is hooked to the cow with a look of determination.

This horse is showing a lot of expression toward the cow.

trimmed one spring morning. No amount of coaxing with grain, which usually did the trick, worked this time. The farrier's friend had a roping horse with him and assured me he could capture the mare in just a few seconds. Thirty minutes later, the roper and his horse were heaving and drenched in sweat. My mare was placidly grazing and not even damp. She had eluded the roper, with little effort, by allowing him to get within striking distance, then trotting just out of range.

The same mare enjoyed challenging my little fox terrier to a match race along the fence line. The tiny terrier ran full throttle, and the bay mare always stayed neck and neck, graciously trading the lead in the spirit of fun and friendship. This ability to rate action is another prerequisite for a good cutting horse.

Penalty-free runs based on good fundamentals will earn money almost every time. But it takes a little extra to win the big ones. Sometimes courage makes the difference. And that is something no amount of training can impart. Peppy San Badger displayed just such courage against a determined cow in Abilene, Texas. His rider, Buster Welch, thought the game was up when the cow ran right straight for them. "I thought that she was going to get away," remembers Welch. "Then he hit that cow so quick, and just dropped off of her. He knew that was the only chance he had, and he took it."

It is natural for a horse to protect his legs and balance by avoiding impact. Cutting horses will do this by giving ground to the cow and maintaining distance. Of course, if he gives too much, the cow will run into the herd and a penalty will be incurred.

A horse can also earn extra points with an attractive style of working that sets it apart from other horses. Cutters refer to this credit-earning ability as "eye appeal."

A horse with eye appeal is very alert and intent on cows that he traps in the center of the arena. He will usually drop down low in a catlike crouch to counter and encourage the calf. Some horses will quiver in anticipation of a calf's next move, and pounce to meet it. Doc Per, NCHA Futurity and Super Stakes Champion, drove spectators to a frenzy with his dazzling style. The flashy chestnut's flaxen tail would whip the ground as he danced with a cow, cheek to cheek, toe to toe.

Another desirable quality in a cutting horse is the ability to entrance a cow without threatening or frightening it. Cutters refer to this attribute as the ability "to draw" a cow. An overly aggressive horse can intimidate a cow and send it running. But some horses seemingly mesmerize cows. The cow is still bent on returning to the herd, but it thinks the horse holds the key to the door. It will duck and dodge in front of the horse, looking for a hole.

The Basics of Cutting 129

Great form for Solid Gold Doc, a Peppy San son.

Handle Bar Hanna shows her grit.

1990 NCHA World Champion Cash Quixote Rio and Kobie Wood. Don Shugart photo.

A horse's ability to draw cattle is closely related to its natural cow sense. Cow sense, in cutting parlance, is the talent for anticipating a cow's actions. Cutters say that a horse is good at reading cattle, or a horse is cow smart. Cow sense is probably linked to the horse's primal herding instincts. Most cutters believe it is an inherited trait, although some think it merely reflects intelligence and natural curiosity. Whatever the source of cow sense, some horses have an abundance of it.

World Champion Cash Quixote Rio cuts cattle without a bridle at NCHA promotional demonstrations. "He's got a great mind," says Cash Quixote Rio's owner, Kobie Wood. "He knows what a cow is going to do to him, sometimes before the cow does." Bridleless cutting, in fact, has been a favorite form of proving the mettle of cow-smart horses for over a century.

Contest cutters are penalized for reining after a horse has been released to work on a cow. The effect is the same as working unbridled. During the 1990 NCHA Open Futurity go-rounds, Little Rey Doc stayed hooked to a wild cow, even though another cow cut in for the action. Most horses would have switched to the closer cow, but the tenacious sorrel mare stuck with the original and earned 220.5 points.

The Basics of Cutting

Non-pro champion Skip Hobbs' mare Peppys Tachita has earned over $200,000 with cow smarts. "It's easy to ride her because she's going to get where she needs to be," says Hobbs. "On tough cattle, it's a little bit of an advantage to her because she is so smart. She'll give herself room to where she doesn't have to make mistakes."

A smart, confident horse wins paychecks if he has his rider's trust. Many riders admit they learned the most about riding from good horses. When Hyglo Freckles won the 1988 World Championship, his owner and rider, Faron Hightower, admitted, "He's better than he's ever been. But, I think a lot of that is me finally realizing that the more I leave him alone, the better he gets."

The Cutting Contest

Cutting contest format is simple: the rider has a two-and-one-half-minute time period to cut and work at least two cows, one at a time, from a herd held at the end of the arena. The rider has four mounted, volunteer helpers—two herd holders and two turnback riders. Herd holders are positioned close to the herd, on either side, and help contain the herd when the rider is driving cattle or working a cow. Turnback riders are positioned between the rider and the judge(s), on either side, and try to keep the cow that is being worked in front of the rider. The ultimate goal for a rider is to cut cows that challenge his horse, but that won't escape back to the herd. Size of arenas and herds of cattle may vary from show to show, but riders forfeit and earn points by specific actions evaluated by one or more judges.

THE RIDER'S ROLE

A rider who learns to relax before competition helps his horse as well as himself. Tension creates rigidity and resistance, which the horse feels through the saddle and in the reins and bridle. The warm-up session, therefore, is as important for the rider as his horse.

Larry Mahan, a former World Champion Cowboy, rides in non-pro cutting competition and likes to listen to music and self-awareness tapes as he warms up his horse. "I listen to a lot of easy-listening music," says Mahan. "I like the way it gets my body functioning and into the animal."

A few minutes before a run, some riders like to put an edge on their horse by taking hold of the reins, backing him up and making him turn over his hocks. More than anything else, this mentally prepares the horse for the run and relays the message "On stage in five minutes."

ENTERING THE HERD

A rider may enter the herd from either side or the middle. Because rules require at least one cut be made deep into the herd, most riders do this with the first cut, riding to the back fence on one side. If you are riding first in a group of fresh cattle, you will want to take more time than you would working last. The cattle may be skittish and tend to scatter. Move slowly and watch the cattle. Judges award credit for quiet herd work. Keep an eye on the leader and any cows you would like to cut. The herd holders will help push the cattle forward, but you are in the driver's seat. Remember, your goal is to separate one cow in the center of the arena—preferably one that is standing still.

Pros often pick their cattle before they ride and go to the herd with a certain cow in mind. It is better for beginners to drive a group of five or ten to the center, wait for them to begin to drift back to the herd and cut one of the stragglers. Cutters refer to this technique as "cutting for shape."

Often there will be two or three cows left and the rider can commit to one by taking a step or two forward. The herd holders should be watching and will hustle the surplus back to the herd. If you get stuck with two cows paired and on the run, keep your action to a minimum until they are separated.

Herd work, so essential on a working ranch, has become basically a credit situation in the cutting arena. If a rider commits to a cow in the herd, then has to switch to another cow, or if the cow runs while he is cutting and he loses it, he forfeits 5 points.

While most riders prefer to play safe and cut what shapes in front of them, they can still often get the cattle they want, with the help of the herd holders. If the herd holders know what cow the rider is after, with a little teamwork it is possible to shape the flow so the selected cow passes front and center. Sometimes the turnback riders will also step in to help.

COMMITTING TO A COW

A rider must signify to the judges his intention to work one specific animal. This commitment may be made in the herd, or the rider may wait until one cow is left standing in front of him in the center of the arena. Once the rider has committed, he will be penalized 5 points if he switches to another cow.

The most obvious sign of commitment is for the rider to drop the hand holding the reins to the horse's neck. But, two steps to the same animal, or one move that clearly indicates a single animal has been selected, will also commit a rider. If the rider steps to a cow to stop a group, then cuts another cow from the group, he will not be penalized for changing cattle.

If the rider has trouble with other cattle running between his horse and

The Basics of Cutting

the cow he has picked, it may be better for him to pick up the reins and reseparate his cow. He will be penalized 1 point for reining, which is preferable to losing 5 points if his horse switches cattle.

THE CUT

The best position for cutting a cow is in the center of the arena. NCHA rules specify that it is desirable and credit will be awarded if the cut is made in the center and far enough from the herd to assure they will not be disturbed by the proceeding action.

Sometimes, if a rider commits to a cow that breaks to one side, he can save the situation by bringing the animal back to the center. Depending on the circumstances, he might even be awarded credit for "courage" in a high-risk situation. At the least, he will not be penalized if he stays with the cow.

Mick McBride encountered such a situation when he placed second in the 1990 NCHA $50,000 Limited Futurity riding Genes Hickory Lady. "I tried to cut one and she didn't shape very well," remembers McBride. "I jumped over there to get her, and I probably shouldn't have done it. I was a little behind, and it took a couple of moves to get her centered back up."

Although McBride, who scored 214 points, did not incur penalty points for his cut, he was penalized for losing working advantage, a 1-point deduction for each move in which the horse does not have control of the cow.

START THE ACTION

Up until this point, all movement has been slow, quiet and relaxed. Once the reins are dropped, however, all hell can break loose. Octogenarian Bazy Tankersly, the owner of Al Marah Arabians, says that riding a cutting horse is more fun than a roller coaster. "You know what a roller coaster is going to do," says Tankersly.

No one knows exactly what a cow will do when she finds herself alone in the center of an arena, surrounded by humans on horses. Competition is based on the premise that she will try to return to the herd. But she may need some prodding. Or she may be so unhinged that she bolts for the turnback riders.

It is the horse's job to follow the cow. Cutters say that good horses can "read" a cow and anticipate her actions. At this point, the rider should have his eyes on the cow and his feet deep into the stirrups. He should be relaxed but flexed and ready to move with the horse. Although he is looking at the cow, his upper body should not turn with it. Only his head should move.

Legs should be relaxed, with heels down and toes out, ready when needed to urge or guide the horse. The reinless hand should have a firm grasp on the saddle horn. The wrist should be straight, but the shoulder and elbow should

Punk Carter sits deep and focuses on the cow (out of photo).

be flexible. Holding the saddle horn is much the same as gripping the handlebars of a bicycle. The only difference is the upright angle of the horn. The hand and arm will be used to push and pull on the horn, and cushion the rider's impact, as the horse stops and turns, then pushes out of the ground.

In the heat of action, really good cutting horse riders look like passive passengers. But appearances are deceiving. The rider is moving in unison with the horse, but the harmony is orchestrated and flexibility is the key.

As the horse moves with the cow, through momentum the rider's seat shifts in the saddle. If he is seated properly, with weight centered, he can use the horn as a shock absorber and help maintain his center of gravity. When the horse stops, the rider pushes on the horn and pushes down with his seat to help the horse sit into the ground. When the horse springs out of a stop or turn, the rider pulls on the horn and rocks slightly forward with his hips to ride forward with the action.

Learning balance is very subtle and elementary. Like riding a bicycle, once you have the skill, you don't lose it. But every horse has a different feel, so there are always adjustments.

Although the rider depends on his horse to follow the cow, he can still influence distance and timing with legs and feet. If the horse is getting too close to the herd, the rider can move him back. If he is too far behind a cow,

The Basics of Cutting   135

Carter pushes on the horn and down into the seat as Handle Bar Hanna gets down into the ground and turns.

As the horse pushes out of the ground, Carter pushes slightly forward with his hips.

he can be urged ahead. The down side of leg aids, especially with beginners and young horses, is that they can put a horse too far ahead of the action. It is best for amateurs to trust timing to the horse.

QUITTING A COW

Knowing when to quit a cow is much like learning balance. It can only be acquired through practice. A beginner can, however, benefit from watching other riders and from understanding the rules. Cutting rules specify that a rider may legally quit working a cow if it is obviously stopped, turned away or behind the time line. Since the penalty for a "hot" or illegal quit is a deduction of 3 points, it is important to grasp the nuances of the rules.

A rider may quit a cow that has stopped, but if the cow stops, then suddenly turns into the rider, the rider will be penalized. If the cow turns away, however, there is no penalty. It is not necessary for a cow to have all four feet on the ground when it stops. But, if it has a forefoot in the air, it is more likely to move again and more dangerous to quit than one that is planted, or turned away.

Sometimes a moving cow will pull a dirty trick by turning away, then ducking back into the rider just as he is lifting the reins for a quit. The best option is to rein the horse back on the cow and take a 1-point penalty for reining rather than a 3-point penalty for a hot quit. Of course, if the cow is too close to the horse, it may be better to quit and take the penalty rather than risk losing the cow—a 5-point penalty.

Good cows are players. Although they want to get back to the herd, they don't panic. They are smart enough to realize the horse and rider are in the way, but naive enough, at this point, to look for an easy way out. With luck, a good cow will duck and dance, looking for an exit, for fifteen or twenty seconds. After that, it will either stop and surrender, or decide to check the sides of the arena.

It is nice to be able to quit a cow before it stops playing, but not always possible. The rider should always be alert for signs that the cow's attention is drifting. It makes a better impression to quit a cow that still has some play rather than be forced to quit one that runs out of gas and drifts away.

If the rider cuts a wild cow, or a sprinter, that wants to run parallel to the herd, it is best to quit at the first opportunity. Seconds can seem like minutes when a rider is committed to a spinning cow that won't connect with his horse and won't give him an opportunity to quit. Knowing when and how to quit a cow can mean the difference between winning and losing. Cutters are sometimes reluctant to take credit for winning rides. But they are ever so thankful for good horses, good helpers and good luck in picking cattle.

SIX
Training Basics

Once you are familiar with the basics of cutting, the more often you are able to ride, the better you will be able to apply what you have learned. Even though you may not have cattle to work with at home, there are other alternatives. Check with local trainers for information on practice cuttings in the area. Some stables provide regular practice schedules. For a reasonable fee you can work your horse on the cattle they provide.

Never miss a chance to offer assistance as a herd holder or turnback rider. You can often learn as much in this position as riding for the cut. Study cattle and their reaction to riders whenever you can.

It is important for the beginning rider to practice the basic techniques and principles of training in order to understand the reasoning behind specific actions, be alert to problems that can easily be averted and avoid creating no-win situations. A beginner does not want to create or reinforce bad habits in the horse, so it makes sense for him to work with a trainer. Trainers know from experience when to anticipate certain reactions from horses.

Tuning

Tuning is a little like renewing your driver's license. You know how to drive, but it's good to review the basics at regular intervals. Stopping is a good example. It's easy to become lax when driving a car. Have you ever tapped the brakes and rolled through a four-way stop rather than stopping completely? It can be almost an unconscious action—until you're ticketed for it.

Horses will cheat at the stop, too. Instead of stopping squarely and parallel to the cow, with hind legs underneath themselves, some horses will roll into

This horse is collecting for a turn from a good stop, with rear legs well under his body.

the cow slightly. When the cow turns, the horse is out of position for a clean, sweeping turn. When a horse stops correctly, with his back legs well under his haunches, he will be ready to turn with the cow and stay in position with it.

A proper stop is the base from which all moves in the cutting arena originate. Ideally, a horse will cut a cow that is stopped in the middle of the arena. Horse and cow are head to head. The horse is balanced with hind legs under his haunches, slightly flexed and ready to push out in any direction.

A horse that cannot stop and turn on his haunches will not make a good cutting horse. Whether the horse travels at a walk, trot or lope, when he stops he must be collected and ready to turn. The faster the pace, the more difficult and explosive the turn. If a horse stops on his front end, he will have to pull himself into a turn rather than springing into it with his back end.

Training starts at the walk and slowly progresses to the trot. The horse is taught to watch the cow, to move when it moves and stop when it stops. He is not asked to be aggressive, but rather to wait for the cow and follow its lead.

It is difficult for a young horse to handle a wild or pushy cow. His body is not yet physically capable of performing the strenuous stops and turns that

Training Basics 139

Getting into the ground for a turn.

are necessary to stay with an offensive cow—even though he is mentally willing to try. Eventually, the stress of being pushed into no-win situations will make him resentful and unwilling.

Expecting a two-year-old, or even a young three-year-old, to work like a Super Stakes champion is the equivalent of putting a second-string freshman in the Super Bowl.

Besides physical dexterity and mental competence, properly timed training imparts self-confidence. A horse that doesn't believe he can handle a cow won't be able to do so. If he has a base of positive experiences and rewards, he will always look to the next cow eagerly.

Proper training also helps a horse develop a sense of distance and timing with cattle. Here again, each cow and each situation is different. A horse must work with a variety of cows to get a sense of when to anticipate stops and turns.

The first thing a trainer does with a young cutting horse is to teach him to look at a cow. He will move one cow around an arena or round pen to teach the horse to focus on a cow. Most trainers use either a snaffle bit or a side-pull bridle so that they can tip the horse's head directly into the cow with their hands and not put too much pressure in his mouth.

140   CUTTING

This is a young three-year-old filly in a snaffle and martingale. She is alert and focused on the cow, and already starting to collect herself.

Head-to-head in a round pen with cattle bunched in the center.

Training Basics 141

Each trainer has his own preference for training setups. Many like a round pen from 100 to 200 feet in diameter, with several gates spaced around the perimeter. The round pen allows a rider to work one cow and keep it moving—since there are no corners where it can hide. This is especially good for a young horse that is just beginning to follow a cow. Later on, a cow can be pursued and worked anywhere in the pen in relation to the cattle. If the rider works with a group of cattle in the round pen, they can be bunched in the middle or along one side. It is not even necessary to have helpers.

Eventually, a horse must graduate to a square or rectangular arena in preparation for showing. Here a horse learns to drive a cow from a herd and to work in front of the herd. At this juncture the physical demands increase because the horse must speed up to stay with a cow that is traveling a greater distance. Now a horse must learn how to turn a cow away from the fence and stay with it in the turn.

When the cow is moving across the pen, the trainer positions the horse parallel to the cow, from ten to twenty feet away. He tracks the cow, pacing the horse slightly behind it. If the cow and horse stop moving, the horse's head is parallel to the cow's back or shoulder. Finished horses move with

Ellen Leonard's horse shows good concentration.

Ellen and her horse still watching and following at a lope.

their heads parallel to a cow's neck. Younger horses are kept back toward the hip—if the cow turns back, it is easier for a young horse to recover position without tremendous effort. The idea at this point is to make everything positive and nothing too difficult.

If the cow stops, the trainer can move it by moving the horse to its head or moving the horse behind it. A cow will turn around when headed and move ahead when trailed. A young horse is to be discouraged from moving into a cow without direction from the rider. The idea is to get the horse to watch the cow and wait for it. The horse should begin to try to outthink the cow, rather than always try to outmaneuver it.

Horses that are working parallel to cows sometimes have a tendency to cheat or "leak" into the cow. This is undesirable because it puts the horse out of position when the cow turns. Sometimes the rider unconsciously makes the horse move into a cow by anticipating the cow's turn and leaning into it, causing the horse to move in the same direction.

Subtle body language can make a good horse into a great one. Misapplied, it can undermine a young horse's security. Seasoned, older horses usually are self-confident enough to do their work the way they know it should be done. They are not easily confused or misguided by amateur riders. Young horses can be easily intimidated by novices, however.

Training Basics

This young three-year-old Colonel Freckles grandson is tracking the cow.

Stepping up the pace.

Beginning riders often grip a horse with their legs when the horse is stopping. The gripping action tells the horse to go ahead rather than stop. Because an amateur rider may be insecure and unsure of his seat, he may unconsciously clamp his legs against the horse, instead of sitting down in the saddle and relaxing his legs—the proper way to ride a horse into a stop.

If this happens in the practice pen or outside the arena, the rider will usually also pull back on the reins. Now the horse is really confused. He is getting two simultaneous, yet conflicting signals—stop and go. The next time the horse is ridden he will be tense and wondering what is going to happen to him rather than what is happening with the cattle. He will probably carry his head higher than normal in anticipation of being bumped. He may even start throwing his head up as he stops.

Young horses need consistent, positive reinforcement and direction. An older, experienced horse, however, can help an amateur rider gain self-confidence and poise. Many veteran non-pros and pros confess that their best teachers have been older horses. It is much easier to learn by experiencing a move or action rather than trying to create one when you don't know how it should feel.

If a new rider leans forward into a stop when he should sit down, an older horse handles the job and is not distracted. A young horse may become frightened, however, with the rider sliding around in the saddle, searching for balance. Imagine how you would feel riding in an airplane piloted by a mechanic. He can tell you how the engines work, but can he fly the plane?

Bad habits in horses are as easy to impart as good ones. They are also harder to break. Trainers are careful to reinforce good habits in order to discourage bad ones from developing.

Quitting creates difficulties for all cutters—even pros. If a horse quits a cow in competition, it will be penalized five points. Horses can develop this habit if the rider habitually quits cows along the fence. Soon the horse associates facing the fence with quitting a cow and will do so on his own.

Trainers have nightmares about fences. If a cow takes a rider to the side fence, turns away, and the rider quits, it may be legal, but it is also asking for trouble. The next time the cow may be moving into the horse and the horse will look at the fence and decide to quit. Practicing outside of the show arena, it is best never to quit on the fence. If you must do so, turn the horse into the center of the arena.

Horses may also anticipate stops at the sides of square arenas and will stop and leak into the cow before the cow stops. This puts the horse in front of the cow and the cow may stop and turn back again—a risky situation for the horse and rider.

Training Basics

The best place to quit a cow is in the center of the arena when the cow is stopped or moving away from the horse. A rider should never turn tail to a cow that he has quit. If he does so one time, the horse may decide to do it on his own the next time. Horses are like small children. You never know what they will remember, but chances are if it's something they shouldn't, they will remember it at the worst possible time.

A horse should be made to face the cow that it has quit until the cow is on its way back to the herd. Then the horse can be turned back to the herd for another cow.

It is not a good idea to cut a cow that is on the move, especially if other cows are still out in the middle of the arena. The horse may become confused and try to cut another cow. It is best to train the horse to cut a cow that has stopped and is alone in the center of the arena.

Knowing when to quit applies to practice sessions as well as arena confrontations with cows. Always end on a positive note. If the horse does well, reward him by ending the session before he is burned out. If the horse is having an off day, find something that he can do well, even if he is just backing a few steps, and end the session quickly. If you end with a positive attitude, he is likely to come to the next session with that same attitude.

Never get angry with your horse. If you feel resentment or frustration building, unsaddle. Horses that are intimidated or frightened by their riders usually end up blowing under stress—not for retaliation, but from fear. Horses that are treated with respect and encouraged with positive reinforcement usually want to please their riders. They are also self-confident in their actions. Horses that are bullied or harassed react to fear and lack the self-confidence to be able to think and act on their own initiative. Training through intimidation limits a horse's potential.

Helpful Hints

STIRRUP LENGTH

Properly adjusted stirrups will help you stay balanced with your moving horse.

- If the stirrups are too long, you will reach for them with your legs and feet when the horse is moving and be thrown out of balance.
- If the stirrups are too short, you will have the tendency to fall forward in the saddle, over the saddle horn or horse's neck.
- You should be able to see about an inch of your toe when you're in the saddle with your feet in the stirrups—don't bend forward, just look down.

- When you stand in the stirrups, there should be three or four inches between your seat and the seat of the saddle.

SPURS
- Spurs are for quick action and positive reinforcement of leg aids. Don't overuse them, or your horse may become resentful and sour. Tail wringing in a horse is often a sign that the rider is overusing spurs.
- Press with the spurs. Don't gouge.

REINS
- Reins should be loose and even. When you raise your hand chest high, they will still be loose, but will pull the bit shanks back slightly.
- If you have trouble remembering the correct rein length, notch your reins so that you can quickly pick them up at the right spot.

SEAT
- Sit deep in the saddle and think about sitting on your back pockets.
- Relax.

BASICS
- Make sure you understand the fundamentals and rules before you show.
- Keep a positive mental attitude about yourself, your horse and your fellow competitors.
- Don't look for excuses. Find solutions.

WARMING UP
- Use this time to relax yourself and your horse.
- Work your horse until he is at least damp under the saddle pad.
- Take this time to check your girth, splint and skid boots, and bridle to make sure everything is properly attached and secured.
- Right before your call to ride, make some demands on your horse to get his attention—back him up, let him feel your legs and hands—and mentally prepare him for the work to come.

HERD WORK
- Don't rush. Take plenty of time.
- Take out a large number of cows for the best selection.

Training Basics

THE CUT
- Try to pick a cow that seems to want to be cut. Cows that look at you are good ones to cut.
- Face the cow that you are cutting.
- Don't cut while your horse is parallel to the cow.
- Don't try to cut on the move.
- If you have two cows and can't separate them, stay quiet and wait for an opportunity to make your move. If you push, you may lose both cows or be forced to cut on the run.
- Keep track of cows that have already been worked in your herd.
- A cow's aggression will usually be in direct proportion to its distance from the herd. The farther away she is from her buddies, the harder she will try to return.
- A bad cow cut properly is better than a good cow cut incorrectly.

COMMITTING
- If you look at a cow and take one step toward it, judges may consider that a commitment.
- If you look at a cow and take two steps toward it, you are definitely committed to that cow.

Kathy Burkett drops her horse on a cow. Kathy is a professor at Austin College in Sherman, Texas.

THE WORK
- Keep your eyes on the cow at all times.
- Never look at your horse.
- Use your legs to urge your horse forward and for position.
- Wait for your horse—don't get ahead of him.
- Don't forget to push on the saddle horn when your horse stops and turns.
- Don't lean into the cow.
- Remember, the center of the arena is where the money is won.
- Don't let your horse leak toward the cow. Be aware of the herd behind you and don't let your horse fade into it.
- It is better, under some circumstances, to rein your horse and lose 1 point, than to lose the cow and 5 points. Weigh your options.

QUITTING
- Pick up the reins with one hand and place your other hand on the horse's neck—there will be no doubt that you are quitting the cow.
- It's best to quit a wild cow as soon as you can rather than run the risk of losing it.
- Try to quit in the middle of the arena—not on the fence.

PRACTICE
- A round pen helps keep the horse moving and the cattle fresh.
- Keep the horse's head tipped toward the cow.
- Keep the horse's nose even with the cow's neck or shoulder.
- Don't let the horse leak into a cow—move him into line with your leg.
- Don't force too much action and stress your horse. Know what he can and can't handle.
- Try to stay an equal distance from the cow when you are tracking it.

One Trainer's Way

Good basic training makes good horses, no matter the endeavor. Cutting horse trainers may vary in technique and intensity, but they all use the same fundamentals.

Most of today's winning cutting horses and riders have been trained in round pens and arenas because that is the most practical, timely and cost-efficient method to turn out competent performers.

Historically, cutting horses learned their trade on the open range. These elite members of ranch remudas were not made, but evolved from the rank

Training Basics

and file. Talent was cultivated with tough and tedious chores. Time and technology, however, have transformed many ranching traditions. Today's rancher is more likely to check his cattle from a four-wheel-drive vehicle than a fox-trotting gelding. A few ranchers still believe there is no better way to work cattle than on horseback—and one cutting horse trainer, Buster Welch, turns out cutting champions that can hold their own on any cowman's range.

Was it fate? Smokey Garrett brought Smokys Little Peppy to the 1990 NCHA Futurity and left with a championship.

The college business major from Stephenville, Texas, also won the Amateur Championship and the Fort Worth Star-Telegram Rookie of the Year Award.

Smokey Garrett and his gelding had been close partners since Garrett hired on with Buster Welch's Double Mountain River Ranch in west Texas. "It was neat because we both got to learn together and I got to know him pretty well," Garrett explains about his summer at Welch's. He rode his horse during the roundups. "I've been around cattle before—but 50,000 acres, that's rough territory. Every day was a different adventure. It was hard work but we had a lot of fun."

Smokey Garrett and Smokys Little Peppy winning the 1990 NCHA Amateur Futurity. Don Shugart photo.

Smokey Garrett rides point on a herd of cattle on the Double Mountain River Ranch.

Garrett and his parents are clients of cutting horse trainer Buster Welch. Welch trained Smokys Little Peppy's full sister Clays Little Peppy who won $165,494 in major limited-age events. Smokys Little Peppy and Clays Little Peppy received the same training as all of Welch's horses.

While Garrett worked for the Double Mountain outfit, Welch often rode three-year-old Peppy Ole during roundups. One morning, as Welch rode up a steep, narrow path above the riverbank, the sorrel stallion lost his footing and slid down the bluff. Welch had anticipated the disaster just in time to step from the saddle.

Easing down the gap on his heels, Welch watched as the horse rolled over backward, still scrambling for balance. The colt sprang to his feet, casting off dirt and debris. Welch collected the reins and swung back into the saddle of one of his most promising contenders for the $1.5 million 1990 National Cutting Horse Association Futurity.

"I just turned around and rode him back out of that creek and came right around that trail again," explained Welch. "There was a real, narrow, little trail, and, boy, he was careful where he put his hind feet that time."

A living legend of the cutting horse world, Buster Welch honed his spurs as a cowhand and bronc buster on the great cattle ranches of Texas. Although he has ridden five NCHA Futurity winners and four World Champions, Welch still opts for sagebrush over the arena for tuning his show string.

Training Basics 151

Buster Welch, five-time NCHA Futurity Champion, four-time NCHA World Champion.

While most of the sorrel colt's peers follow a daily routine from stall, to arena, to hot walker, Welch's horses are likely to chase cows through thickets, trail herds across cedar brakes or clamber down rocky ravines in seach of missing strays.

The Welches' children—Ken, Greg, Ruth Ann, Georgia, Nina and Dolan—have all been involved with ranching and horses. Greg, who rode World Champion Tenino San and Reserve World Champion Haidas Little Pep, polished Smokys Little Peppy and schooled Garrett for the Futurity, after his summer sojourn with Buster.

On the day the sorrel colt lost his battle with the rocky bluff, Welch and a crew of twelve cowboys were rounding up cows and calves. I was the greenhorn, invited to learn, firsthand, how and why Welch trains and conditions his arena champions with rigorous ranch work.

"I love to work cattle a-horseback," says the trainer-cum-rancher. His horses love it, too. Ranch work not only sharpens their cutting skills, it

Welch and Peppy Ole stop for water after a morning of chasing cows through the brush.

relieves the monotony and pressure of intensive training. Arena education is tap water compared to Welch's "Rocky Mountain spring water" approach. Both are pure in technique, but Welch's method comes from the source.

"There is something about doing things with a purpose on a horse that is different," reflects Welch. "I can ride to check windmills and ride straight from one to the next, and there is something that a horse learns from that. More than just going out and wandering around or loping in circles. His mind is more alert. He seems to sense that I am doing something with a purpose."

Welch never wanders in circles. If a missing cow and calf are in a thicket, he rides straight ahead, making his own trail. The world's most celebrated cutting horse trainer rides into brush the same way he rides into a herd of cattle—with assurance and authority.

One of the areas where we gathered cattle, during the five-day roundup, is appropriately named Big Rough. It is wonderfully rich in native grasses, nestled, along with cows and calves, among the cedar, cactus and mesquite.

While Big Rough is a sanctuary for cows, it swallows cowboys, then spits them out with tattered shirts. I felt like Br'er Rabbit in the briar patch as I followed the cowboys, hunting for strays. I also developed an appreciation

Training Basics

for leather chaps, which guard legs against mesquite thorns and cedar spears. Besides the carnivorous Big Rough thickets, there are deceptive shallows in the river bottom that suck horses down to their hocks. On several occasions I was astonished to see cowboys sink to their stirrups, while my horse stood in the same stream of water, ten feet away.

It amazed me, at the end of the day, to see all of the cowboys' horses, sporting four sound legs and most of the hide they had left with at five in the morning. Welch has no qualms about using his show horses in all phases of ranch work. "You don't see many cats getting crippled catching mice," Welch says, "And I just very seldom ever, ever cripple a horse, no matter what the surroundings. They're bred to do this."

Although Welch's horses are started under saddle in an arena, they are introduced to ranch work soon after they respond to basic hand and leg pressures. While Welch checks windmills, his mounts develop a sense of balance and footing. "There's been many a-winning horse developed without this," admits Welch about his ranch regime. "I don't say that it can't be done the other way. But it's not a horse that I would enjoy. I wouldn't enjoy my cow work near as much if I didn't have these horses."

Welch remembers back to a confrontation between Peppy San Badger and a determined cow at a show in Amarillo. "In just that split second that I saw what was unfolding, I thought, 'She's gonna get away.' Then he so quick hit that cow and just dropped off of her," Welch recalls of Peppy San Badger's defensive maneuver. "But when he hit her, he knocked her ten feet away from him. I'd never had him do that before, and never had him do that since. But it was just some of that old ranch working that came through. He knew that was the only shot he had at it. And he took it."

Although Peppy San Badger was an exceptional athlete, Welch believes ranch work helped develop his keen mind and abiding self-confidence. "I rode him a lot outside," says Welch of the 1977 NCHA Futurity Champion. "I could drag calves on him and he'd figure out where the branding fire was and the shortest way to get there. He was always thinking, always looking, always watching. I rode him many times, all day on the ranch, in some rough country. It never took him long to figure out what the plan was in anything he was doing."

Welch's horses learn timing and control by trailing cattle and holding herd in vast open pastures. The ballet of a cutting arena begins as a two-step on the plains. A cow's tentative advance is subtly thwarted with posture as much as position. A smart horse intuitively understands conservation of energy. The slow student learns vigilance and control after chasing innumerable slipaways.

Welch cuts a longhorn steer just for the fun of it.

Most cow work is done at the walk or jog. Because cattle are potentially volatile, they cannot be hurried or pushed. When we gathered cattle from the far reaches of Welch Ranch, we trailed cows for hours at a plodding walk, then stood quietly holding while Welch cut dry cows and strays from the herd.

A fretful horse is a nuisance to the rider and a powder keg around cattle. Stallions must comply with the rules, as well as mares and geldings. This was illustrated during a lunch break when Peppy Ole, whom Welch had hobbled near the chuck wagon, mounted another horse. Within seconds he was roped, head and heels, and thrown to the ground. Welch climbed into the saddle immediately after the incident, and if the stallion had further amorous thoughts, he kept them to himself for the rest of the day.

After a horse demonstrates proper constraint around cattle, Welch advances to cutting individuals from a herd. Stripping calves from cows occurs on a large scale during branding and shipping, semiannual events on Welch's ranch. In addition, large herds are often separated into age groups and other classifications. Hardly a day passes without the need for cutting horses.

No matter the number of cattle, Welch glides into a herd. Cows quickly melt away, exposing the quarry. So slick is the move, a cow will often volunteer for the cut. But Welch and his horse monitor every move, ready to counter confederates.

At this point, Welch's horses have been schooled for quick, straight stops and turns. Now they are asked to apply technique and talent, relying on their own judgment for distance and timing. This is a watershed for Welch's horses and the third stage that leads a special few from cow horse to cutting horse to contest horse.

Cutting offers a savvy observer the chance to combine experience with action. Already fit from many miles of ranch work, Welch's promising show prospects are primed for a challenge. Restraint is still a cardinal rule, however.

Peppy San Badger was a master at combining combustion and control. "He was so strong and yet so controlled," says Welch. "He never had to slam himself around. Like the golfer's prayer: 'Lord grant me the strength to hit the ball easy.' He had that unique way of being fierce, and then when the time came, shut down and be just soft and pretty."

Disdainful of show horses trained to perform rather than reform, Welch says, "I'm not against a real cow horse headin' a cow and then just making four or five real hard moves, maybe even after she's stopped, just to say, 'I gotcha! I gotcha!' I love that. But I hope our judging doesn't get to where it looks for something that's not real cowhorse—like a cow standing still and a horse doing all kinds of acts, maybe lying on the ground. I would like to see cutting kept pure, a true show of a cowhorse, and not ever see it revert to a circus act of some kind."

Efficiency, pure and simple, is at the core of all good cutting performances, whether on the range or in an arena. To Welch it is as clear as choosing leather over silver stirrups. Razzle dazzle will tarnish. But classics endure.

Riding with Style

THE RIDER

The single thing that sets NCHA events apart from other championship horse shows that are also held at the Will Rogers Coliseum in Fort Worth is an aura of professionalism. It pervades the atmosphere along with the soft jingle of spurs.

Cutters are serious about their horses and serious about their own performances. They know there are no shortcuts to success. From first-time amateurs to the seasoned professional, cutters are always trying to learn and improve. Generally, the most accomplished riders are the most humble. They know winning requires teamwork, as well as skill, and a good horse. They also respect the capriciousness of cattle and the luck of the draw.

Next to a good horse, a positive mental attitude is the greatest asset for a cutting competitor. Not only will the judges read self-confidence into the posture of a confident rider, but the horse will also be receiving the same message.

"When a person is having a hot streak, I think the biggest thing they have going for them is the confidence in their horse," says Non-Pro Hall of Fame Rider Carl Crawford. "They feel like—'Just point me to the cattle, and if we can get one cut, we can win.' When you have that confidence, everything makes a prettier picture. You are confident, the horse is confident, and consequently, that is the picture that you present to the judge."

If you think you are beaten before you cut the first cow, you probably will be. Riding with a positive outlook is akin to posturing in nature. Duelling cats bristle and howl to appear large, formidable and fearless. Stallions do the same by trumpeting and strutting. Black belt karate contenders are masters of intimidation. This is not to say you should ride into the arena with hair standing on end, screaming like a banshee. But riding with an aura of confidence can get you noticed. As impartial as most judges try to be, they are still human, and the subconscious message of a winner comes through just as clear as that of a loser.

One way to calm pre-show jitters is to remember you're part of a team. That kind of thinking helped sixteen-year-old Millie Bouget win the 1988 World Youth Championship. She said, "Words couldn't describe the faith I have in my horse. Every time I went to the herd, I had all the confidence that she was going to be there. She was going to give out her best."

If you want to build self-confidence, look for opportunities rather than excuses. Cutters have dozens of excuses, many of them valid. But the best way to succeed is to view every ride as a learning experience. So what if the cattle are soft? Step up and try one. At least you can work on perfecting technique in the center of the arena.

So what if you draw up first in the bunch? Or last? It's bound to happen and it's part of the law of averages. Make it a challenge. Never surrender before you have tried.

Non-Pro Hall of Fame Rider John Paxton says, "Anyone will tell you that no matter how old or experienced they are, that they learn something every time they show a horse."

If you think you have a legitimate complaint against a judge, you may file a protest with NCHA. It will cost $50 to do so and your money will be refunded if you are found to be right. Usually, complaining about judging is as futile as railing against the weather—and just as commonplace. Just enjoy the sunshine when it comes, and let new growth follow the showers.

Do listen to constructive advice and criticism from fellow riders. Seek it out and let it sink in. Sometimes the obvious can be elusive. Maybe your horse missed that cow because you were out of position on the previous move. If you are an amateur and if there is a problem, ninety-nine times out of one hundred it will be with the way you are riding. Blaming the horse or cattle is easy, but it won't solve problems.

Style and sportsmanship are one and the same in the cutting arena. Most successful cutters are horsemen who respect their fellow riders and the animals they ride. Gene Suiter, owner of NCHA Hall of Fame Champion Montana Doc, remembers sitting in the Coliseum at Sweetwater, Texas, watching Buster Welch, Shorty Freeman, Leon Harrel, Pat Patterson and James Kenney, among others, prepare their horses for the NCHA Futurity.

"What was neat about it is that they showed everyone how to develop a horse without cruelty. None of that went on there. The people that were rough, they were embarrassed because fifty guys were treating their horses right. I saw some of the great horses developed there through the influence of Buster Welch. He was one of the first guys to really show how to develop these horses without harshness."

Many show and performance horses, of all breeds, suffer abuse at the hands of owners and trainers who are willing to sacrifice integrity for money or an ego boost. Fortunately, this behavior is not well tolerated by cutters. NCHA has rules against animal abuse and will suspend violators' membership privileges.

The Horse

Horses are no different from human artists or athletes. While training develops their talents, it is style that sets them apart and earns that extra point or two. NCHA guidelines for judging state that one of the ways a judge can determine differences in cutting runs is by considering the "eye appeal" of the working horse. According to NCHA rules, "Runs that are attractive because of the style of the working horse and the correctness of the overall performance shall receive credit."

All That Jazz is a gritty sorrel mare that works a cow with her ears aggressively pinned flat against her neck. "This mare is a real ill-working mare toward cattle," explains her owner Spencer Harden. "She's very pleasant until you drop your hand, then the ears go back and she drops to the ground." Judges like All That Jazz's spunk. Her menacing appearance projects her determination.

When a cutter says that a horse has "a lot of look," or is "bright," he means the horse concentrates on the cow being worked with head low to the ground and ears pricked forward.

Bella Coquette has lots of look. The petite bay is owned by Sandy Bonelli, who rode her to the 1990 NCHA Non-Pro Futurity Championship. "She traps a cow," says Bonelli of Bella Coquette. "She always wants to get to the head and hold a cow. It's something she does just naturally."

Former Futurity Champion Doc Per would get his nose in the dirt and tremble in front of a cow. Trainer Ronnie Nettles remembers the sorrel stallion lying down in front of a numb cow on one occasion. "I think superstars are superstars the first time you ride them," says Nettles. "You have to have a lot of admiration for horses like that because they just want to perform so bad."

Some horses are very physical in their intensity. Kingstream, a four-time World Champion, wouldn't let anything come between him and the cow he was working. His former owner, Billy Otto, remembers the time a huge steer lumbered between the gelding and his quarry, a Brahma calf.

According to Otto, "The Brahma tried to get behind the steer and run into the corner. But old Kingstream hit that steer and knocked him plumb down. He was on his belly on top of that steer, and he just rolled it up behind him, and held the calf. It was the most amazing thing I ever saw a horse do."

NCHA judges also give credit for "amount of courage" shown by a cutter in a tough situation. Millie Montana should have earned a medal of honor for her performance in the 1990 Futurity Finals. The gutsy sorrel mare, ridden by Joe Suiter, pinned her ears and defended the line against a bovine hellbender turned kamakaze, earning the winning score of 221.5 points.

"The cow ran right under my mare's neck," says Suiter. "About the last two turns, it got in my mind that I didn't think we could hold it. But she never missed a lick."

Horses are instinctively protective of their legs and bellies, so it is truly amazing to see one hold and not give ground to a calf that is trying to run underneath it.

Smart Play, who was second to Millie Montana in the 1990 Futurity, has a style cutters refer to as "get down" or "crouch." While some horses get down in front, with their hindquarters elevated, Smart Play crouches all over. When he traps a cow and stops, the ground appears to swallow his legs and his belly nearly kisses the dirt. As soon as the cow moves, however, Smart Play is catapaulted out of the ground and on the run.

If a cutting horse has a weak stop and a poor impulsion, he had better be able to cut a cow clean and keep it in the center of the arena. All cutters

Training Basics

place a high value on a horse that can get up and go after a cow. These are the horses that pick up extra credit for "degree of difficulty" in trying situations.

Jae Bar Fletch has the style and the physical ability to stick with four-legged drag racers. This small but powerfully built World Champion can fill his rider's boots with dirt on turns. "You're not quite sure that you saw it happen," Fletch's owner Ernest Cannon explains about the turns. "It's all one fluid motion. He doesn't have to put an extra step in there. He just sticks it in the ground, and the next instant he's turned back around."

Commandicate, who lost the 1989 NCHA Futurity by one-half point, has his own brand of explosive style. "He's one of the strongest horses I ever put a leg across," says leading trainer Bill Freeman. "He's a lot stronger and more explosive than Smart Little Lena. Smart Little Lena was really a thinking-type horse. This horse is too, but everything he does is explosive."

Some horses seem more adept than others in catching and holding a cow's attention. Horses with this style are said to be able to "draw a cow."

Poco Lena was a sorceress with cattle. "She always seemed like she had control of a cow," said trainer Pine Johnson about the immortal mare. "She seemed to play with cattle and was so quick and smooth that a cow kept thinking that he could see daylight behind her. He'd keep trying to go behind her, and she just kept blocking him and pulling him to her."

There is no doubt that a stylish horse can be a point stealer. In the sixties, the mare Royal Jazzy used to send crowds into a frenzy with her routine. "When she would stop a cow and it would turn to look at her, she'd get lower and lower, and pound her feet and tremble all over," says her owner, Bubba Cascio.

Spectators are attracted to cutting by the superstars. Judges award points for the style and daring that draw applause, but most of the horses that earn paychecks year after year are "solid" troupers who don't make mistakes. These campaigners are well trained and confident about their work. They are cow-horses who could work a pasture as easily as an arena. And they never quit.

Kingstream had more miles on him than a garage full of bald tires. The NCHA Hall of Famer earned over $250,000 at $200-added cuttings, which net the winner $300 or $400. "He was just a cow-minded, smart, hard-knocking type of individual," says Kingstream's longtime owner, David Gage. "That's the way I found him to be, day in, day out, under all kinds of conditions."

Take It from a (Non)-Pro

Cutting is like any other endeavor—you get out what you are willing to put into the sport. Nothing takes the place of hours in the saddle, but experienced riders can smooth the way for beginners.

Following are insights, suggestions and advice for first-time cutters from some of NCHA's non-pro and amateur riders.

Dee Dee Reichers of Trabuco Canyon, California, is the mother of two small children. She showed hunters and jumpers as a junior rider, and was a nationally ranked wind surfing competitor until she began riding cutting horses in 1988. Although Dee Dee had not ridden for twenty years before she bought her first cutting horse, she was $50,000 Non-Pro Champion of the 1990 NCHA Futurity.

"With three-year-olds, if you're not knowledgeable, you can get yourself into a heck of a lot of more trouble than it's worth," Reichers says. "Why pay a trainer? I don't try to say that I know anything. I just get on and go. I like cutting a lot. I don't want to ride hunters and jumpers anymore because I don't want to get hurt. You can do cutting without riding them. It fits my program better than any other equestrian event. And I really like the people a lot. That had a big draw for me. With hunters and jumpers, I feel like you have to ride every day, because your timing is so critical and your eye. With a cutter as long as you have the balance and a little bit of horsemanship, I think you can show one."

Steve Gantenbein, a forty-three-year-old real estate developer from Ione, California, began riding cutting horses in 1988, although he had owned them for several years before that. In 1990 Gantenbein won the NCHA $10,000 Non-Pro World Championship, and was $20,000 Amateur Non-Pro World Champion. He says of cutting horses, "You should stay out of their way, not hamper them at all, not clamp on them. Learn to let them do their job, and just help them."

I get a thrill out of any horse that's cowing up and trying its heart out, whether it's the great one or not. Of course, if you're on the great one, that's what it's all about. But I get a thrill out of all of them, even some horses that can only do a little bit; when they do that, I'll give them a holler.

"I think I idolized some of the horses more than the people at first: Smart Little Lena, Little Peppy. Actually, a mare of my own, Sly Chex, inspired me more than most of the people or horses around."

Training Basics

* * *

Ben Ingram, a thirty-three-year-old contractor from Springville, Indiana, got hooked on cutting when he attended an exhibition at the Indiana State Fair. He was ranked among NCHA Top Ten non-pro riders in 1989 and began showing with his wife, Pam, in 1990.

"I didn't even realize that horses could do that," Ingram says. "After I once got on one, there wasn't no getting off. I bought an old horse, an eighteen- or nineteen-year-old gelding and started showing it. I've had several since then. Trying to learn cattle was probably the biggest problem. The old gelding got me started and give me some confidence. Quit over-riding was probably the biggest piece of advice I got. That works the best."

Ken Smith, Jr., is a thirty-five-year-old real estate broker from Hopkins, South Carolina. Although he began riding when he was nine, until 1986 he rode American Saddlebreds except for a one-year stint with cutting horses when he was fifteen. In 1990 Smith ranked fifth in the NCHA Non-Pro World Champion standings, earning $39,087 in fifty-six shows.

"When I was fourteen or fifteen, there weren't many other fourteen- and fifteen-year-olds fooling with it in this part of the country. Everybody likes to show with their peers," Smith says. "Most of the cuttings were out in the middle of a cow pasture somewhere, tough conditions, tough cows, in the mud or the rain. Now everybody has these covered arenas, and that makes it a lot nicer. It's changed a lot in the last twenty years here. When I was doing it before, it was pretty much a new thing here.

"The riding part wasn't that difficult, but I would have to say the cattle would be the biggest variable and still is to this day. Compared to racehorses, gaited horses or almost any other kind of show horse, it's usually just the horse, the rider and a time clock or judges. With this deal, you throw in thirty head of cows.

"The most difficult thing for a novice cutting horse person is learning how to handle the cattle, which cattle to try to cut. If you've got good help, they tell you which cows to cut, but getting it done is a trick. You can be mounted on the best horse in the country, but if you can't bring the variables together, you may never get a check. Some people less mounted, but who really know what they're doing, can go in there and win quite often.

"Every time I rode in the herd, John Starrak was telling me to let it happen, not make it happen. I think I finally started listening to him some and it started happening, instead of forcing the issue.

"Patience is such a virture in this deal. Two and a half minutes sounds short, but it's all the time in the world you need. Sometimes it's more than you want. When I started letting it happen, things started falling together, and it got a lot easier. You get some confidence built up and you can start making it happen a little bit, start being more aggressive.

"If you're a novice rider, you don't need a novice horse. Too many people want to buy a four-, five-, or six-year-old horse that hasn't been worked much and say 'We'll learn together.' That doesn't work. I think one of the two of you has to know what's going on, either the horse or the rider.

Most people starting off would be better with an aged horse that's got a lot of experience, but not to the point that he's sour headed, or won't help you out a little bit. One that will take care of you some. If you can develop some confidence, maybe you can move to a better horse that might not be quite as solid.

"I've seen too many novice people who can afford it, yet they'll buy the cheapest horse they can—which is usually not the best horse for the job—and they say, 'We'll just learn together.' They get disgusted, and unless someone gets ahold of them and says, 'Look, you need to get a little better mount,' those people aren't in the business very long. They get discouraged.

"Then you see people who can't ride go out and buy a $100,000 horse and they get discouraged, too. The horse can't do it all, and they say, 'I spent all this money, why am I not winning?'

"You don't need to go overboard. You don't need to be stupid about it, but you do need to buy a horse that knows what it's doing. You'll find out if you have any acumen for it. Not everybody does. Not everybody's going to be totally successful at this thing—but it sure is fun trying."

Eddie Fergerson is a fifty-year-old rancher from Anahuac, Texas, who bought his first cutting horse in 1981. In 1990 he won the NCHA $20,000 Amateur World Championship riding Docs Real Un.

"I think the hardest part is they all have to stop on their back end," Fergerson says. "When you get one that really wants to be a good cowhorse, they all want to stop on their front and look at a cow, but you've got to remind them to go on their butt.

"The first thing a person needs to do is find a good trainer to help him, somebody that can be honest, and get an old, seasoned horse, and start showing. That's the only way to do it, as far as I'm concerned.

"There's no sense in a fellow just starting out to spend $100,000 on a real good horse, because he couldn't ride him. But you need one to be good and solid. I'm talking about in the price range of $5,000 to $10,000.

"I had Dell Bell showing a horse, Miss China Bell, and she could mark a 72, 73 almost every time he rode her. Man, I thought I could just crawl on this horse and we could win cuttings every time I went out. It was so frustrating to know that she could mark it, but I just couldn't get marks like that. That all comes with experience and knowing your cattle. You don't learn it overnight. You could be on top today, and tomorrow . . . it's a real humbling sport because there's so many variables."

Ned Huntt, a fifty-two-year-old landscape contractor from Laytonsville, Maryland, has ridden horses since he was eight years old. He showed pleasure and reining horses, as well as hunters and jumpers, before being introduced to cutting in 1963. He now trains his own cutting horses. In 1990 he placed twelfth in NCHA Non-Pro World Champion standings with $19,431 earned in thirty-five shows.

"The hardest thing to do is cut cattle clean," Huntt says. "It's a challenge every time you go in there because there's all kinds of different variables. You've got turnback men, cattle, your horse, yourself.

"For newcomers coming in, I would suggest you get an older horse and get with a reputable trainer, one that you've got some confidence in. I'm talking about an eight- to twelve-year-old horse, maybe even older, that's just as solid as he can be, and something that can teach you. Those horses are few and far between. Horses will range from $10,000 to $20,000, in that bracket. You can buy some cheaper horses, down around $3,500 to $7,500 range, but I think they'll get you in a lot of trouble.

"The initial cost of the horse is not as expensive as the cost of going down the road and showing him. You want one that can win a little money and help with the expenses, and of course build your own ego. You want to be in the money at least 20 to 30 percent of the time when you start out, and you have to have a good, well-trained horse to do that.

"We have levels of entry in cutting that allow just about anyone to come in on the bottom floor and work their way up. We have a $2,000 any horse level where you don't have to buy a horse. You can get started and get the feel of cutting. The next stage is your $10,000 Non-Pro and $20,00 Amateur. Because they're jackpotted classes, they'll last you a long time. After four to five years of experience, you can get up to the Non-Pro where you need to grade up, get yourself a better horse.

"Once it gets you, you've had it.

"It's an expensive deal to train your own horses. It's actually cheaper to spend it out to a good trainer, because of the amount of cattle you need. It would take 250 to 350 head of cattle to train one horse. There's others who will tell you you can do it on a lot less, and I'm sure they've been successful at it, but I think the vast majority will take 250 to 350 head of cattle.

"It's consuming, too. You've got to ride those horses five days a week to get where you want to go. I say it takes almost a year and a half. Patience is a virtue you'd better have when you get into cutting training.

"You meet the greatest people in the world in the cutting industry."

Michael Orr of Texas City, Texas, became intrigued with cutting in 1982 when he attended a cutting event at the Houston Livestock Show. In 1984, after less than a year of showing, he placed third in the $7,500 Amateur Gold and Silver Stakes and earned $7,400. Riding Gay Bar Cee in 1990, he placed seventh in NCHA Non-Pro World Champion standings, with $28,768 earned in fifty-eight shows.

"I saw that it was a team effort between rider and horse, and the phsyical and mental involvement by the rider intrigued me," Orr says. "I later found that it also demands a well-trained horse. The attraction hasn't changed, it has only increased. I have found it to be a great escape from the mental stress of the business world.

"Ninety-nine percent of the advice I got in the very beginning was bad advice, and it cost me thousands of dollars. If I was the type of person who was easily discouraged, I probably would have quit. I have seen this happen to people since my involvement with cutting horses, because they couldn't handle the financial mistakes—mainly through bad advice.

"I can only advise someone who is wanting to show a cutting horse, because I'm not involved in breeding or the other aspects of cutting. Newcomers should take their time before making any decisions. Go to as many cuttings as possible and meet and talk to as many people as you can. The great majority of cutters are friendly and willing to share their experiences. If people do their research, they will find a trainer who will help them get started in the right direction.

"Don't chose a trainer only because he is the closest one to your home. Be willing to drive a greater distance to achieve a greater goal.

"Be willing to buy quality, because it's better to pay more for a good one in the beginning than to spend less and go through three or four average horses and end up with nothing. Good horses hold their value.

"A beginning rider will make a lot of mistakes, but a solid, well-trained horse will get that rider through most of them. If you don't know the horse well that you're considering buying, try that horse for a minimum of two weeks under the supervision of your trainer, to see if the horse is consistent and fits you.

"One last bit of advice—start showing at weekend shows, and stay there for several years before attempting to show young horses at the big aged events. Save your money. At the weekend shows, if you're not scoring well after a period of time, resist the temptation to blame others and other things, such as bad judging, poor help or bad cattle. Take that energy back to the practice pen and use it to improve your abilities. Remember—the sport of cutting is not competition of people versus people, but rather horse versus cattle."

Mary Crist, a fifty-six-year-old grandmother of five from Hereford, Texas, had never ridden a horse before 1982. Since that time she has become successful in amateur and non-pro classes. Mary and her husband, Ron, own Commandicate, 1989 NCHA Futurity Open Reserve Champion, ridden by Bill Freeman.

"I started riding when I was forty-seven years old," Crist recalls. "My husband taught my two daughters to ride. I might have been frightened off when I was a kid. My mother would never let us have pets. She had me so frightened of horses that I just felt like I needed to keep house and raise my family.

"The first cutting I saw was the Futurity the year Diablo won it. Right after that, we got into the cutting horses and I learned to ride on the old cutting horse Freckles Booger. The first cutting I ever went to, I won, and I won a saddle as the year-end award for the $250 novice rider. It was kind of a joke to Ron and me because I was so green at it.

"It's really a thrill. I had never cared for horses, but when I watched that first Futurity, I thought that was the prettiest thing I'd ever seen in my life. I thought I'm just too old to get into that—I have five grandchildren. After I watched Ron ride in 1982, I thought, man, I've got to do this. It really got to me, and now I'm addicted.

"A lot of people say that they wanted to start because I was an inspiration, starting at that age. These thirty- or forty-year-old people say I don't know whether to start or not. That's foolish. If you like it, you need to do it."

Susan Adkisson of Aubrey, Texas, began riding cutting horses when she was thirty-five in 1981. Before a neighbor introduced her to cutting, she owned pleasure horses. In 1990 Susan placed third in the NCHA Amateur Classic Challenge.

"The hardest thing was becoming humble when I thought I knew more than I did," Adkisson says. "You don't know it because you can't see it until the little light goes on and you say, 'My goodness! I really don't know what I'm doing.' I think when you learn that, you start learning.

"When you first start showing, you blame yourself more than you should. You learn later on that it's not always you, it's not always the horse—it's a combination of things. There are so many variables, but to the beginner, it always seems the horse is great and they're bad, which is not always true.

"Go ride for somebody. Exercise horses for about a year. And watch. Unless you've got a lot of money, the best advice I could give you is to go exercise horses, because that's about all you're going to get to do. Maybe you'll get to ride one once or twice if you're lucky. You'll learn the most that way.

"If you bought yourself a cutting horse and you've never ridden one, you'd better find a good trainer. Keep the horse tuned up. Not all trainers are non-pro trainers. Find one that fits you."

SEVEN

The First Show

You must be an NCHA member or affiliate member to participate in NCHA-approved shows. A membership covers the spouse and minor children of the holder. As of January 1990, the annual membership fee was $50, with a $10 additional fee for new members. Cost of membership includes a subscription to the *Cuttin' Hoss Chatter*, the official monthly publication of NCHA, which includes calendars and schedules of all upcoming NCHA approved events.

The *Chatter* lists locations and time of shows, classifications, entry fees, office and cattle charges, purses, classes, judges, addresses and phone numbers of show secretaries.

Classes, Conditions, Entry Fees

Every rider competing in an NCHA non-pro or amateur class must have a nonprofessional card issued by the NCHA. Forms may be obtained at no charge from NCHA and must be endorsed by two NCHA non-pro card holders or by one currently active NCHA director. Every member of a competing family must have an individual card.

Non-pro card holders must not show, train or assist in training a cutting horse or rider for remuneration, directly or indirectly. In addition, non-pro and amateur riders may only show horses that they own, or that are owned by their spouses, parents or minor children. Proof of ownership will be required by show management.

There are nine classifications for NCHA shows, in addition to youth classes. The *Cuttin' Hoss Chatter* carries monthly lists of the top fifty horses in each category:

Open and Non-Pro Championship Classes   These contests carry added money purses of at least $200 per day, and points are awarded toward NCHA Horse of the Year awards.

Open and Non-Pro Cutting Horse Classes   These are jackpot contests and shows with added money purses of less than $200.

$20,000 Limit Amateur Classes   The rider must be a non-pro card holder with lifetime NCHA non-pro and/or amateur earnings of $20,000 or less.

$10,000 Limit Non-Pro Classes   The rider must be a non-pro card holder with NCHA lifetime non-pro earnings of $10,000 or less.

$3,000 Limit Novice Classes   Open to all horses having NCHA lifetime earnings of $3,000 or less.

$1,500 Limit Novice Classes   Open to all horses having NCHA lifetime earnings of $1,500 or less.

Open Gelding Classes   Open to any gelded horse.

$2,000 Limit Any Rider Any Horse Classes   Open to all riders with NCHA lifetime earnings of $2,000 or less. Any horse may be ridden without jeopardizing non-pro status. NCHA membership is not required.

Limited-Age Events   Limited to horses between three and six years of age, with individual classes for each age or combined age classes.

Entry fees vary depending on classes and purses. Some fees are as low as $30 and range to about $100. Limited age event fees, however, may be as high as $1,500. Of course, the stakes are higher, with larger purses and more added money than open shows. They also usually have payment schedules with penalties for late payments. If you are interested in entering a limited age show be sure to check your calendar and the payment schedule.

Besides entry costs, most shows charge cattle fees and a nominal office and video fee. For example: The MSCHA held a show on December 16, 1990, in Jackson with $200-added open and non-pro championship classes. Entry fee was $50, plus a $50 cattle charge for each class. The non-pro class had nineteen horses with a total purse of $1,046, from which $313.800 went to the winner. The first five horses earned money over their expenses.

The $100,000-added 1991 Memphis Futurity cost $1,300, plus a $200 cattle charge for open and non-pro entries. The non-pro division paid $14,472.73 to the winner from a purse of $78,520. Thirteen of the fifty-nine entries won enough money to pay for their entry and cattle charge, with a bonus, depending on placing.

Travel Arrangements

Whether you are traveling five hundred miles or across town, you will want to plan ahead for each show. Most championship events do not close entries until an hour before the show starts. But some require advance payment of fees, so it is always wise to check before you start from home. If you are late, some shows will still let you enter for an additional fee.

Contact the show secretary, whose phone number will be listed with the conditions in the *Cuttin' Hoss Chatter*, for overnight accommodations. Some hotels offer discounts for local show participants. Several national and regional travel guides are available that list overnight horse accommodations.

If you are traveling out of state, you will need a health certificate and current Coggins test for your horse. The show management may also require these papers, so it is best to have them at all times when you travel. The Coggins test involves a blood sample and certification, so you have to allow time for the results. This cannot be obtained at the last minute.

Traveling with a horse in tow requires a few special considerations, not the least of which is the care of your horse trailer. Always check lights, brakes, hitches and latches before and after each trip. In addition, clean the flooring and pull out the rubber floor mats each time the horse is removed. Never travel without floor mats. They protect the floor and provide stable footing in a moving trailer.

Always check the wooden floor under the mats and repair or replace it if there is any sign of rot. There are too many true horror stories about horses falling through trailer floors. Also check for any rough edges on the feeding bins or the partition. Some horses travel better without the partition, even if there is another horse in the trailer, while others prefer the security of a partition.

It is a good idea to wrap your horse's legs for travel, even for a short distance. If you are forced to make a sudden stop or sharp turn, a horse can do a lot of damage to his legs and feet by stepping on himself to recover balance. Padded leg wraps (shipping boots) with Velcro fasteners are a good insurance for trailering.

If your horse is groomed and clean before you leave home, be sure to put a blanket or cooler on him for the ride. It is also a good idea to wrap his tail in case he leans against the butt bar.

Do not water your horse immediately before loading. If you are traveling a long distance, stop every few hours to water him and allow him to get out of the trailer and urinate. This will save your floors.

Assuming your horse loads easily, walk him to the trailer door, encourage him to step up, throw the lead rope across his withers, and let him jump in. If it is a two-horse trailer or if you have an escape hatch in front, you may lead the horse in and tie him. When he is in the trailer, secure the chain or butt bar behind him, and close and latch the door. Tie the lead rope in front only after the butt bar and door have been secured, then close and latch the window.

Be confident about loading your horse. If you are hesitant and he is unsure of you, he may balk. Sometimes a horse can be enticed into a trailer with a little grain. Some will load after another horse is already in the trailer. Do not get into a battle with the horse if he refuses to load. You will only reinforce negative feelings, and tension will be doubled the next time you try to get him in the trailer. Ask an experienced horseman to show you how it is done.

Remember you have an extra passenger when driving with a trailer. Take the turns more slowly and wider than you ordinarily would, and avoid abrupt stops. Try to plan the route to bypass rough and bumpy roads or a lot of stop-and-go traffice. When you are ready to unload your horse, always untie him first, then unfasten the butt bar and open the door.

Check List for Shows

It is a good idea to keep a check list of items you will need when you travel to shows. Eventually most of this will become second nature, but it never hurts to take inventory. A well-stocked first-aid box should be kept in the truck or trailer at all times. Keep a separate one in the barn.

Papers Health papers, proof of ownership, proof of entry, non-pro card, important phone numbers, reservations.

Trailer Check lights, hitch, brakes, tires, latches, floor.

Tack Besides your saddle and regular tack, take an extra saddle blanket, halter, lead rope, cooler, horse blanket, leg wraps, shipping boots.

The First Show

Grooming Shampoo, coat conditioner, insect repellent, baby oil, rubber bands for mane and tail, curry, brushes, combs and hoof picks, liniment, hoof dressing, clippers.

Feed In addition to grain or pellet rations and hay, Karo syrup for water if your horse refuses to drink, salt brick.

Stall Buckets, snaps and hooks, hay net, fan, manure rack, shovel, trash bags.

First aid Twitch, wound spray, antibiotic ointment, rubbing alcohol, cotton balls, hydrogen peroxide, thermometer, gauze bandage, cotton rolls, adhesive tape, Vet-rap, scissors, dosing syringe, 10 or 20 cc syringe for flushing wounds, saline solution or salt, one- or two-cup measure, flashlight.

Extra key For truck, trailer, tack room and trailer hitch, stall tack room padlock.

What to Expect When You Arrive

If you have entered a show that lasts more than one day, check with the show secretary to see when your stall will be available. Some shows charge stall fees by the day and others charge one flat fee for the length of the show. If you have more than one horse, or if you are traveling with friends, you may want to rent an extra stall for feed and tack. If you do, be sure to take a padlock. If you are familiar with the facility and barns, you may be able to request specific stall locations.

Sometimes bedding is provided or it is available for a price. You can usually find hay and grain for sale. Most horsemen, however, prefer to bring their own. Show horses do not need the added stress of new or different rations. Be sure to bring feed, water buckets, hooks, snaps, and hay nets. Some stalls may have hay racks, but do not depend on it. You do not want your horse eating off the floor even with fresh bedding.

Never feed grain from wooden stall troughs. It's hard to tell what bacteria or mold may be lurking in the corners. Also, use your own buckets to water your horse. Don't let him drink from a common trough.

It is always a good idea to inspect the stall before you leave the horse.

Kick the flooring around to make sure there are no sharp objects. Also check the walls and door for sharp edges. If you hang an electric fan, be sure there are no loose wires for the horse to pull or chew.

Most facilities with stalls will also have special setups or shower stalls for bathing horses. If you want to bathe your horse at the show, take your own hose. You may need it. You may also want to take an extra mat to put on the floor of the shower stall to keep your horse from slipping.

If you are attending a one-day show and will use your trailer as headquarters, make sure you have a safe arrangement for tying your horse. It is better to tie at the horse's nose level or above. Never tie a horse to the tailgate of a pickup. Watching a horse cast and struggling underneath a tailgate is not a pretty sight.

Check hitching rails before you tie your horse to make sure they are secure. It takes just one horse to pull back on a rickety rail and set it flying. Once it is loose, the horses will back away from it and will be more frightened of the rail than what is behind them.

Always slip a halter on your horse before you tie him. Never tie him with the bridle reins. If a horse becomes frightened and pulls back, the bit can cause severe damage to his tongue. If you ever see a tongue that has been damaged by a bit, either in the hands of an ignorant or irresponsible rider, or because the horse spooked while tied by the reins, you will never forget it.

Before you leave the barn, check at the office for your work order schedule and to make sure that all your paperwork is in order.

Helpers: Turnback Riders and Herd Holders

One unique aspect of cutting is that participants must rely on four helpers in the arena. The helpers, two herd holders and two turnback riders, are usually recruited by the contestant. If you are new to cutting and do not have helpers, do not hesitate to ask another rider for assistance. Cutters are always ready to lend a hand. Someday you may be able to return the favor.

The herd holders are stationed at the end of the arena, on either side of the herd. When a cutter enters the herd, the herd holders help "shape" the cattle by flanking the bunch being driven into the arena. Once the cut has been made, herd holders move stragglers back to the end of the arena and remain positioned alongside to prevent "shooters" from joining the rider's cow.

Turnback riders help contain the cow that has been cut. On the open range, a cow is separated from the herd and driven to the "cuts," the animals which have already been cut from the original group. It is the rider's job to prevent the cow from returning to the herd, if it tries. In show arena cutting, a challenge by the cow is necessary for the horse to earn points. Turnback riders try to contain the cow within the far boundaries of the working area, which is in front of the judges and the time line.

Because of their relation to the cow being worked, turnback riders are in position to offer more assistance to the rider than just serving as backstops. Good helpers know the horse and rider, and because they watch the cattle, they probably know the cow. They can help keep a cow moving in front of the cutter, and they can move in on a cow and force it close to a horse that works well at close range. If the horse needs room to maneuver, turnback riders will keep their distance.

Non-pro riders, especially, rely on their helpers for support and assistance. "I couldn't have won without my helpers" is a common refrain among successful non-pro riders.

Sherry Wolfenbarger won the 1990 NCHA Non-Pro Breeders Cutting with a gutsy stand against an especially aggressive cow. But it was her helpers who gave Wolfenbarger the confidence to stay with the cow.

"They helped me win," admitted Wolfenbarger after the Breeders Cutting. "They all knew my mare could hold that bad cow. I worked for forty seconds, and the last twelve, the cow was right in her face every turn-around. I went until the buzzer sounded."

Working with the same team every event gives seasoned performers like Wolfenbarger a definite edge. But there are many good helpers willing to ride for beginners, as well as veterans. Chances are your turnback riders will be helping another rider in that set of cattle and will appreciate the chance to look over the cows at close range.

NCHA Non-Pro Derby winner Scott Fleming of Ocala, Florida, learned about cutters' hospitality on his first trip to Fort Worth in 1988. "Every time I went down there, I had top hands helping me," remembers Fleming. "None of those people knew me very well, but they all helped me as well as they could. They had no obligation to me. They had other clients that were non-pros. They all helped me to the best of their ability."

Do not wait until the last minute to ask for help. Talk with your helpers before you enter the arena. Listen to their assessment of the cattle. If they are helping other riders in your group, they will know which cows have already been cut, which ones to avoid and which ones might be good to cut.

Let the turnback riders know how your horse works. Does he need to have a cow pushed into his face? Does he need room to work? If you are new to cutting and are riding an experienced horse, your helpers may know more about him than you do. Listen and learn.

It is always nice, when you cut your last cow, to know how much time is left on the clock. You may choose to stay with a difficult cow and gain a point or two, rather than quit, if you know the buzzer will sound in a few seconds. Your helpers can see the clock and advise you on time remaining.

Although it is too late for training once a rider is in the arena, it usually helps to heed your helpers' advice. The instruction most often given to amateurs during a run: sit down and relax.

Warming Up

The warm-up you give your horse before a cutting event serves several purposes. The cutting horse, like every athlete, requires a period of gradually intensified physical activity to prepare his muscles and cardiovascular system for the rigorous demands of competition.

Asking a cold horse to perform is asking for trouble. The horse may give, but so will the muscles, ligaments, joints and tendons. Begin the warm-up session at least thirty minutes before your performance. Horses vary in the amount of time they need to warm up and relax. The more you ride your horses, the better you will be able to judge how much time to spend. Most cutters have their horses in the warm-up ring, at the show grounds, at least one hour before they are scheduled to ride.

Since the warm-up ring is usually adjacent to the cutting arena, the warm-up period gives the rider time to look over the cattle, as well as time to relax. Begin by jogging. When the horse is loose and relaxed, move to the lope. You will have plenty of company in the warm-up ring. This is a good opportunity to meet other riders and become familiar with names and faces.

Some riders use the warm-up period to take the edge off a nervous or "fresh" horse. This is also a good idea for new cutters. Even if your horse is experienced and unflappable, it will sense your tension and anxiety. Relaxing your hips, back and shoulders as you jog around the warm-up arena is good therapy for both you and your horse.

Non-Pro Hall of Fame Rider John Paxton spent a lot of time in the saddle preparing Doc's Otoetta for performances. "I think I rode her six hours before I showed her in the National Finals," he recalls. "Not riding her into the ground, but just keeping the edge off her. You have to keep the horse from being too tense. It's tough to find where that is sometimes. They have to have their body ready and they have to be mentally ready to work also."

World Champion Hyglo Freckles, on the other hand, is so easy going he requires minimal preparation.

"Somebody asked me about working him before a show and they said I was lying when I told them I didn't," says Faron Hightower, the horse's owner and rider. "Ringo [Hyglo Freckles] is the only one that knows how much he really needs, and we just turn him out in the pen and let him exercise himself. You can tell almost by the look in his eyes—that little cocky look. When he's got that little look about him, when his eyes are sparkling—then he's ready to go."

Fifteen minutes before your run, practice a few steps and spins and back the horse in a straight line. Take a deep breath, relax.

You are ready to perform.

Arena Etiquette

Because cutting is mentally demanding, it is easy to forget everything but your own run. Be considerate and respect other riders. Make sure that when your name is called you are ready to ride and that your help is ready.

Remember, other riders will be using the same cattle. Do all you can to avoid disturbing the herd. Do not correct your horse in or near the herd. Any unnecessary movements can create havoc. The biggest favor you can do for other riders is to be prepared when you ride into the arena. If you and your horse are prepared, there will be little need for "schooling."

When the buzzer sounds at the end of two and one-half minutes, quit the cow you are working as soon as possible. You will not improve your score by continuing, but you will needlessly tire a cow someone else might be able to use.

Walk quietly out of the arena to wait for the score. If you are finished riding, loosen your horse's cinch and remove his protective boots.

EIGHT

The Contest

The thrill of watching a cutting horse get down face to face with a cow is incomparable. The only thing better is to be riding the horse. Buster Welch calls it "the best seat in the house."

Each horse is allotted two and one-half minutes to display his ability to the judge or judges in a cutting contest. Cutting is very much a team effort between horse and rider, with two turnback riders, stationed near the time line, helping to keep the cattle in motion. Scoring begins as soon as horse and rider approach the herd, which is held at the end of the arena by two herd holders, one on each side. There should be a minimum of two and one-half cows per horse, per go-round. If there are ten riders in one go-round, there should be at least twenty-five cows.

The rider is the conductor entering the herd. He must select one cow and drive it away from the others, toward the center of the arena. The herd holders help move unwanted cows back to the herd. The cut is accomplished once the cow is isolated. The rider then loosens the reins and the horse is in control.

Performance is judged by the way the horse enters the herd, the finesse he displays in moving the cow away from the herd, and the skill with which he prevents it from returning. Each rider must cut at least two cows.

Judging

NCHA-approved judges are association members who fulfill exacting requirements, including regular attendance and testing at judging clinics and seminars. They are also classified by experience and judging record. Judges who are employed for major events with large purses, where five judges are required, are also monitored for errors and discrepancies in scoring during the shows.

The NCHA pays judges $300 to $500 per day, depending on the event, for working at the association's major shows. Local associations typically pay from $150 to $350 per day for each judge at their events, depending on the judge's rating and experience, and on the affiliate's guidelines and expenses.

Depending on the number of show entries, one to five judges may be employed. If five judges are used, the high and low scores for each contestant are discarded and the middle three scores are totaled. Judges view the proceedings facing the cattle and behind the time line and turnback helpers, seated in stands, on the back of a horse or in the back of a pickup truck.

Although judging may seem complicated and obscure because of the variables involved with cow, horse and rider, it is amazing how close five judges will be on the scores of hundreds of riders for a major event.

Timing begins for the contestant when he crosses a designated line about ten horse lengths in front of the herd. Judges score from 60 to 80 points, with half points allowed. Each "run" evaluation is started from a median score of 70 points and may be increased for certain positive actions on the part of the horse or rider. Penalties, ranging from 1 to 5 points, are subtracted from the run content value, to arrive at the score.

The highest score ever posted in an NCHA-sanctioned limited-age event was 230 points by Hall of Fame Rider L. M. "Pat" Patterson of Tecumseh, Oklahoma, on San Jo Lena in the 1987 NCHA Classic. Greg Welch scored 232 points on Tenino San in the World Championship Finals. The winning score in open classes at eight major NCHA aged events in 1990 ranged from 218.5 to 223, and averaged 221.

There are several reasons why winning scores at weekend cuttings, which offer modest purses, sometimes run higher than those for the glamour events. For instance, the great older horses, which have hooked every type of cow imaginable in their years on the road, have an edge in experience over the younger horses in the limited-age events. Another reason is that the high and low scores are thrown out in the closely monitored five-judge system at the major events.

At events with more than one judge, cutters often refer to average scores from a go-round. A "70" translates into a score of 210 where three judges' points go on the board, a "75" equals a 225, and so on.

Evaluation begins as soon as the horse approaches the herd. By entering a herd quietly and driving one animal away from the herd and toward the center of the arena, the horse demonstrates its restraint and its driving ability. Although the rider may cut as many cows as he wants within the time limit, at least one cut must be made "deep" into the herd. In other words, a rider will be penalized if he selects all of his cattle from the edge of the herd. He must ride into the herd so that the horse is surrounded.

Quiet dependability in the herd is an absolute necessity. There is no place for a high-strung, prancing horse when cattle are gathered and held in an open pasture. The soft approach gets the job done most efficiently. Cattle cannot be kept together if they are rushed. Ramrodding through a herd is like fanning a grass fire.

Once a cow is selected and cleared from the herd, it should be driven to the center of the arena. This is not always possible, but it is desirable. In actual ranch work, a cow is cut from the herd and pushed out past the herd holders to the "cuts." In the arena, the cuts are represented by the turnback riders, who push the cow back into play.

When the rider has made a cut, he must drop his hand to release any pressure on the bit and ride with loose reins until he quits that animal. This particular rule evolved for arena cutting. In ranch work, a rider needs to have ready contact with the bit. But cowboys have always loved to demonstrate the resourcefulness of their horses by riding without a bridle in the arena. Today's slackened reins create the same effect.

Early-day cutting contestants held their reins high in the air with their elbows out, to demonstrate slack. It was verboten to hold the saddle horn in those days.

Once the rider has committed to a specific cow, he will be penalized for switching to another. He will also be penalized if he is not able to separate the cow he has chosen—unless he is saved by the buzzer, which signifies the end of the ride.

When the cow begins to move after it has been cut, the horse must keep it from returning to the herd. If the cow dashes for the herd but is stopped or turned by the fence, the horse will be penalized. Each show will have a designated area of fence, referred to as "back fence," to gauge this penalty. If during the course of action the horse goes far enough past a cow to lose momentary control, or "working advantage," a penalty will also be incurred.

Working advantage is the essence of arena cutting and ranch work. A savvy cutting horse has an innate sense of distance and timing. This is something that is difficult to fake and separates the stars from the performers.

The rider may stop working, or "quit," a cow without penalty only if the cow stops, turns away or is behind the turnback helpers and time line.

Quitting a cow can be trickier than it sounds. Amateur June Roberts has a fear of cows that turn tail and run from the horse. "That's my nightmare," admits Roberts. "When they run way far away and then make a run straight back at you."

That was the scenario in the Finals of the Bonanza Cutting when Roberts quit a cow as it turned away. The judges considered the quit legal but it was a close call. "If I had been first, or if it had been a tough cutting, I might not have done that," said Roberts. "But I was just playing it safe and it worked out great."

If a horse turns completely away from the cow being worked, a 60-point score will be posted, and all credits lost. An automatic 60-point score also occurs if the rider is thrown or if the horse falls to the ground. If the horse lets the cow return to the herd, a 5-point penalty will be assessed.

Additional penalties, from 1 to 3 points, will be given for disturbing or scattering the herd of cattle; training or abusing the horse; spurring or hitting the shoulder with toe, foot or stirrup; and pawing, biting or kicking cattle.

Although two horses may both have penalty-free runs, the performances will not be identical and might receive different numerical scores. Judges will give credit for skill, style and guts. Because of the individuality of each horse's working style and the reactions of each cow, there is no absolute standard for awarding credit. There are criteria, however.

Credit will be given for quiet and efficient herd work; ease and proficiency in driving an individual cow to the center of the arena and holding it there; and working with loose reins.

Horses that control difficult cows, those that break and run and turn quickly, will score higher than a horse that controls a slow-moving cow. Cutters refer to this factor as "degree of difficulty," and will try to select challenging cows.

Subtle differences in style can have a positive effect on a horse's score. Judges like to see a horse work with enthusiasm—with ears pricked, on the alert. It is always a thrill to see a horse drive an unsuspecting cow to the center of the arena, then wait crouched and trembling in anticipation of the cow's first move.

Often cutters will talk about the prudent practice of aiming for "correct" runs, especially in a first series of go-rounds leading to a Finals. As horses are eliminated and go-rounds progress, the scores get higher because riders begin to take more chances, like staying with a really tough cow, instead of legally quitting. These risks qualify for extra credit under the category "amount of courage."

Lindy Burch and Mis Royal Mahogany earned the all-time record high score, 225.5 points, for the NCHA Futurity with just such tactics. "When the Finals came, I just took no prisoners," explains Burch. "I dropped all holds and really went for trying to have great work. I didn't want to be conservative."

Working time, within the two and one-half minute time period, varies from run to run. Some cutters will spend just a few seconds working a cow, or as many as sixty, depending on the circumstances. The average is probably close to twenty seconds per cow. But some riders will stall in the herd, allowing time to run out, especially if the run has been solid and penalty free. All other things being equal, the rider who spends more time actually working cattle will score highest.

Leon Harrel rode Smart Date through the herd of cattle in the 1987 NCHA Futurity, to find a paint cow that was hugging the chutes. Smart Date eased the cow through the herd to the middle of the arena, then held it dead center, seemingly bouncing it back and forth between her front feet. When the calf finally turned toward the judges, as if in defeat, there were twenty four seconds remaining on the time clock. Smart Date had worked the cow for nearly fifty seconds. She won the Futurity with 225 points, the second highest score in Futurity history.

The Ideal

The ideal cutting scenario involves a quick, cow-smart horse with lots of expression, hard moves and a dirt-plowing stop. Add to that a bunch of spunky cows with enough courage to face a horse, enough desire to return to the herd and enough brains to create a challenge.

Some cutters like to work two types of cows in one performance—one quick and snaky, and the other slow and deliberate. A horse will need a full range of resources to handle both.

Other riders try to pick cows that are best suited for their horse's ability. A big, muscular horse may intimidate cows too easily for a waltz in the center of the arena, but will be dynamite when stopping and turning a sprinting cow. Conversely, a small, catty cutter may be a regular Svengali at center stage, but not have quite enough bottom to get out of the ground with a wheeling wrangler.

Peppy San Badger, who won the NCHA Futurity and Derby, "could be a classy, pretty horse with lots of style," explains his trainer, Buster Welch, "and then he could immediately turn into a fierce working horse. He was so strong and yet controlled that he never had to slam himself around."

The blaze-faced sorrel mare Smart Date possessed an abundance of style and cow sense. After she won the NCHA Futurity by holding a spotted cow in the center of the arena for nearly a minute, her rider, Leon Harrel, bought the cow. He retired it to a lifetime of unlimited grazing on his ranch in Kerrville, Texas. In Harrel's estimation that cow was a perfect "ten."

Since cattle are never predictable, consistency is essential in a truly successful cutting horse. Some horses seem to have a knack for going with the flow, no matter the circumstances. Poco Lena, honored as Number One in the NCHA Hall of Fame, was such a horse.

"You never had to go in on her and pick up a cow," explained Poco Lena's trainer, Pine Johnson. "You just went in and cut a cow and she'd handle it. She seemed to play with cattle and was so quick and smooth that a cow kept thinking that he could see daylight behind her. He'd keep trying to go behind her and she just kept blocking him and pulling him into her."

Poco Lena's son, Doc O'Lena, had the same knack for consistency. The little bay stallion is the only horse in the thirty-year history of the NCHA Futurity to win all four Futurity go-rounds. He is also a leading sire and grandsire of cutting horse performers, as was his maternal grandsire Poco Bueno.

Common Penalties and Mistakes

One penalty situation that probably causes the most confusion and discussion among competitors is the "hot quit." According to the rule, a cutter may legally stop working a cow he has cut if it is "obviously stopped, obviously turned away or is obviously behind the turnback horses, and the turnback horses are behind the time line."

Differences of opinion most often occur over the definition of "obvious." It is not unusual for a cutter to quit a cow, then worry until the score is posted, wondering if the judges agree with his assessment of the situation. Because there are many viewpoints, the judges do not always agree, but must review videotapes of the action, shot from several perspectives, to be certain.

The difficulty exists with cows that twist and turn suddenly, one moment moving away from a horse, the next turning back. If a cow stops while facing a horse, and then moves into the horse while the cutter is in the process of quitting, a penalty will be given. Sometimes it is almost impossible to read what a cow will do. If in doubt, it is best to stick with the cow until it surrenders, backs up or runs off in the opposite direction.

Many cutters get into trouble when a cow runs up to a fence, stops momentarily, then wheels into the horse. The rider, expecting the cow to turn away, will lift the reins to indicate a quit, just as the cow barrels ahead.

Feints are a bane to cutters. Sometimes a cutter can save points by dropping his hand back down after a hot quit. If the cow turns away in the next move, and the cutter stops his horse, he will only be penalized 1 point for reining. If, however, the cow turns into the horse, the cutter will receive 4 penalty points—1 for reining and 3 for a hot quit.

Another area of confusion exists with the 5-point penalty for switching cattle. According to the rule the penalty is applied "if a rider changes cattle after visibly committing to a specific cow."

Here again, the problem exists with the definition of one word: "commit." If the rider makes two moves toward a specific cow in a group, or alone, or one obvious move, that move will be considered a commitment. A cutter is allowed to stop a group of cattle however, and then cut from that group. In order to stop a group, one cow is usually stopped in the flow. If that is the situation, the rider will not be penalized.

If a cutter commits to a cow and the horse attempts to switch to another, the rider will not be penalized if he has not yet released the horse to work. If the horse has been released, the cutter will be penalized.

Cows that shoot out from the herd into the path of a cow being worked can cause problems for a cutter if his horse becomes confused and switches to the "shooter." If the rider anticipates a problem, he may rein the horse to prevent a switch and receive a 1-point penalty for reining, which is better than 5 points for switching. If his horse switches anyway, he will be penalized 6 points—1 for reining and 5 for switching. On the bright side of this situation, if the rider does not rein the horse and the horse stays with the original cow, in spite of a confusing situation, the horse will be awarded extra credit.

It is the rider's obligation to show the judge a penalty-free run. Competitors should try to avoid close situations that will force the judge to make a decision.

While many aspects of judging may seem confusing to a beginner, the best way to get a feel for what is acceptable and what is not is to attend as many cuttings as possible. Observe and ask questions. If you are performing in a show, watch as many runs as you can before your performance. This will give you a feel for the judging. In addition, judges' cards are posted after every go-round. If you do not understand how a run was scored, check the score cards. This should provide an insight. Do not attempt to converse with the judges, however. This is against the rules, and if you are a contestant, you may be fined and/or suspended.

As noted earlier, a contestant may protest a judge's decision by submitting a written request for review to the NCHA director of judges within seven days of the closing date of the show. There is a fee for a review, but it is returned to the contestant if the judge is found to be in error.

Do's and Don'ts

One of the best ways to become familiar with the rules of cutting is to study the *NCHA Rule Book*, which is revised each year and sent to all members. Hand in hand with the *Rule Book* is the *Case Book*, which provides interpretations of the rules and examples of application.

After you have studied the rules and the *Case Book*, try to watch a cutting as if you were judging it. Compare your scores with the judges' scores. Note discrepancies. Then look at the posted judges' cards and go back over the performance in your mind.

You can also purchase an excellent videotape from NCHA of the 1989 Judging Seminar with film clip tests and answers, run content evaluations and explanation of rules and applications.

Remember that judges are rated according to number and size of shows worked, as well as numerous other standards. Not all judges on the local weekend show circuit will be as experienced as the judges at the NCHA Futurity, Derby and Super Stakes. You can learn something from every show experience, however, regardless of size.

Listen to your helpers. Then, sit in the stands and watch other non-pro and amateur riders and listen to the advice they are getting from their helpers. By watching them you may gain insight into your own performance. The most frequently repeated advice is simple, however—relax!

It is also helpful to be able to watch your performances on videotape. At the larger shows private video companies set up booths where you watch your performance for a small fee. Or you may want to purchase the tape. You can also recruit a friend to tape for you. It is much easier for good advice to sink in if you are able to see your mistakes and weaknesses. Solicit criticisms.

Give yourself a chance. Pat yourself on the back for improvement and work to correct your weaknesses. Know your horse and what you can expect. If you have a solid horse, trust him.

NINE

Campaigning

Ask cutters how they became involved in cutting competition and you will get similar answers. There are variations, but the gist is the same. "It's like your first kiss," says NCHA Non-Pro Hall of Fame member Carl Crawford. "You'll never forget it, and from then on you're hooked."

The lure of cutting draws riders from 50 states and 13 foreign countries, to over 1,500 annual NCHA-approved cuttings. Most are sponsored by 109 NCHA affiliate clubs, which are listed, along with club secretaries' addresses and phone numbers, in the *NCHA Annual Yearbook*. Riders also accumulate points in 25 NCHA-designated geographical areas. Area leaders compete for National Championship standings each spring in Jackson, Mississippi.

Affiliate shows are conducted under standard NCHA rules, using NCHA-approved judges. Show results are compiled and tabulated by NCHA to determine World Championship year-end standings in each classification. NCHA standings are also used to determine annual affiliate and area standings.

The majority of NCHA members compete at local and area shows. Entry fees are relatively low—a $200-added money class will cost in the neighborhood of $55 for entry fees and $55 cattle charge. Entry fees, minus a small percentage for show administration, are added to the purse. The more entries, the more places awarded money. Usually you can register when you arrive at the show grounds.

If your horse is registered with a breed association, you are eligible to participate in that breed association's shows. Not all breeds offer cutting competition, however. Contact the registry for information.

Championship classes fit all ages and levels of riders, as well as horses. Many riders begin competing in local shows and discover midyear that they rank in championship standings. The top fifteen competitors from each category are eligible to perform in the NCHA World Championship Finals held in Houston, Texas, every February. This show offered prize money of $126,400 in 1990, with $50,000 added to the purse. It is possible for a non-pro rider to earn over $15,000 in the NCHA World Finals.

Those riders who aim for the very top must commit themselves to as many as one hundred shows in one year. Cutters who compete for World Championship standings refer to this effort as "hauling." For most it is a busy year of carefully coordinated schedules.

Winnings can be impressive. For example, Cash Quixote Rio holds the record for World Championship earnings. In 1990 the bay stallion earned $121,731, breaking the record of $108,114 set in 1985 by Ball O'Flash. George Glover of Bay City, Texas, holds the record for highest single-year Non-Pro World Championship winnings—$99,062 earned in 1985.

Limited-Age Events

Cutting is the world's richest equine arena sport. Although the stakes are higher, limited-age events, for horses between three and six years old, offer the heftiest purses. In 1989 limited-age events paid contestants $8 million.

Because cutting is physically and psychologically stressful to young horses, NCHA set a precedent for limited-age events with their Futurity for three-year-olds. The NCHA Futurity was conceived, in 1962, as a tool to market the cutting horse industry. Owners, breeders and trainers agreed to debut their cutting prospects in December of their three-year-old years. To ask more, sooner, would jeopardize a horse's soundness and well-being. It is against the rules for an NCHA Futurity horse to have performed in any previous shows. This policy has created as aura of excitement about the Futurity that is unmatched in any other event.

Before the Futurity, the same horses monopolized cutting events. They just got older and better, and occasionally changed hands. But the Futurity guaranteed a new crop each year.

In 1990, the NCHA Futurity carried a total purse of $1,216,000, with $200,000 added money, from 584 entries. Millie Montana, the Open Champion, earned $87,468, and Non-Pro Champion Matt Gaines won $35,454. Entry fees, paid in installments, added up to $1,500 for open and non-pro entries.

The NCHA Super Stakes ranks second, to the NCHA Futurity, in prize money. Unlike the Futurity, the Super Stakes is limited to horses that are sired by subscribed stallions. Held late spring of each year, the Super Stakes is limited to four-year-olds, with a separate event for five-year-olds.

The Gold & Silver Stakes is another stallion progeny event with limited age restrictions. In 1989 the Gold & Silver offered a purse of $884,822, with half the total in added money. In 1987 Poco Quixote Rio earned $1.09 million as the winner of the event from a total purse of $1.86 million.

The trick for an amateur rider who wants to compete in limited-age events is to find a horse with enough maturity to offset the rider's inexperience. Three-year-olds are really not suitable for beginners, although there is always the exception. The beginning rider should try to find a solid five-year-old. After a season of competition, he may be ready for a younger horse. Most amateurs and non-pros who ride in limited-age events rely on trainers to keep their horses "tuned" and to offer advice.

Because good younger horses stand the chance to earn considerably more money than older horses, they are more expensive to buy. They usually require time with a trainer, and are therefore more expensive to maintain. If a rider has the time and money to spend up front, however, a limited-age-event horse can recoup costs many times over.

Breeding

One of the biggest pitfalls for enthusiastic new horse owners is the breeding business. The profits might look enticing, but the facts are sobering. Very few people make money breeding horses. Those who do are knowledgeable horsemen with the ways and means to promote their horses. Economically, buying ready-made cutting horses makes more sense, for the average rider, than breeding them. For horse owners who have the proper facilities, raising a foal can be a gratifying experience.

If you do not own a mare, several options are open to you if you would like to raise a foal. Some breeders lease mares. Arrangements vary, but usually the lessor pays for breeding and veterinarian fees and maintains the mare through weaning of the foal. Be sure to check the breeding history of a mare and have a veterinarian check her reproductive system before you sign a lease.

Should you decide to purchase a mare, consider one already in foal, providing you approve of the sire. Usually you can find some relative bargains, compared to the price of an open mare (a mare not in foal), for which you will pay veterinarian, boarding, breeding and handling expenses. By purchasing a mare in foal, you are assured that she is capable of conceiving.

There is always a risk in buying maiden mares. If the mare is young and healthy, the risk is minimal. If she is six or older, and has never conceived, do some detective work. Nothing adds up faster than veterinarian and board bills at a breeding farm. If your mare does not conceive within a reasonable period of time, your expenses could outweigh the stud fee and the value of the future foal.

Pedigree is a major consideration in breeding. If you attend cutting events, you will begin to get a feel for successful and popular bloodlines. Send for auction sales catalogs and study the pedigrees and produce records of the horses. Attend as many sales as you can to get a feel for prices. Or contact the sale company for results.

Talk with other owners, riders and trainers. Learn the characteristics of different bloodlines to determine which pedigree best suits your interest. Just looking at the sires of non-pro horses in event programs will give you an idea of which stallions produce easygoing dispositions.

Always keep salability in mind when buying and breeding. Bargains are sometimes difficult to resist, but it is usually best to stay with popular and proven pedigrees. Prices may be higher for good breeding, but they will hold at the other end of the line should you decide to sell.

Be especially careful in selecting a stallion. Do not waste your time and your mare with offers from friends and acquaintances who are trying to prove their stallions with free breedings. Study your budget and bloodlines. Look at the stallion's performance and sire record. Check the breeding farm and talk with other mare owners to see if they were satisfied with the mare care and charges. When you have narrowed your choices, look at promotion. If the stallion owners put a lot of effort into marketing and advertising, so much the better for your future foal.

Most stallion services come with a live-foal guarantee, although some syndications do not offer this. Be sure to inquire. If you don't have a guarantee and your mare aborts, you lose the stud fee. Also ask about chute or handling fees and standard veterinarian expenses. Some farms encourage mare owners to ship mares in after they have been palpated and are ready to ovulate. This cuts boarding costs. It also reduces stress for mares that are sensitive to changes in environment.

Breeding farms usually offer options for mare care. Open mares, those not in foal, are referred to as dry mares if they do not have nursing foals. Nursing mothers are called wet mares. If your mare needs to be in a stall or pen by herself, this can usually be arranged, but it will cost more.

In 1990 stud fees for top cutting horse sires ranged from $1,500 to $7,500, with chute fees from $250 to $500. Some farms do not charge chute fees. Most require a booking fee, from $250 to $1,000, payable when the breeding contract is signed, and deducted from the fee. The balance of stud fee and other expenses are due when the mare leaves the farm, unless other arrangements have been made.

Mare care costs per day are generally between $6 and $25, depending on the type of accommodations—pasture, stall, wet (mare with foal at side), dry (mare without foal), etc. Veterinary and palpation expenses are usually additional.

Because accidents can happen anywhere, make sure your mare is insured before shipping her to the breeding farm.

Selling

In time, as you become more experienced in cutting, you will probably be ready for a new horse. This is a natural progression. Just as an art student begins with charcoal and advances to a full palette of colors, you will want to broaden your range.

If you are actively riding and doing well, word-of-mouth may be the only advertising you need. After the purchase of the first horse, most non-pros tend to buy horses they have seen perform and have competed against. Let it be known that your horse is for sale.

Be realistic about the asking price if you really want to sell. Check the market for horses of similar age, sex, breeding and show record. You may be able to get what you paid for the horse, but be prepared to be flexible. Do not expect to recover expenses you have put into the horse unless you have been very successful in the show ring.

Often it is wise to find a trainer who will act as an agent in selling your horse. The percentage you pay will be well worth eliminating the bother of trying to sell on your own, especially if you do not have cattle. Showing horses to prospective buyers requires a lot of time and patience.

Another alternative is a public sale, which auctions horses for a consignment fee and percentage of the sale price. Many sales are scheduled during major cutting events, at or near the cutting facility. Consignment fees begin at $200 and commissions run from about 5 to 10 percent.

The nice thing about a sale is that it will be advertised and promoted, and catalogs with pedigrees and performance information on each horse are available to prospective buyers. The *Cuttin' Hoss Chatter* provides information on upcoming sale dates and contacts.

If you consign your horse to a sale, you may enter a reserve bid so he will not be sold for less than a fixed price. You will forfeit your consignment fee if you do this, however. If the sale is a well-known annual event and well attended, trust that you made the right decision to sell to the highest bidder.

If you are determined to sell your horse yourself by advertising in a local newspaper or trade publication, remember that you may be liable for accidents. You know your horse, but you won't know the people you put on his back. Be cautious. If it is obvious that a prospective buyer can't ride, don't take a chance.

Make sure that you are present when someone comes to look at the horse. I had someone wander into a pasture to look at a filly without my knowledge. She brought along a bag of carrots and was knocked down by four greedy youngsters jostling for a handout. Her arm was broken. I had told her she could stop by to see the filly, never dreaming she would climb into the pasture, which had a locked gate.

TEN

The Enthusiasts

Buying three-year-old cutting prospects before the NCHA Futurity is like shopping for Christmas. Prices are at a premium and it's hard to be sure of a fit.

There are plenty of Neiman-Marcus shoppers in the cutting industry, and hundreds of high-dollar horses. But fancy price tags do not guarantee success. Grassroots, backyard cutters are the mainstay of the industry. Most of them compete close to home and ride good horses with modest pedigrees and market values.

Grass Roots Cutters

Harold Franklin doesn't have much time for cutting horses. He works as a feed salesman and farms soybeans, corn and wheat on four hundred acres near Columbia, Missouri. He thinks he's lucky if he can attend half a dozen shows a year.

Making the trip to Forth Worth for the 1987 NCHA Futurity was a big venture for Franklin. "It was something that I had always dreamed about doing," says Franklin. "But I didn't think that I could ever get it done."

A self-taught rider and trainer, Franklin hardly ever ventures farther than Iowa or Nebraska for a cutting, but he had a three-year-old in 1987 that was too good to keep under wraps.

Baldy Freckles, a white-face sorrel gelding, won the 1987 $10,000 Non-Pro Futurity for Franklin and the 1990 NCHA Non-Pro World Championship for Lee Garner, who paid Franklin $40,000 for the horse in 1989.

"I trained the horse all along," says Franklin, who purchased Baldy

Freckles as a two-year-old for a very modest sum. "I just have an outside round pen and I worked him all alone.

"I'm real short on cattle and I usually buy twelve at a time. I just work one calf at a time. Sixty days before I was going to Fort Worth, I started working out of the herd. I tied two horses in the pen on either side for the herd holders. Then I would just work my horse. I've got a turnback dog, and that's how I did it.

"I never worked Baldy more than once a week on cattle ever since he was a two-year-old. I just let him run out all that summer."

"Someone like me takes a big NCHA event one step at a time," says Scott Fleming, a dual champion of the 1988 NCHA Derby. "I didn't have any idea how much money was there until it was over. I didn't want to know."

The Derby was the second NCHA event the Ocala, Florida, veterinarian had ever entered. Raised on a small ranch in Anson, Texas, Fleming always had an interest in cutting horses, but never had the money or connections he thought he needed to be able to show. As a student at Texas A&M University, he worked summers for Norman Bruce of Rutledge, Georgia, and learned how to ride cutting horses.

Fleming works mostly with Thoroughbreds in his Florida equine practice and raises a few racehorses of his own. One mare that has given him a number of nice race claiming and allowance horses is Sculptors Whim, the dam of his NCHA Derby Champion, Squeak Toy.

Sculptors Whim seemed to be the right choice for a cutting horse producer. She had good conformation and her foals had shown a lot of early speed and maturity. In addition, she was an older mare, and Fleming had a better chance of getting her in foal by artificial insemination, which is sanctioned by AQHA but not allowed by The Jockey Club.

"I really like Thoroughbred horses and I like an outcross," says Fleming, who bred Sculptors Whim to the Quarter Horse Docs Sugs Brudder, hoping for a cutting horse he could ride.

Tied to his practice and ranch during the breeding and racing season, Fleming decided on a do-it-yourself program and began learning all he could about riding and training cutting horses.

"I've watched all the Joe Heim, Tommy Lyons and Bill Freeman videotapes," says Fleming. "And it's actually all there if you just take the time and watch close. I also go to one or two of the major events every year and just sit around the practice pen. I probably do that more than the show ring.

"The first year and a half I was doing this was a wreck," Fleming admits. "I didn't know what I was doing and the horses didn't either."

Everything began to fit for Fleming in 1987, and in the spring of 1988 he placed third on Squeak Toy in the Southeastern Cutting Horse Non-Pro Futurity and won the Classic on another Thoroughbred-Quarter crossbred horse.

The NCHA Derby seemed a logical step for Fleming, who felt competent for the $10,000 Non-Pro class, but thought the Non-Pro would be a long-shot. With his double victory, Fleming became the first rider to ever win both the Non-Pro and $10,000 classes in an NCHA limited-age event.

Roy Carter was in the right place at the right time when Smart Peppy Lena pitched his new owner Rob Parker.

Parker had gotten the sorrel gelding in a package deal for $400 because he was so wild. As a Smart Little Lena son, Smart Peppy Lena had the pedigree of a good cutting horse—if he could be ridden. Parker called on his friend Roy Carter.

"Rob bought him and he bucked him off, so he called me and said, 'You've got to come get this horse,' " recalls Carter of his first acquaintance with the gelding. "He bucked right up until the Futurity, but he finally got it out of him."

Carter, a champion bull rider, had recently retired after sixteen years, and some serious injuries, with the Professional Rodeo Cowboys Association and hoped to make a living training cutting horses. It was a logical choice, since Carter had grown up watching his father John Carter ride some of the legends of early cutting, including Poco Mona, Hollywood Cat, Doc's Starlight, and Jewels Leo Bars (Freckles).

"Smart Peppy Lena has really encouraged me to go on and do the cutting," says Carter of the 1990 NCHA Challenge Open Champion. "Otherwise, I'd still be running around rodeos."

"It's one of those stories that you'd like to see happen all the time, but very seldom does," says Rob's father, Tommy Parker, a livestock broker from Anderson, Texas. "The little horse helped Rob and Roy both. They were riding bulls. This horse got their minds off the bulls and onto the cutting horses."

Ron Crist is a rancher from Hereford, Texas, who dabbles in cutting when he has a chance. He likes to buy a few young horses for a modest price each winter, start their training, and sell them as three-year-old Futurity prospects.

"I bought a two-year-old Doc's Hickory filly for $5,000 and took her home and trained on her myself for a year," explains Crist. "Then I took her to Kathy Daughn, and within forty-five days Kathy had her sold for me for $26,000. That's an example of how my program works."

When Crist saw Commandicate, a Smart Little Lena son, in the catalog of a small livestock sale in Roswell, New Mexico, he hitched up his horse trailer and headed west.

"I saw the way he was bred," says Crist. "I went to the sale expecting to get a good deal and, sure enough, I did."

Crist started working Commandicate on cattle, but it was soon evident the gelding belonged with a professional trainer.

"We took him home and he had never seen a cow," remembers Mary, Ron's wife. "He was just barely green-broke. The first time Ron got on him and ran him across the arena and stopped him—he looked down and his back feet were in front of Ron's in the stirrups. He said, 'Mary, I think we've really got something here.'"

Bill Freeman, a leading trainer of aged-event champions and Smart Little Lena's pilot, was the rider Crist wanted to see on Commandicate's back. He came within one-half point of winning the 1989 NCHA Futurity and was Reserve Champion. In 1990 he won the NCHA Breeders Cutting.

"This horse kind of broke my program because he was a super horse," says Crist. "He's the best horse that I've ever owned. I decided I'd better not sell him."

Everyone loves rags-to-riches stories, and Ball O'Flash's is one of the most spectacular.

Choice horse flesh for foreign markets brought fifty-five to sixty cents a pound, on the hoof, at Texas slaughterhouses during the mid-seventies. Horse thievery was rife, and "killer buyers" haunted every small horse auction in the state—like the one in Mesquite, Texas, in 1976, where a little grey gelding with an undistinguished pedigree went through the ring.

"The killer buyers had offered $225 for Ball O'Flash, but I gave $350 for him and saved his life," remembers Bud Evans, who liked the four-year-old gelding's pretty grey coat. Shortly after, Evans sold him to V. D. Adair.

Veteran cutter Charlie Ashcraft trained Ball O'Flash. "We showed him for about a year and won several saddles," Ashcraft recalls. "Then Adair decided to take him home and Ball O'Flash became a family horse. They ran barrels on him, showed him in reinings and at pole bendings, and he did well in everything."

In 1980 Adair sold Ball O'Flash to Ashcraft. Five months of training put the gelding back in form for cutting, and Ashcraft and his daughter Connie Sue began showing him.

"A child could ride him, he was that gentle. But he was so quick when cutting cattle. He could turn a rider's face red from trying to hang on to him."

Ashcraft smiles as he remembers one man who wanted to buy the gelding but was afraid he couldn't ride him.

"How do you expect to win first place if you can't ride a first-place horse?" asked Ashcraft.

Ball O'Flash, a $350 gelding, had a head for cattle and the heart of a champion. He was 1984 and 1985 NCHA World Champion Gelding, ranked NCHA Open Top Ten for six years running and held the record for single-year earnings until 1990.

When he died in 1988, Ball O'Flash had NCHA lifetime earnings of $476,558—nineteen hundred times the price Bud Evans paid to rescue him from the killers.

Vive la Différence

Cutting horse riders are gender conscious. They refer to "my mare," or "your colt," or "this gelding," as if to acknowledge nature's scheme. There is no bias—just an acknowledgment. Mares and colts are on equal footing in the cutting arena. So are men and women.

Cutting is very democratic. What other sport offers over $15 million in annual purses to men, women, and children competing in the same event, under the same rules?

Men will be the first to agree that women cutters are just as competitive as men. In fact, some think women have an edge. "Some of the best riders are women," says Buster Welch. "They seem to have a gentle touch that men just don't have."

Welch's wife Sheila (pronounced Shay-la) has been a top competitor for over a decade and has such a graceful, effortless style of riding that it's hard to remember to watch the horse working instead of Sheila riding.

A former World Champion, Sheila has earned nearly three-quarters of a million dollars riding cutting horses as a non-pro. "This is something I truly love to do," she says. "People ask me about the rules. I don't even know what half the rules are. That's my two-and-a-half minutes. I bought and paid for it and I just try to get my horse shown. I love to win, but I don't go out to beat anybody."

Lindy Burch of Carmel, California, was the first woman to win the NCHA Open Futurity riding Mis Royal Mahogany in 1980. Burch was studying for a masters degree at UCLA, in hopes of attending veterinary school, when she started training cutting horses in 1978.

Although her win stands as a watershed for women in NCHA limited-age events, Burch looks at it from a different perspective.

"I've never made a big woman-man thing about what I do," says Burch. "I want to do it because I'm a good hand, not because I'm a good hand that's a woman. I think everybody wants the best horse to win no matter who is on it—man, woman or child.

"I had a feeling of being marked down at times, maybe because I was a woman. But it was no different than the young guy who gets marked down under the old tough. I never made an issue out of it. When I was beat I just tried harder."

Kathy Daughn of Clements, California, began riding horses when she was thirteen. During the summer of 1979 she was introduced to cutting horses through a summer job and has been riding professionally ever since. In 1985 Daughn won the NCHA Futurity riding The Gemnist.

Daughn, like Burch, puts her focus on the horse and her fellow competitors. "I have had the benefit of working with some outstanding people in this industry," says Daughn. "There's a real feel of team play in there because of the people who are helping you. It's just an outstanding sport."

Barbra Schulte of Brenham, Texas, is a working mother who spends her days in front of a cow, instead of behind a desk. Schulte, a former teacher of the hearing impaired and a speech pathologist, won the 1988 NCHA Open Derby on Freckles Son Ofa Doc. She also teaches non-pros and amateurs how to ride.

"I felt stifled in a traditional career," says Schulte, whose sister Mary was a top non-pro rider. "Now my husband and I have our own business that is very family-oriented."

One of cuttings' toughest non-pro competitors is Mary Jo Milner of Irving, Texas. Milner, a two-time World Champion and three-time Reserve World Champion, was raised on a ranch and began riding cutting horses with her husband, Jim, founder of a national fast-food chain. Between the two of them,

Model and actress Christie Brinkley owns and rides cutting horses. Don Shugart photo.

Mary Jo and Jim have won every NCHA non-pro title and $1.4 million in prize money.

"To be successful in cutting it takes dedication and perseverance, the same qualities it takes in any business," says Mary Jo. "Even though it is our hobby, and we like to play at it, the fun and satisfaction is the success of it. Maybe that comes from the way we were raised. We started out with nothing and accomplishment was our goal. That is the way we were taught. I sometimes wish I could just relax. Yet, that doesn't satisfy me."

Sandy Bonelli is another Californian who earns big bucks riding cutting horses. In 1989 she won the NCHA Non-Pro Futurity riding Bella Coquette, a mare she raised and trained herself. Bonelli was a horse-crazy kid who grew up on the back of a pony. When she was old enough, she began showing western pleasure horses, but switched to cutting when she met Tom Lyons and Doc's Oak, the sire of Bella Coquette's dam.

"I like to ride and I love horses," says Bonelli, who has earned $585,000 with her string of non-pro limited-age-event horses.

Country-western star Tanya Tucker is a winning cutting competitor. Don Shugart photo.

Debbie Patterson of Tecumseh, Oklahoma, was born to the sport. Her father, L. M. "Pat" Patterson, has trained cutting horses for over sixty years and is a member of the NCHA Riders and Members Hall of Fame. Debbie, 1987 Non-Pro World Champion, is a member of the Non-Pro Hall of Fame. Her brother Kenny is a professional trainer and rode 1989 World Champion Cutting Horse Jae Bar Fletch, a full brother to Debbie's World Champion mare, Jae Bar Maize.

"I was like every other kid," says Debbie. "I wanted to do what I wanted to do. Then I realized that there was considerably more money in cutting than rodeo and I decided to make the switch."

Sherry Wolfenbarger of Malibu, California, earns a living teaching pleasure riding to clients like Hollywood producer Steven Spielberg and actor Michael Keaton. For fun she rides cutting horses and has earned over $281,000.

"I like to introduce people to the equine world," says Wolfenbarger.

Actor Michael Keaton, riding here in the NCHA Celebrity Cutting, takes pleasure riding lessons from Non-Pro champ Sherry Wolfenbarger. Don Shugart photo.

"When my clients from California come to watch me ride cutting horses, they just can't believe something like this exists. Really, it's the last of the Old West. They just think they're living their cowboy dreams."

June Roberts dreamed cowboy dreams as a young girl growing up outside of Los Angeles.

"I was your basic California, city-girl horse nut," says Roberts, who owns 1990 NCHA National Champion Gelding Monkeys Formula. It wasn't until I was a senior in high school that my parents bought me a horse—a $400 gelding. Everyone was barrel racing then. Sammy Thurman was having a barrel racing clinic and everyone was going. I couldn't go, so I took the notes out of the trash can."

Roberts perservered. She earned a scholarship riding in high school rodeos and later placed sixth in the Women's Professional Rodeo Association on her $400 gelding.

On a whim, in 1988 Roberts traded a car for a couple of cutting horses. Riding in small weekend cutting events, she enjoyed moderate success on a four-year-old mare, Doc N Bars. One day, at a cutting event in Fort Worth, Roberts and Doc N Bars came to an impasse. When Charlie Ashcraft, who was campaigning Monkeys Formula, offered to help, Roberts unloaded.

"Get rid of her," she told Ashcraft. "Colorado isn't big enough for the two of us."

Ashcraft, a veteran trainer who rode World Champion Ball O'Flash, knows how to make a winner. He worked with Roberts and Doc N Bars and helped the pair get back in the money.

During one weekend cutting, shortly after the trainer and amateur met, Ashcraft loaned Monkeys Formula to Roberts for an amateur class. It was the first time she had ever ridden the gelding, and nearly the last.

In spite of her rocky ride, when Roberts learned the horse was for sale, she threw caution to the winds. Monkeys Formula, with $200,000 in lifetime earnings, seemed a sure bet for paychecks—if Roberts could learn to ride him. She sold her mare and signed a note in order to pay for the eleven-year-old gelding.

Family and friends were skeptical, but Roberts' confidence was buoyed by the lucrative, unsolicited offers she received. One non-pro, well known in the Quarter Horse industry, was incredulous when she refused his $50,000 offer.

Monkeys Formula had never packed a non-pro, much less an amateur, but he was as solid as bedrock. The only problem in riding him was staying on his back.

"The only way I can stay on him is to ride with two hands on the saddle horn. I look like a monkey on Monkeys' back."

While Roberts is the first to ride the gelding with both hands braced for action, she is not the first to experience his whiplash action.

"I rode him and I scored a 76, and I looked like a puppet," one well-known trainer sheepishly admitted.

"He gets his neck really low," explains Roberts, "and snakes it around like, 'You think I'm going left? But, no! I'm going right,' I feel like I'm at the end of a dish towel when you crack it."

In spite of the effort involved in staying on Monkeys Formula's back, Roberts is not overly self-conscious about her appearance or apprehensive about her performance. There is a certain amount of pressure that comes with riding a champion, however. Roberts is conscious of high expectations.

"Everyone knows he's a great horse," says Roberts. "If I don't win they think that I'm stupid. And if I do good, they think he does good in spite of me. And it's true. I can kick him in the ear and he still does the right thing."

When they're not on the road, Roberts, her six-year-old son, John, and Monkeys Formula are at home on a sixty-acre ranch thirty miles north of Fort Worth. Even with her recent success, Roberts is taking it one day at a time.

"My immediate goal is not to fall off," says Roberts. "But I figure I'm going to ride him and show him as long as I'm winning. Then the kids can take him and be World Champions. I think he's going to make a champion out of anyone that rides him."

Saddling Up to Let Down

Cutting is a great leveler. Boardroom achievements don't carry over into the arena. The CEO may control corporate millions but can't do a thing about the wild-eyed calf that ducks beneath his horse—except try again.

Executives and professionals leave the high pressure deadlines behind when they slide into the saddle of a cutting horse. It's a place where effort counts and there is always next time.

A rider redefines himself when he looks into a herd of cattle. It's not so much the outcome that matters, but how he uses his resources. It's a little like poker, with the luck of the draw, yet there is scant room for bluffing. Instinct and competence maintain a fine balance in the cutting arena, perhaps one reason it is such a popular sport with businessmen. Caution wins money, but inspiration earns more. Perfection is the goal that everyone chases, but most riders are satisfied to occasionally catch a glimpse.

"You can't win every time," says Lee Garner of Batesville, Mississippi. Logistically, cutting is Garner's kind of game. The 1990 NCHA Non-Pro World Champion played linebacker for Ole Miss in the late sixties when the team's defensive line was rated tops in the nation. Sacking quarterbacks take talent, but playing defense against baldies and Brahmas demands skills Garner never had to hone playing football.

"Cutting is a game of percentages," says Garner, who manages a family-owned private-duty nursing business. "You can't win every time because you have too many factors. You have the human factor—your help and yourself. Then you have the animal factors—your horse and the cattle. And, you have all the judging factors. All those things are not going to gel every time."

Although Garner has ridden since he was a toddler and rodeoed as a

1990 NCHA Non-Pro World Champion Lee Garner on Baldy Freckles. Don Shugart photo.

teenager, he didn't start cutting until he was forty-three and his children were already showing horses.

"I guess I was an over-achiever father," admits Garner. "One day I told my son Lee I was buying the best horses I could afford and he wasn't doing as good as I thought he should, so I was going to do it myself."

Garner admits to trying more than a few mounts before finding one that fit him—a 1984 gelding, Baldy Freckles.

"I know that I'm not good, but I know that Baldy Freckles and I are good together," says Garner, who doesn't like anyone else to even lope the gelding for him.

The only differences Garner and his gelding have are in the herd. "He can read cows better than me, and he and I will usually have an argument right before we cut one," says Garner. "He thinks certain cows will be better, and I hate to say that a lot of times he's right."

Much of cutting's appeal is the special working relationship between human and horse. Ernest Beutenmiller, who owns a meat packing business in St. Louis, has owned three world champion cutting horses. His favorite was Kingstream, a gelding he paid $60,000 for in 1978. Although Kingstream had earned two world championships before Beutenmiller bought him, he was a confirmed bronc.

"I never even rode him before I bought him," says Beautenmiller, who mounts a horse with the aid of a footstool. "I have two artificial hips, so I ride with a seat belt. When I bought him, most people were willing to bet I'd never ride him. But, when you want something bad enough . . .

"I shook like a leaf the first time I showed him. I had him over a month before I took him to a show. I wanted to make sure I could get along with him. I sure didn't want to embarrass him. There are a lot of expectations out of an animal like that. When he went to the herd, everybody expected him to be the greatest.

"He was a bronc the whole time I had him, I never could ride him except to show. I would just ride him to the herd and cut a cow and get out. But I enjoyed every minute of it."

Most executives and jobholders have little time to ride outside the show arena, but they can still be competitive with the right horse and a good trainer.

James "Skip" Hobbs II, a building contractor from Germantown, Tennessee, was the first NCHA Youth Champion, back in 1973. School, work and family took him away from the sport until 1987, when he hooked up with trainer Faron Hightower.

Because of his demanding work schedule, Hobbs relies on Hightower to keep and train all of his horses, and rarely climbs into the saddle until just minutes before a performance. Hightower, the lanky Texan who rode World Champion Hyglo Freckles, knows how to turn out horses that fit Hobbs, who is 6'8".

"With forty-inch inseams, I'm going to hit them somewhere," Hobbs explains about the signals he gives his horse. "Faron trains them so that I can make a mistake and the horses will adjust and not mess up. He uses a lot of leg on a horse, where you can bump them. There's no buttons, no gimmicks. They just go where the cow goes."

Previous riding experience is not a prerequisite for cutting. Some trainers prefer teaching inexperienced students who don't have to unlearn bad habits.

• • •

CEO of his own Chicago-based systems management firm, George Stout never mounted a horse until he was forty-five years old. Stout felt more at ease on a putting green than in a cutting arena.

"I was a golf degenerate," says Stout. "I was looking for an outlet from the pressures of the corporate world. I was a student and fan of the Old West and had always had fantasies as a kid about being a cowboy someday."

Stout began showing cutting horses in 1983 and was champion of the 1989 Non-Pro Super Stakes. His home base is Oak Brook, Illinois, but he maintains a ranch for his show string and their trainer in Santa Ynez, California. Stout is a top competitor at all the major limited-age events.

George Hicks hadn't ridden a horse in nearly thirty years when he discovered cutting. Now co-owner of an aircraft business in Aubrey, Texas, Hicks has a new lifestyle that includes a barn right next to his office.

"I got tired of traveling, stress, too many people working for me," says Hicks. "Now I've slowed the pace down. My partner and I can plan how busy we want to be. We have an arena right next to our office. So we can actually be working a cow and get a customer phone call and take the call while we're still riding on the horse.

"I guess cutting horses and the cattle are my psychiatrist. My health has improved. I'm happier, and I'm a more well-rounded person since I started cutting. It just brings you down to earth—you're working with something very basic."

Dan Lufkin has spent a lifetime studying stock. Co-founder of the well-known Wall Street firm Donaldson, Lufkin and Jenrette, and former chairman of Columbia Pictures, these days Lufkin prefers Black Angus to blue chip.

Lufkin began investigating cutting horse pedigrees in the mid-seventies in an effort to upgrade the quality of horses used for work on his 100,000-acre Oxbow cattle operation in Prairie City, Oregon. Today Lufkin owns some of the cutting industry's finest broodmares and maintains breeding and training facilities in Weatherford, Texas, and Carmel, California.

An astute horseman and accomplished non-pro competitor, Lufkin is as much an innovator in the horse world as on Wall Street. He engineered the pedigree of 1986 NCHA Derby Champion Miss N Cash by breeding his cutting mare Doc N Missy to Dash For Cash, a racehorse whose runners have earned over $30 million.

"Dash For Cash is about as balanced and athletic a horse as I've ever seen," Lufkin explains. "We felt that the rewards would be great . . . the cutting industry really does need an outcross that would go well with Doc Bar bloodlines."

Jim Milner, retired founder of the Taco Bell chain of restaurants, is cutting's richest non-pro. He has amassed over $800,000 in twenty years of competition. He is also a World Champion and has won non-pro championships in all but one of NCHA's major limited-age events.

"I like the aged horses," says Milner, who faced the demands of a fast-paced business world with the same intensity he focuses on a cow. "It's a real challenge to work with young horses."

Milner and his wife Mary Jo, a two-time Non-Pro World Champion and formidable competitor in her own right, were high school sweethearts, raised to ranching and farming in New Mexico. They operated a feedlot in California before venturing into the fast-food business and cutting competition.

Bill Gunlock was a football coach at Ohio State University during the reign of legendary Woody Hayes. He became president of an Ohio service corporation, then built his own indsutry-leading corporation. Fascinated by horses all his life, Gunlock never had the opportunity to ride until 1989.

"It's a little more difficult for me since I didn't start riding until I was sixty," admits Gunlock. "But I get personal enjoyment from the horses.

"There's very much a parallel between football and cutting. I think that's what atrracted me to the event. That two and one-half minutes you're out there is like playing football. You just don't have to hit anybody."

Involvement means spending money, as well as earning it. The payout is usually a lot more than the income, but the payoff is a matter of perspective.

"You spend an awful lot of money for two and one-half minutes out there," says Dan Craine, a beer distributor from Fort Worth, Texas. "But I think that's the thrill of it."

Craine, who was Amateur Champion of the 1989 NCHA Derby, got hooked on cutting by watching the NCHA Futurity. He and his wife Sally started with one horse. They now have over twenty and a ranch to keep them.

Sally Craine, who is also an amateur champion, rode hunters and jumpers when she was in her twenties, but now prefers cutting. "This is the most exciting thing I've ever done," she says. "It's by far the most rewarding event."

Kids and Cutting

She was a typical horse-crazy teenager growing up in the early sixties. Since that time, Kay Floyd has won the NCHA Non-Pro Futurity and earned the NCHA Non-Pro World Championship. The former Hoosier also owns Freckles Playboy, one of cutting's leading sires.

"Kay came to Texas as our babysitter," remembers Charlie Boyd, owner of NCHA's first two Futurity Champions. "Kay simply did it on what I call desire. Nobody ever pushed her. Anything we'd let her ride, she'd jump on it and ride it."

Most kids love horses. Little League, soccer and gymnastics keep parents on the sidelines, but cutting's appeal is universal. Because it can be learned at any age, parents often follow their children into the sport.

"We went and watched my daughter for years and finally got tired of sitting in the bleachers," says Gordon Glasmann about the introduction he and his wife Joyce had to cutting. "We finally went and looked at a horse and rode it. We tried it on a flag the first time. Several weeks later we tried a stale calf and we got hooked."

Glasmann, a former newspaper publisher and communications director who lives in Twin Falls, Idaho, is retired and devotes full-time attention to horses. Although he competed in jumping and polo as a youth, cutting horse competition is his real passion.

Now it is Jo Woodbury who cheers her father and stepmother from the stands. Woodbury has something to cheer about. She knows it's a miracle that the Glasmanns are able to walk, much less ride horses.

The evening before the Glasmanns were to be married in 1977, they were struck by a car traveling forty-five miles per hour as they walked across a city street.

The impact broke both of Joyce's knees and severed the main arteries of her legs. She rides today with plates and bolts in her legs, as well as leg supports.

"This sport of cutting is many things to many people," says Jo Woodbury. "But to Dad and Joyce it made the difference between existing and leading a full life. The cutting horses have given them much to live for and a reason to keep trying. It was the light at the end of the tunnel for them.

"Joyce has shown what courage is. She knows that if she ever damages her legs, she truly will never walk again. But every time she goes out, she gives it all. She never holds anything back."

Gordon Glasmann has another explanation for the couple's enthusiasm and dedication.

"I like to win and I like to have fun," he admits. "I don't think any of us like to go into a competition when you don't try to win. We sure as heck wouldn't be doing it if we didn't enjoy it."

NCHA has benefited from the Glasman's enthusiasm. Because of his love for the sport, and his personal commitment to youth and education, Glasmann established a $200,000 scholarship trust through Cutters in Action, a beneficent organization of NCHA members.

Like other CIA scholarships, the Glasmann Scholarship is available to students under the age of twenty-one with an immediate family member who has been an NCHA member for three years. Scholarships are granted on the basis of academic records, extracurricular activities, and financial need.

The Cox family raises Limousin show cattle on their farm in central Indiana. While attending a cattle show in South Dakota in 1985, the Coxs made a side trip to a local horse show. Fifteen-year-old Jason was so enthralled with a cutting horse event he decided he wanted a cutting horse for Christmas.

Younger brothers Jay and Jared didn't want to be left out when Jason rode his horse, so in 1986 the three brothers traveled 160 miles round trip, twice a week, to learn cutting from Marlin Eggers of Markleville, Indiana.

Since Jason had received a cutting horse for Christmas, Jay was next in line. For his sixteenth birthday on June 1, 1986, he received Dry Oil, a nineteen-year-old stallion by Dry Doc. Dry Oil, 1983 World Champion Novice Horse, had been shown four months in 1983, the extent of his career until J. V. Cox purchased him for Jay.

"We heard all kinds of stories about this horse," says J. V. Cox. "I was advised not to buy him, that he was a killer, a maneater that had put a guy in the hospital. I kept him in another barn the first six months I owned him. I didn't want my kids around him because of all the stories I had heard."

Jack Liedister, who boarded Dry Oil for Cox that first six months, told him that as far as he was concerned, the stallion was safe for anyone. He also told Cox that although he had ridden hundreds of horses, Dry Oil was the best one he had ever saddled.

"He may have been aggressive and mean," Cox says. "I'm sure he would be if you abused him. But all you have to do is talk to this horse and he'll do anything for you."

By January 1987, all three of the Cox brothers decided to aim for a place in the NCHA Youth Top Ten. Jay rode Dry Oil. Fifteen-year-old Jason was mounted on Miss Scenic Tagbar, 1983 World Champion Paint Cutting Mare. Sadie Red Lace belonged to thirteen-year-old Jared.

Father and sons traveled every weekend, covering 100,000 miles during that year. Because of school, the Coxs concentrated on shows in the midwestern and southern states.

Jay, Jason and Paige Alexander traded the lead for World Champion all year. In early December 1987, Jay and Jason pulled ahead with a comfortable edge. It was just the two of them racing for the championship. Jay had a 20-point lead at one time; by mid-month he was only 1 point ahead of Jason.

Although Jay and Jason were still talking, things were tense.

"At the last show in Indiana, I was 1 point ahead of Jason," Jay recalls. "It was seven in the evening, and Carter Dillman and I decided to go to Lufkin [Texas] for a show the next day."

Jay and Dillman drove all night, Jay and Dry Oil won the next day, and Jay pulled ahead of Jason by 4 points.

There was still one show left.

"The Louisiana State University show was on December 28, 29 and 30," Jay remembers. "Jason won the first day and got ahead of me.

"All during this time, all four of us boys [Dillman included] were calling NCHA every day to see if the points were right."

Jay won the last day and ended the season with 5 points more than Jason. For the first time in the history of NCHA, two brothers placed Champion and Reserve Champion of the World. Jared finished fifth.

Jay and Dry Oil were the only pair in 1987 to qualify for both Open and Non-Pro NCHA World Championship Finals. Dry Oil competed in 488 shows in 1987—more times in one year than any other horse in NCHA history.

Jay and Jason curtailed their showing in 1988, but still earned enough points to stay in the Top Ten. They were saving themselves for 1989.

"When I started, I was just going to try to make the Top Ten," Jay explains about the 1989 season. "Then I got a pretty good lead, so I decided I wasn't going to back off. If my brothers had beat me, it wouldn't have bothered me that bad. But I wasn't going to let anyone else beat me."

Jay and Dry Oil seemed nearly invincible in 1989. Although they attended fewer shows than Jason and Jared did the first half of the year, when they went to a show they won.

"The highest I ever scored was that year," says Jay. "I marked 77.5 points in Danville, Indiana. For some reason Dry Oil never would lose the cow. It about killed me, but he stayed in there."

Persistence paid. By year end, Jay was again World Champion Youth. He is only the third youth rider to capture the title twice. Jason and Jared tied for the Reserve Championship.

Dry Oil has an amicable disposition and is willing to do everything that is required of him, including breeding and showing sometimes in the same day. "We bred Dry Oil to twenty-five mares in 1989 and he never missed a weekend showing," says J. V. Cox. "Sometimes we bred him on Friday evening before we left. A couple of times we took mares to shows with us and bred them there."

Sixteen-year-old Millie Kay Bouget of Branch, Louisiana, showed her first cutting horse at the age of five. In 1988 she was NCHA World Champion Youth, $10,000 Non-Pro World Champion and ranked fourteenth in Non-Pro standings.

Although Millie is a Non-Pro, she's no amateur when it comes to riding and showing cutting horses. The daughter of professional trainer Bob Bouget, Millie can't remember when she wasn't riding horses.

There is nothing *but* cutting for Millie. She has earned over $79,000 and enough scholarships for several college educations with her performances. More than anything else, Millie loves the sport and her horses.

"Words can't descibe the faith that I have in my horse," said Millie after winning the World Championship. "Every time I went to the herd, I had all the confidence that I knew she was going to be there. I don't get nervous when I show and I don't worry too much about the cattle. My horse can handle anything."

Millie's 1991 mount, Smoke On Echols, also looks out for her. When she accidently dropped a bridle rein riding the gelding in the National Finals, she held her breath.

"I still had two cows out there, trying to separate them," remembers Millie. "Holding one bridle rein was not too easy. I finally got the cows separated and stayed on the cow for almost a minute, then quit. The rein was flying. But he didn't do anything but stay in position and work that cow real good."

How many eight-year-olds earn thousands of dollars having fun during summer vacation *and* beating adults in a sports arena? That's what Cassye

Carter of Celina, Texas, did when she won the 1978 NCHA $1,500 World Championship. She was by far the youngest rider to ever do so, and she rode against competitors like country-western singer Lynn Anderson. She was also Reserve Champion Youth the same year.

Cassye was born to cutting. Her grandfather John Carter has ridden some of the sport's legends, including World Champion Mare Doc's Starlight. Punk, her father, is an accomplished rider and teacher who preps movie stars and sports heros for the NCHA Celebrity Cuttings.

Cassye rode in her first cutting event at five, her next one was a few years later, when she was seven. "We had her on Booger Man," says Carter. "Me and Daddy, we had drilled her. 'When we tell you to stick him, you stick him.' "

Booger Man was actually Man's Toughy, who got his nickname when John Carter called to tell Punk he had purchased a horse for Cassye. He was ugly as the booger man, John reported, but could cut fly specks out of pepper.

"They sold Booger Man out there during the circuit, remembers Punk. "So we put Cassye on Careless Trouble, the turnback horse. The next day Daddy called and said Cassye had won the Youth on him and the $1,500 Non-Pro."

Glossary

ACHA   American Cutting Horse Association (P.O. Box 999, Burleson, TX 76028).

Added money   Money added to the purse in addition to owners' and breeders' nomination and entry fees.

Adjusted score   Score that has been reviewed and changed under the rules of the Adjusted Monitor System.

Alligator   A cow that is difficult to control.

Amateur   A novice rider.

APHA   American Paint Horse Association (P.O. Box 18519, Fort Worth, TX 76118-0519).

ApHC   Appaloosa Horse Club, Inc. (P.O. Box 8403, Moscow, ID 83843).

AQHA   American Quarter Horse Association (2701 I-40E, Amarillo, TX 79168).

Argentine Snaffle   A bit with a broken mouthpiece and hinged shanks that is used with a curb chain.

Babysitter   A cow or horse that is gentle and easy to control.

Back fence   A designated area of the fence behind the cattle. A horse will be penalized 3 points each time the cow being worked stops or turns within three feet of the back fence.

Bad cow   See Alligator.

Baldy   A white-faced cow.

Barrel turn   A turn executed on the front end rather than the back end. This is an undesirable turn for a cutting horse.

Blow up   Said of a horse or cow that panics, as in "My horse blew up the first time he saw a cow."

Break   Said of a horse or cow that turns and runs, as in "That cow is going to break for the gate."

Bright   Alert as in "That horse is really bright on a cow."

Brindle   Streaked or spotted coat color on some cows.

Chaps   Protective leather leggings that are usual show attire.

Cheat   To look for an easy way out of working correctly, as in "If I don't watch my horse, he will try to cheat on the turns."

Check   To half-halt or stop a horse while riding.

Collected   Refers to a horse that is balanced and working on his haunches for easy maneuverability.

Commit   To show intention to work a specific cow by looking at it and stepping toward it.

Corrected score   Score change due to a simple error in calculation.

Cowing   Describes a horse that is focused on a cow.

Cow sense   The mental ability and aptitude of a horse to focus on cattle and work them.

Cow smart   The ability of a horse to anticipate a cow's actions, as in "That horse is so cow smart it knows what a cow is going to do before the cow knows."

Curb bit   A bit used in conjunction with a curb strap (a strip of leather, sometimes with a chain, attached to the bit and positioned behind the horse's chin) to exert pressure on the bars of a horse's mouth. The reins of a curb bit are attached to shanks leading from the mouthpiece.

Cut for shape   To drive cattle into the center of the arena, wait for them to flow around the horse and back to the herd, and cut the one that is left.

Glossary

Cutter's slump Describes the posture of a cutting horse rider whose seat is deep in the saddle and who sits on his back pockets with his back relaxed and curved slightly forward.

Deep Cut A cut made when the horse goes far enough into the herd of cattle to be completely surrounded by cows. NCHA rules require one deep cut for each two-and-one-half-minute ride.

Derby An event for four-year-old cutting horses.

Die in the herd To go into the herd of cattle for another cow when the buzzer sounds to end the run.

Draw cattle Describes a horse's ability to make cows look at him and come toward him, as in "My horse can really draw a cow."

Drift To slowly lose position, as in "His horse always drifts back into the herd."

Drive To push cattle forward while maintaining control.

Drop on a cow The crouching posture of the horse when a cow has been cut and separated and the rider drops his rein hand to the horse's neck.

Dry work Training maneuvers performed without cattle.

Expression Alertness shown by a horse in front of a cow.

Eye appeal A horse with lots of expression when working a cow is said to have eye appeal.

Fade back A cue from the rider to the horse to back away from a cow being worked while still staying hooked.

Fresh Frisky and full of energy. Also used to denote cattle that have not been used for cutting, as in "We will have fresh cows to work."

Futurity An event for three-year-old or early four-year-old cutting horses.

Get down The action of a horse lowering himself down to the level of the cow being worked.

Get into the ground Refers to a horse's ability to stop hard on its rear end.

Good cow A cow that acknowledges the horse and rider when cut but does not panic and bolt.

Gouge To make a quick, hard jab with a spur.

Grazing bit A curb bit with shanks slanted back to make it easy for the horse to graze.

Green A term used to describe a rider or horse just beginning training. A green-broke horse has a minimum of training.

Hackamore A headstall with a rigid noseband and knot under the jaw. Popular as a training bridle because there is no pressure in the horse's mouth.

Haul To travel to world championship shows, as in "I'm going to haul for the Top Ten this year."

Heading Getting in front of a cow to stop it or turn it.

Heart Denotes a great degree of willingness and courage in a horse, as in "That horse has a lot of heart."

Heifer A young female cow.

Herd bound Refers to a horse that is reluctant to move a cow away from the herd.

Herd holder A rider who is positioned on one side of the herd of cattle, close to the fence. Together, two herd holders contain the cattle at the end of the arena close to the fence.

Honor Refers to a cow that will acknowledge and look at a horse and rider.

Hooked Refers to a horse that has his total attention focused on the cow he is working.

Hot walk To walk a horse to cool him off after a performance or workout.

Hot-blooded Refers to a high-strung, nervous horse.

Hunt A horse is said to hunt a cow if he follows it with his eyes.

IAHA International Arabian Horse Association (P.O. Box 33696, Denver, CO 80233).

Inside leg The rider's leg closest to the cow being worked.

Jackpot Prize money made up from entry fees.

The Jockey Club The organization in the United States that maintains the Stud Book and approves Thoroughbred registration.

Leak To drift out with the front end into a cow, as in "Don't let your horse leak when he stops at the end of the arena."

Glossary

Limited-age events Events that are restricted to horses between the ages of three and six years old.

Long on a cow Refers to a horse being too far ahead of a cow when traveling parallel across the arena. If the horse is long, the cow can easily gain advantage by turning or ducking back.

Look Used to denote a horse's expression when facing a cow, as in "That horse has a lot of look on a cow."

Lope Three-beat gait of the horse, also called a canter. Cutters lope their horses to warm them up for a performance or a training session.

Martingale Training device attached to the girth and breast collar that loops around the horse's neck. Attached straps have rings through which the reins are fed. This device helps to keep the horse's head low without excessive bit pressure.

NCHA National Cutting Horse Association (4704 Highway 377S, Fort Worth, Texas 76117).

Nominate To pay a fee to make a horse eligible for a special event. Nomination fees are part of the purse money.

Non-Pro Nonprofessional rider. An NCHA non-pro rider must have a non-pro card attesting to the fact that he does not train cutting horses for profit or for any other renumeration. (See NCHA rule #8.)

Numb Refers to a cow that is not threatened or challenged by a horse and shows little desire to return to the herd.

Open Events or classes in which any rider is eligible to perform.

Outside leg The rider's leg that is on the opposite side of the horse from the cow.

Over-ride To push a horse and not wait for him to react to a cow.

Paint A spotted cow.

Peel To drive a cow away from the edge of the herd. Also refers to the action of a herd of cattle when a rider drives through the middle—the cows flow out and away from the rider and back to the rest of the herd.

Penalty points Points deducted from the run contest score because of penalties.

Purse Prize money consisting of nomination and entry fees, plus money added by sponsors.

Push-button Refers to a horse trained to respond to a rider's signals, not necessarily related to the action.

Quick-stop A training bridle that exerts a great amount of pressure under a horse's jaw and is used sparingly to get a horse to stop quickly on its haunches.

Quit To stop working a cow.

Rate A horse is said to rate a cow when it paces its actions and timing with that of the cow.

Read cattle The ability of a horse or rider to anticipate a cow's actions.

Ride your horse To use your body and legs to assist the horse—aggressive riding as opposed to passive riding.

Round pen A training arena usually from 100 to 200 feet in diameter.

Run Refers to the two-and-one-half-minute contest time period allotted to each cutting contestant.

Run through Refers to the action of a cow that tries to run under a horse to return to the herd. May also be referred to as "running over a horse."

School a horse To train a horse.

Settle cattle Spend time quietly working a herd of cattle at the end of an arena in preparation for cutting.

Shape cattle To manipulate cattle to flow in a specfic direction.

Shooter A cow that bolts from the herd for no apparent reason and interferes with a performance.

Short on a cow Refers to a horse's parallel position in relation to a cow that is moving across an arena. If a horse is short on a cow, it is too far behind to influence her movements.

Sidepull A training bridle with reins attached at the side of a noseband.

Skid boots Protective leg wraps that are fastened to a horse's hind legs below the hocks and covering the fetlocks.

Snaffle A widely used bit, especially in training. It usually has a jointed mouthpeice attached to circular or D-shaped rings to which the reins are also attached.

Glossary 217

Soft   Describes cattle that have little play and are easily tired and distracted.

Solid   Describes a well-trained horse with lots of show experience.

Sour cattle   Cattle that have been used for cutting too often and do not respond well for training and cutting.

Spin   To turn a horse back over its hocks.

Splatter   Refers to the action of a horse that drops down in front of a cow.

Splint boots   Protective leg wraps that are fastened to a horse's front legs below the knees and covering the fetlocks.

Spurs   Worn as a pair, they are metal devices that are strapped to a rider's boots and when used, reinforce a rider's body signals to the horse.

Stakes   An event in which purse money consists of nomination and entry fees, plus added money from sponsors.

Stale cattle   Cattle that have been used too often for cutting and will no longer challenge a horse.

Steer   A castrated bull.

Stick   To prod with a spur.

Sticky   Refers to cattle that bunch closely together and are difficult to separate.

Style   Refers to the flare with which a horse works cattle, as in "His horse shows lots of style in front of a cow."

Sweep   The action of a horse when it sits back on its haunches and moves its front end, with front legs extended, to track a cow.

Tight on a cow   Refers to a horse that is controlling a cow in a close confrontation.

Time line   A designated line along the arena wall. When a rider crosses the time line, the clock starts for his performance.

Tune   To give a horse a short refresher course.

Turn tail   Refers to a horse turning away from (quitting) a cow that is working. This is a 5-point penalty action.

Turnback riders   Riders stationed between the rider and the time line and positioned to be able to turn cows back toward the rider.

Unhooked   Said of a horse that loses a cow's attention.

Wait on your horse   To wait for your horse to react to the cow.

Warm up   To physically and mentally prepare a horse for a performance.

Whistle   Judge's action to stop a performance.

Working advantage   Describes the position from which a horse is able to influence the actions of a cow.

Youth   A rider eighteen years old or younger.

Index

Figures in *italics* refer to illustrations.

Age of the horse, 89, 97, 98
Amateur riders, 144, 167, 168, 186, 190–205; suggestions for, 160–166
American Appaloosa Cutting Horse Association, 85
American Jockey Club, 14, 87
American Paint Horse Association, 85
American Quarter Horse, 83
American Quarter Horse Association (AQHA), 5, 7, 13, 21, 22, 23, 24, 32, 33, 39, 43, 44, 45, 47, 48, 49, 50, 83, 85, 86, 87, 98; formation of, 15, 21; registration, 87
American Quarter Racing Association, 83
Angus cattle, 123
Appaloosa Horse Club, 84
Appaloosas, 84–85
Arabians, 4, 5, 50, 60, 82, 84, 85, 86–88
Arena cutting. *See* Contest cutting
Arena etiquette, 175
Arraff, 87–88
Assault, 15
Attire, riding, 106–107

Backing, 121, *121–122*, 123
Balance, in riding, 109, *110*, 111, 119, 134

Ball O'Flash, 193–194
Bareback riding, 109, 111
Bar Socks Babe, 68–69
Basics of cutting, 108–136; cattle, 123–136; contests, 131–134, *134–135*, 136; gaits, 119, *120*, 121; hands, 117, *117–118*, 119; herding instincts, 125–131, 141–142, 144–145; leg pressure, 111, *112*, 113, *113*, 117, 123, 134, *135*, 144; locomotion and balance, 109, *110*, 111, 119, 134; seat, 113, *114*, 115, *115–116*, 117, 123, 134, *134–135*, 144, 146; stopping and backing, 121, *121–122*, 123, 137–138, *138*
Bedding, 171
Bella Coquette, 95–96, 196
Bits, 97, 102–103, *103*, 104, *104*, 108, 109, 139, *140*, 172
Blanketing, 105
Boots, 107
Brahman cattle, 123–124
Breast collar, 100–101
Breeders Cutting, NCHA, 54
Breeding, 90, 98, 186–188; business, 186–188
Breeds, selection and types of, 82–88
Bridle path, 105
Bridles, 97, 102–103, *103*, 104, 109, 139, 172
Buying horses, 97–99

Case Book, 183
Cash Quixote Rio, 130, *130*, 185
Cattle, 123–136; breeds, 123–124; committing to, 132–133, 147, 178, 182; in contests, 131–134, *134–135*, 136, 176–183; fees, at shows, 168; horses and, 125–126, *126–127*, 128, *129*, 130–136; offensive, 138–139; quitting, 136, 144, 145, 148, 178–179, 181–182; traits and temperament, 124–125; and tuning the training basics, 137–145, *138–143*
Celebrity cutting competitors, *196–198*
Chaps, 107
Chickasha Ann, 53, 58, 59, 61, 63, 71
Chickasha Dan, 53, 61, 63, 71
Chickasha Glo, 53, 57, 58, 59, 60, 71
Chickasha Mike, 58, 59, 60–61
Children, and cutting, 205–209
Cinches, 100, *101*
Classifications for NCHA shows, 167–168, 184–186
Clays Little Peppy, 150
Climbers, 97
Coat, 105
Coggins test, 106, 169
Colonel Freckles, 70
Cols Lil Pepper, 77, 102
Committing to a cow, 132–133, 147, 178, 182
Conformation, 91–93, *92–93*, 94
Contest cutting, 11–12, 131–134, *134–135*, 136, 176–189; committing to a cow, 132–133, 178, 182; do's and don'ts, 183; entering the herd, 132, 178; the ideal in, 180–181; judging, 176–183; NCHA Futurity, 52–81, 180–183, 185; penalties, 179, 181–183; quitting a cow, 136, 178–179, 181–182; rider's role in, 131; starting the action, 133–134
Cost of the horse, 97–99, 163
Cribbing, 96
Curb bits, 102–103, *104*
Cut, the, 9, 133, 147, *147*, 154, 178
Cutting for shape, 132
Cutting horses: buying, 97–99; and children, 205–209; contests, 11–12, 52–81, 131–134, *134–135*, 136, 176–189; definition of, 1; first show, 167–175; ranch, 7–11, 82, 83, 86–87, 148–155, 178; riders, 52–81, 100, 108–136, 155–157, 176–183, 190–205; riding and contest basics, 108–136; selection and types of, 82–107; tack for, 97, 99–105, *99–104*; training basics for, 137–166
Cuttin' Hoss Chatter, 10, 97–98, 167, 168, 169, 189

Dandy Doll, 47–48
Dan Tucker, 14
Derby, NCHA, 54, 191–192
Disposition of the horse, 94–96
Doc Bar, 30, 33, 44, 46–47, *47*, 48–51, 57, 63, 64, 66, 67, 73, 82, 83, 87
Doc O'Lena, 30–31, 32, 49, 51, 55, 64, 65, 67–69, 74, 181
Doc Per, 75, 128, 158
Docs Diablo, 72
Doc's Marmoset, 66–67
Docs Okie Quixote, 74–75
Drawing a cow, 128, 130
Dry Doc, 31, 49, 66, 72

Ears, 93, 94, 105, 125–126, 179
Entry fees, 168, 184
Exercise, 106
Eye appeal, 128, 157
Eyes, 93, 94, 105

Farrier, 106
Faults of the horse, 96
Feed(ing), 97, 106, 171
Fees, show, 168–169, 184
Feet, 105–106
Fences, 144, 178
Fetlocks, 105
First aid kit, 171
First show, 167–175
Foals, 18, 125, 186, 187
Freckles, 18, 44
Futurity, NCHA, 52–81, 180–183, 185; of 1962, 55–58; of 1963, 58–60; of 1964, 60; of 1966, 61–62; of 1967, 62; of 1968, 62; of 1969, 63; of 1970, 64–

Index

65; of 1971, 66; of 1972, 66; of 1973, 66–67; of 1974, 67; of 1975, 67–70; of 1976, 70–71; of 1977, 71, 153; of 1978, 72; of 1979, 72–73; of 1980, 73; of 1981, 73–74; of 1982, 74; of 1983, 74–75; of 1984, 75; of 1985, 76; of 1986, 76; of 1987, 76, 180, 190; of 1988, 77–78; of 1989, 78–80, 159, 165; of 1990, 78, 80, 81, 149, 150, 158, 160; rules, 54

Gaits, 119, 120, 121
Gay Bar King, 46
Gay Jay, 17–18
Geldings, 90, 154
Gemnist, 76, 195
Gender of the horse, 89–90, 194
Grain, 97, 106, 171
Grazing bit, 104
Grooming and conditioning, 105–106, 169, 171, 172

Hackamore bridle, 102, 103
Halter horses, 83
Halters, 97, 172
Hands, rider's, 117, 117–118, 119
Hats, 107
Hay, 106, 171
Head, 93–94, 144
Headstalls, 102, 104
Health of the horse, 106, 169
Heat, mares in, 90
Herd, entering the, 132
Herd holders, 131, 137, 172–174
Herding instincts, 125–131, 141–142, 144–145
Herd work, 146, 178
Hereford cattle, 123
Hickory Bill, 13, 14
Hindquarters, 109
Hocks, 93
Hollywood Gold, 40, 53
Hollywood Sana, 87, 88
Hooves, 105–106
Horns, saddle, 118, 119, 133–134
Hot quit, 181–182
Hunters, 160

Ima Little Lena, 84–85
Injuries, 106

Jazabell Quixote, 25–26, 79, 80, 86
Jazalena, 79, 80, 86, 95
Joe Reed II, 34–35, 35, 36–37, 39, 40
Joints, 91, 106, 174
Judging contests, 176–183
Jumpers, 115, 160

King, 21, 21, 22–24, 27, 43, 46, 56, 77, 83
King Glo, 23, 53, 56, 57, 58, 59, 61
King Ranch, Texas, 7, 13–20, 40, 41, 71
Kingstream, 158, 159, 202
Knees, 92

Leaking into the cow, 142
Leg pressure, rider's, 111, 112, 113, 113, 117, 123, 134, 135, 144
Legs, 92–93, 158; protected for travel, 169
Leo, 37–38, 38, 39–40, 44, 67, 77, 83
Leo San, 40–41, 53, 82
Leota W, 37–38
Ligaments, 91, 106, 174
Lightning Bar, 48, 49, 50
Limited-Age Events, 168, 177, 185–186
Little Fanny, 36, 37
Locomotion of the horse, 109, 110, 111
Lope, 121, 142
Lynx Melody, 72, 90, 91

Mane, 105, 117
Mares, 18, 53, 90, 125, 154, 194; and breeding business, 186–188; heat cycles, 90; maiden, 186–187
Marion's Girl, 18, 55, 57, 71, 88
Martingales, 101, 140
Millie Montana, 80, 81, 125–126, 185
Mis Royal Mahogany, 73
Miss Silver Pistol, 1–2, 3, 24, 40, 126
Money's Glo, 55–58
Monkeys Formula, 198–200
Morgans, 4, 5, 82
Mouth, 97, 139; abuse, 103, 104

Mr San Peppy, 18–19, *19*, 20, 30, 41, 53, 55
Muscles, 91, 93, 94, 106, 174

National Championships, NCHA, 54, 184
National Cutting Horse Association (NCHA), 11–12, 18–20, 23, 24, 25, 26, 30, 31, 32, 33, 34, 40, 44, 45, 46, 49, 50, 51, 85, 86, 87, 88, 89, 90, 91, 98, 101, 102, 123, 133, 155–165, 167, 176–209; Breeders Cutting, 54; classes, conditions, and entry fees, 167–169, 184–186; competition prerequisites, 88; Derby, 54, 191–192; and first show, 167–175; Futurity, 52–81; judging contests, 176–183; limited-age events, 168, 177, 185–186; membership, 167; National Championships, 54, 184; registration, 184; Super Stakes, 54, 185–186; World Championships, 54, 184, 185
NCHA Rule Book, 183
National Quarter Horse Association, 83
Neck, 92
Nipping, 125, 126
Non-pro riders, 160–166, 167, 168, 186, 190–205

Old Fred, 7
Old Mike, 58
Old Poco Bueno, 27–28
Old Sorrel, 6, 7, 13–15, 16, 17, 40, 83
$1,500 Limit Novice Classes, 168
Open and Non-Pro Championship Classes, 168
Open and Non-Pro Cutting Horse Classes, 168
Open Gelding Classes, 168
Open mares, 187
Oriental horses, 3–4
Oxbow stirrup, 101, *101*, 102

Paint horses, 85–86
Paperwork, 170, 172
Pawing, 96
Pedigree, 88, 97–98, 187, 203–204
Penalties, contest, 179, 181–183

Pens, training, 141, 148
Peppy Belle, 40–41
Peppy San (Little Peppy), 9, 20, 40–41, 53, 55, 63, 71, 77, 86, 92, 94–95, 128, 153, 155, 160, 180
Peter McCue, 5, 6, 7, 13, 14
Poco Bueno, 23, 24, 26–27, *27*, 28–29, 32, 33, 34, 42, 49, 56, 64, 65, 83, 100, 181
Poco Champ, 34
Poco Lena, 26, 29–31, *31*, 32, 33, 49, 64–65, 159, 181
Poco Tivio, 29, 32, *32*, 33, 48, 49, 64, 65, 66
Pretty Boy, 27, 29

Quarter Horse News, The, 98
Quarter Horses, 4, 5, 7, 14, 15, 27, 28, 29, 33, 35, 37, 39, 41–44, 46, 48, 49, 61, 82, 84, 85, 88; selection and types of, 82–83
Quitting a cow, 136, 144, 145, 148, 178–179, 181–182

Racehorses, 83, 99
Ranchero, 16, 17
Ranch horses, 7–11, 82, 83, 86–87, 148–155, 178
Registration of horses, 87, 98, 184
Reins, 104, *121*, 146, 178; hands on, 117, *117–118*, 119
Rented horses, 98
Rey Del Rancho, 16, 17
Rey Jay, 15–16, *16*, 17–18, 61–62, 71
Rey Jay's Pete, 18, 61–62, 88
Riders, 100, 108, 155–157, 176–183, 190–205; amateur, 144, 160–166, 167, 168, 186, 190–205; and basics of cutting, 108–136; in the contest, 52–81, 131–136, 176–183; first-time, suggestions for, 160–166; style of, 155–157; and training basics, 137–166
Riding attire, 106–107
Rooster, 11
Royal Jazzy, 24–26, 105, 159
Royal King, 24–25, *25*, 26, 79, 82
Royal Silver King, 76

Index

Saddlebreds, 4, 82
Saddle pads, 102
Saddles, 97, 99, *99*, 100–101, 119, 146; horns on, *118*, 119, 133–134, 178; sitting in, 109, *110*, 111, 113, *114*, 115, *115–116*, 117, 134, *134–135*, 144, 146
Seasoned horse, 89
Seat, rider's, 113, *114*, 115, *115–116*, 117, 123, 134, *134–135*, 144, 146
Selection of the horse, 82–107; age of horse, 89, 97, 98; conformation, 91–93, *92–93*, 94; disposition of horse, 94–96; faults and vices of horse, 96; grooming and conditioning, 105–106; popular breeds, 83–88; sex of horse, 89–90; size of horse, 91; tack, 99–105, *99–104*; unsoundness, 96–97
Selling horses, 188–189
Setups, training, 141
Sex of the horse, 89–90
Shanks, 103, *104*
Show cutting, 167–175, 184–189; arena etiquette, 175; classes, conditions, and entry fees, 167–169, 184–186; equipment, 170–171; travel arrangements, 169–170; turnback riders and herd holders for, 172–174; warming up, 174–175
Show horses, 83, 89, 94, 98, 106–107, 167–175
Side-pull bridle, 139
Sires, 5–7, 187–188
Size of the horse, 91
Skid boots, 105
Smart Date, 76, 180, 181
Smart Little Lena, 74, 76, 77, 79, 80, 84, 86, 159, 160, 192, 193
Smart Little Senor, 77, 90
Smart Peppy Lena, 192
Smart Play, 80, *93*, 94, 126, 158
Smokys Little Peppy, 149, *149*, 150, 151
Snaffle bits, 102, *103*, 139, *140*
Solid Gold Doc, *129*
Solid horse, 89
Solis, 14, 16
Splint boots, 105
Spurs, 107, 146
Stallions, 18, 89–90, 154, 187, 194

Stalls, show, 171, 172
Stirrups, 99, 101, *101*, 102, 115; length of, 145–146
Stock horses, 99
Stopping, 121–123, 137–138, *138*
Stud fees, 187–188
Sugar Badger, 20
Sugar Bars, 44, 45
Super Stakes, NCHA, 54, 185–186

Tack, 97, 99–105, *99–104*, 108, 109, 139, *140*; bits, 97, 102–103, *103*, 104, *104*; bridles, 97, 102–103, *103*, 104; saddle pads, 102; saddles, 97, 99, *99*, 100–101; for shows, 170, 172; splint boots, 105; stirrups, 99, 101, *101*, 102
Tail, 105
Teeth, 97
Tendons, 91, 174
$10,000 Limit Non-Pro Classes, 168
Texas Dandy, 47, 48
Thoroughbreds, 4, 5, 7, 14, 15, 16, 27, 39, 41, 43, 44, 50, 84, 85, 87, 88
Three Bars, 41–42, *42*, 43–46, 48, 63, 77
$3,000 Limit Novice Classes, 168
Tie-downs, 101
Tracking the cow, 141–142, *142–143*, 144, 146
Trailers, 97, 169–170, 172
Trainers, 98, 137, 141, 144, 148–155, 162, 163, 164
Training basics, 137–166; committing to the cow, 147; the cut, 147, *147*, *154*; helpful hints, 145–148, 160–166; herd work, 146; and the horse, 157–159; pens and arenas, 141, 148; practice, 148; quitting the cow, 144–145, 148; reins, 146; riding with style, 155–157; setups, 141; spurs, 146; stirrup length, 145–146; suggestions for first-time cutters, 160–166; tracking the cow, 141–142, *142–143*, 144, 146; trainer's description of, 148–155; tuning, 137–145, *138–143*; warming up, 146
Travel arrangements, for first show, 169–170
Traveler, 5
Triple Crown, 54

Trot, 119, 138
Turnback riders, 131, 132, 137, 172–174
Turning, 139, 141–142
$20,000 Limit Amateur Classes, 168
$2,000 Limit Any Rider Any Horse Classes, 168

Uno's Princess, 62
Unsoundness, 96–97

Vaccinations, 96, 106, 169
Veterinarians, 96–97, 106, 186, 187, 188

Walk, 119, 138, 154
Warming up, 146, 174–175
Water, 170
Weavers, 96
Wee Darlin, 69–70, 88
Wimpy, 7, 13, 14
Working advantage, 178
World Championships, NCHA, 54, 184, 185
Worming, 97, 106

Zantanon, 21–22, 27, 28, 56